HISTORY AND BIOGRAPHY

To the reader of this manual, what becomes immediately apparent when first glancing through the pages, is that by the very nature of the structured exercises, this is not a 'novel' which can be read from cover to cover. Nor is it a reference book, to be picked up now and then to do one or two exercises here and there, simply because they are interesting.

This manual, and the subsequent ones - The Armour of Light - Part II and The Magnet - has been written as a result of serious and dedicated work by the author, Olive Pixley, during the first part of this century. As she is no longer with us, the following is given by way of a brief explanation as to how Olive Pixley came to bring this work into the format as it is presented now. More importantly however, the reader needs to be made aware of the fact that there is a specific and correct method to undertake these exercises because, as is the case with all scientific procedures, precision and accuracy are of paramount importance, and Light is a scientific process.

These conscious, meditative exercises, focused on Light, were given to Olive Pixley over a period of

of tin consci believ given she wa task during her lifetime was not only to *receive* this unique knowledge of the Light, but also to *give* this knowledge to all who seek the Light, which is for the healing of oneself, the healing of others and the whole of our natural world. These books on The Armour of Light are a culmination of a step by step process of revelation to Olive Pixley. It is often referred to as the Technique, but was originally described by Olive as The Christian Initiation.

Biography

A biography of Olive Pixley, from the information she revealed or recorded concerning herself, is very brief. Olive clearly emphasised that the reason for this was because she believed the purpose of her life was to reveal and demonstrate the Light, and that she herself was not to be seen in any way as a charismatic figure or personality leader of a 'cult'.

Olive Pixley believed herself to be an ordinary person, and was described as a very direct, frank and even forthright woman. Nor was she credulous, but maintained a healthy critical attitude to the experiences that had befallen her, with no seeking on her part. However, it would not be an exaggeration to say that her psychic gifts were above the ordinary.

Born in November 1888 (just within Scorpio), Olive Pixley was one of a family of six children, three boys and three girls, who lived in a typical English country home in Wooburn Green, Buckinghamshire. As a child she suffered from poor health and so received much of her early education from governesses, until she later went to finishing school in France. A close relationship existed between Olive and her younger brother Jack, both of whom apparently shared psychic abilities. This close bond was to be the key which began to open Olive Pixley's gifts. After the tragedy of Jack's unforeseen and premature death in the First World War, came the first of Olive's communication with the spiritual world, and which began her training as a channel.

"Listening In"
Olive did write a personal account of this significant time in her life in a small book called *"Listening In"* which details the communications she received from her brother, and the information Jack wanted her to know

of the spiritual realm he found himself in after he died. It is a moving and enlightening personal account of the universal experience of bereavement.

Olive believed this relationship with her brother formed the basis of what is required as a foundation within one's self as a Christian Initiate, and that is the act of voluntarily submitting oneself to the state of *receptivity* through the *link of love*.

"The Trail"
In 1924 came the next stage of Olive Pixley's training in sensitivity, when she met and formed a friendship with an artist, Madame Jill Raoul-Duval. The experiences which they so unexpectedly encountered are more fully outlined in another publication *"The Trail"*. This short book is also highly recommended reading, as it does give a greater insight into the personal process Olive Pixley underwent to reach the point of the Christian Initiation, and describes what that really does mean.

"The Trail" is a compilation of lectures presented by Olive Pixley during the 1930's. It begins with an explanation of the development of her gift of psychometry, and that of Madame Raoul-Duval's talent as a recording artist. Apparently it all began quite casually when the two

8

THE ORDER OF THE NEW COVENANT

THE

ARMOUR OF LIGHT

PART I

VOLUME I

A technique for healing the self and others.
Revealed through, and presented by,

OLIVE C.B. PIXLEY

First Published 1957
Re-issued 1961
Reprinted 1971
Reprinted 1974
Reprinted 1978
Reprinted 1983
Reprinted 1992
Revised 1999

ISBN   0-9536630-0-0

Published by
The Armour of Light Trust Council

Printed by
Waveney Print
College Lane, Worlingham, Beccles, Suffolk NR34 7SA

INDEX OF CONTENTS

Page

VOLUME I

The Exercise and Talk on:-

*These Exercises are presented with an illustration.

3

INDEX OF CONTENTS

VOLUME II

INDEX OF CONTENTS

Page

VOLUME II

NOTE:

These talks were presented as correspondence course notes by Olive Pixley, but are no longer available.

++ These talks have been recorded on cassette tape.

friends were sitting in a garden having coffee after lunch. Olive Pixley found herself doing a little sketch, which Madame Raoul-Duval immediately recognised as relating to a private incident in her own life.

Next morning they were sitting together when Olive was made to put down the pen and book she was holding and, to quote her own words, "I got up slowly and unhesitatingly started gestures and postures, Egyptian in character. I never walked with my feet side by side, but toe to heel, and all arm movements were with stiff wrists. I had never been to the East but I found it just as easy and quite as quick to walk this way. I never made a mistake and I had to take positions which were extremely difficult for a Westerner to take."

From then on each morning Olive Pixley was taken through a different ceremony while in the afternoon she and Madame Raoul-Duval recorded in freehand design the structure of the movements. This experience lasted for six weeks after which they returned to Paris where they were guided to read Budge's *"Book of the Dead"*, wherein they found they had gone through the Ceremony of the Opening of the Mouth.

Olive Pixley returned to England,

bringing with her an amazing collection of drawings and hieroglyphics, hoping to find someone who could tell her what strange language she had been transmitting. There then followed another stage during the following year, of being taken through other rituals of ancient mystery schools, beginning with the Hermetic mysteries. Olive, again working with Madame Raoul-Duval, was guided to model forms and animals in plasticine and wax, which were used in ceremonies; as well as undertaking other interesting and detailed work.

Having been taken through the ancient ceremonies of the worship of the Light, Olive Pixley then firmly believed the climax of her work commenced in 1932 when she began to follow instructions for the development of individual consciousness, and was made aware of what she could only call "The Christian Initiation."

In her own words Olive Pixley said:-

"I realised that Christ was Conscious Man: that He knew scientifically how to apply the laws of this world to the service of mankind. His miracles were not haphazard evidences of a sporadic power, but a scientific application of His knowledge. He knew what He was doing. I was convinced that understanding and controlling the elements, walking on water,

9

disappearing into space, transmuting His physical atoms in three days, were examples - not of His Divinity - but of His perfect manhood: the highest expression of life in matter that the world had ever seen. It is the perfect equilibrium of earth (magical) and spiritual forces.

"I was made to understand, without a fragment of doubt in my own mind, that to reach the ultimate understanding and fulfilment of life, one must follow the Christ line of teaching. The old philosophers will take one far ...., but the Christ has the spiral - height, depth and inter-penetration; that was the Truth I had to apprehend before I was ready for further instruction."

Olive Pixley did in fact receive a great deal of further instruction and revelations in Light, the first of which are now recorded here in this book, The Armour of Light - Part I, as a series of exercises. These are the exercises and talks Olive Pixley began to teach to groups of people, small classes and also by correspondence course with any person who sought the Light of Christ.

The process of training and development was firmly established and continued to grow. Olive Pixley's depth of understanding of where this extraordinary experience was leading her was then consolidated in her third narrative, a book called, *"Human Document"*.

"Human Document"

This book was written several years after Olive Pixley began teaching the Armour of Light and can only be described as her most comprehensive understanding of this training she describes as the Christian Initiation. Any attempt to precis it would not do any justice to the depth to which Olive was able to understand and express the mission and the achievements of Christ. It is a profoundly enlightened book which brings a new perspective and revelation to Christ's life and resurrection, and is an inspiration for all who seek oneness with God.

The reader may be interested to know that all three books - *"Listening In"*, *"The Trail"* and *"Human Document"* are now published as one volume, as *"Olive Pixley's Spiritual Journey"*.

"The Armour of Light"

From the 1930's until her death in 1958, Olive Pixley conducted tuition on the exercises she received through conscious revelation. While the exercises remained consistently the same, the talks she gave on each one were sometimes different, often giving complementary information.

In this latest revised edition of The Armour of Light - Part I, the manual has been divided into two parts. The first part - Volume I - explains each exercise with a talk; while in the second part - Volume II - a compilation of additional talks to each exercise has now been added for the first time. This has been done for the sake of the reader who may find these additional talks give a greater depth of understanding and insight into their daily practise of the exercises.

Today, a small number of groups of people continue to meet, but often this Technique is usually practised on an individual basis. By practising the exercises one comes gradually to live consciously in Light. Consciousness is not in this sense, a state of mind, but a state of *being*. It is achieved not just by thinking good thoughts or even doing good deeds, but by linking up with the Source of Light; an accurate process of visualisation of Light whereby we are to completely recharge our light, or soul, body so that it is revitalised and shines through the physical body.

This important process makes us into channels for the Light, so that the Light may radiate through us doing the work that is required, whether it be healing work, helping through sound or music, saying the right thing in counselling, listening to others, or earthing the Light where ever we are. Above all, this Light will work in us, showing us up to ourselves, helping us to follow that rather uncomfortable injunction "know thyself", and it will very gradually transmute the particles of the physical body.

Starting in a very small way, a step at a time, and as with all true growth, the results may well be almost imperceptible — it is not a spectacular way of working, but it *does* work! After practising, after visualising, after deliberately tuning your mind and inner vision to the Light for some time, you will come to realise that you are in Light, as you are in the air of this world. Light is the condition and substance which you *become*, and which you live in, and you now cannot imagine living without.

Revised Edition, Easter 1999

METHOD OF PROCEDURE

♦ The *sequence* of the exercises, as listed in the Order of Learning the Exercises - *must* be followed.

♦ From the beginning, undertake *only one exercise at a time* and work on it for at least a *minimum* (longer if you wish) of a fortnight, before undertaking the next exercise. This is to ensure a thorough conscious integration has taken place. Once each exercise has been learned and absorbed, it should continue to be practised along with the new one, so that by the end of the manual, *all* the exercises are practised daily - morning, midday and night.

♦ It needs to be understood that sensational psychic happenings are not to be expected or encouraged.

♦ This conscious technique of visualisation of Light *works* at the speed of light, and can therefore be performed quickly, anywhere. All light, both materially visible and spiritual light, functions in a scientifically measurable manner.

♦ The visualisation process brings the functioning of the spiritual light into manifestation, and so accuracy in the performance of the exercises is as important as if one were working with electricity or lazer beams.

♦ The Armour of Light, Part I, must be practised and fully absorbed before embarking on Part II, which is a more advanced stage of the Technique.

ORDER FOR LEARNING

The correct order for learning the complete set of exercises is as fo

1. Ritual of Light
2. Conscious Breathing
3. Ah Meh — A E Ooo
4. Shafts of Light
5. Spirals and Circles
6. The Needs
7. E.O. Lihum
8. Transmuting Light
9. The Name
10. The Rhythm over the Head
11. Soul Body
12. Ah-Lah-Hième
13. The Throat
14. Equilibrium of the Name
15. The Infinite Eight
16. Sah-Veh
17. Rhythm of the Name
18. Hi-You-Meh
19. Cross of Breath
20. Ah-Mou

THE DAILY ROUTINE
The Daily Routine should be as follows:-

MORNING	MIDDAY	EVENING
Ritual of Light	Transmuting Light	Spirals and Circles
Conscious Breath	The Throat	Ah-Lah-Hième
Ah Meh — A E Ooo	Equilibrium of the	Sah-Veh
Shafts of Light	Name	
The Needs	The Infinite Eight	
E.O. Lihum	Rhythm of the Name	
The Name	Hi-You-Meh	
Rhythm over the Head	Cross of Breath	
Ah-Mou		

NOTE: Revision on the Spelling of Sounds
Over the course of the years and after several reprints of The Armour of Light a number of variations on the spelling of the sounds associated with the exercises, as revealed to Olive Pixley, have evolved. In this revised edition, it was decided to revert to all the original spelling as was initially recorded. Readers may find the following words appearing in previous editions:-
Ah-Mer: Ahlah-Heay-Ve: Sah-Vay: Hi-You-Mer: Ah-Moo.
The reader is encouraged to pronounce the words as instructed in this manual.

INTRODUCTION

"My thoughts are not your thoughts, neither are my ways your ways," saith the Lord. That truth, revealed through the mind of Isaiah, was also my experience. One cannot have any idea of His thoughts and ways since they are not ours, unless He reveals them to us. The Armour of Light was shown me as a way of life which would train my mind to receive His thought, and this training proved a Light unto my path; a path on which the Light was revealed just one step at a time.

In 1917 a greatly loved brother went on ahead, and started a personal wavelength of communication between his world and mine, through his heart into my heart. That experience you will find in detail in a little book, *"Listening In"*, which I wrote ten years later. In 1924 the impersonal work started. My receptivity had developed, and I was able to receive in conscious vision the rituals of the ancient worship of the true Light. That meant going through the experiences of both priest and neophyte of the Egyptian, Hermetic, and Mithraic initiations. Several lectures that I gave of my conscious experiences are incorporated in *"The Trail"*. Finally I was started on the Christian Initiation.

It is difficult to remember now those early stepping stones of revelation, when the action of the cosmic rays on matter was made clear to me. I knew then why it had taken Jesus thirty years to perfect His humanity. Step by step I was made aware of the power of blood. I was shown how humanity had polluted its bloodstream by fear, greed, cruelty and worry, and that it could be regenerated only if some great entity, who had never fallen at the Adamic crisis, would voluntarily take on that contaminated condition and by utter selflessness, fearlessness and love, purify it. This Jesus did, and His purified blood has become available for the whole world to contact.

We know in our day, as Jesus knew in His lifetime, the power of propaganda, and how the enemies of freedom and progress make use of it with all the force of fear behind it. How, after His death, could twelve faithful men stem it? They needed reinforcement, and got in the person of St. Paul.

To change the focus of the mind is the most difficult part of this training, and so the *volte face* of Paul of Tarsus concerns us closely. His academic mind could not accept revelation. He had resisted and reacted strongly against the unorthodox teaching and behaviour of Jesus the Nazarene. He approved of the crucifixion, and did his best to prevent the news of the resurrection from being spread or believed. Then out of the blue came a Voice, on a sound wavelength from the Source to the personal receiving instrument. It was such a shock to Paul's orthodox system that he lost consciousness, but his wonderful moral courage after this experience, in making a public avowal of it, gives every academic and scientific mind the knowledge that the capacity for such revelation is universal.

It was a shock to me to find out that what I had fondly hoped was an enthralling personal experience was to be shared publicly or privately with anybody wishing to receive it. This health-receiving Technique in Light can be universal and is in line with the scientific discoveries of our day. We take the telephone, radio, and television instruments for granted. We turn knobs, and voices speak; other knobs, and faces and figures appear. The prophets of the Old Testament were connected with cosmic sound wavelengths. St. Paul is important only as a disbeliever, and yet, because of his capacity, he was called and chosen.

Christ calls and needs us, for He cannot work without us. Some of us respond; some of us do not. He cannot force us.

I found that out quite early in my training. When it was personal and private, I was thrilled with my secret experiences, but when later on I was shown that I must share and pass on to all who asked, then indeed I realised that my way was not His way. When the disciples found His command that they should eat His flesh and drink His blood, a saying that confounded them, many of them felt that they could follow Him no further, and went off. Christ did not attempt to persuade them to stay, but they also found they could not endure to stay away, and returned to experience the reality of His teaching. So in the same way, when I wanted to turn aside and follow the normal social routine of a young woman's life, I found I could not break away from the Technique, and started to share it. As soon as I made that sharing the most important factor in my life, other activities fell into their right place. He has never asked me to give up anything. What He needs of all of us is that we should be normal, practical people, efficient in both worlds, enjoying both worlds, but being self-indulgent in neither.

Self-indulgence and self-pity are corroding conditions, and insulate one's receptivity. One must never be a "duty martyr", making the recipient of a service conscious of the effort. Love is serving of need. When these daily lessons in Light become part of our physical substance, we shall find we can discern between need and demand. When it is a need, our heart will satisfy it; when merely a demand, our minds can receive the inspiration to refuse without hurt. That is why I must keep on asserting that the Technique must be thought and felt with the speed of light, must be done every day, and cannot be discussed or debated. It must be lived, and can only be lived by daily experience. The sun and the stars have their daily and nightly visibility whether we see them or not. They shine because of their radiant nature. Whether you ever actually see the Light that you will draw daily into your flesh and blood is immaterial. When you think of it, it is there, whether you register it consciously or not, and you are bound to feel different.

Feeling and seeing in Light seem often identical. The feeling is so vivid, it corresponds to sight. It is not a comparative condition. Never compare your experiences with those of another person, for we all react individually to the Technique. Some exercises seem easier than others, and one is apt to do the ones one likes, and ignore the others. Please do not do this, for the Technique is a very exact formula for the freeing of every part of our mind and body from conscious and unconscious fear and egotism. By leaving out the lessons that do not appeal to you, you will find yourself wondering later on why others can heal and you cannot, although you may have done them (the ones you liked!) as long in time as they have.

Do not think that just by reading you will become a channel. Think of your blood like the oil in a lamp, and set it alight every day. Do not merely read the instructions but, as it were, strike the match. Remember the poor foolish virgins. They left it too late. It never entered their superficial minds that they must light them every day in case He came that day. How do we know which day the light in the temple of our bodies will be checked? We cannot be too young, and we cannot be too old to start our daily lessons in Light. One thought, one breath, one flash, and the contact is made.

We must teach the young that they have television sets in their heads, and that God has a daily programme to show them. The old must know that radio wavelengths were discovered by the prophets in the Old Testament, and that the greatest scientist of all ancient and modern times earthed in His physical body the first atomic generator, and made the first conscious interplanetary space journey from His airport on the Mount of Olives.

We have to bring Jesus Christ alive in our modern civilisation, because He is the same, yesterday, today and for ever. Einstein's and Marconi's knowledge, and the secrets of modern atomic power research were embodied in His flesh and blood. He could, when needed, control the elements. We must learn how to contact His all-knowledgeable mind to solve our terrible modern problems. Do not start the Technique out of mere curiosity. Christ never pandered to intellectual curiosity. Becoming a channel is a living experience and satisfies the heart.

Do not be greedy and read all the lessons and talks, and then put the book aside without beginning to practise them. I was given these lessons one at a time, and there was a long interval before I received the next. I had to become familiar with the shape, substance and functioning power of each lesson in Light, and feel a reaction in my body before I received a further lesson. It is because we must not make it just a mental exercise that I stress the need of at least a fortnight's interval between one exercise and another. Do not even read a new one until you have thoroughly absorbed the old. As you progress, retain the same sequence, but speed them up as much as you can. The more lessons you learn, the less time I hope it will take you to do them.

Although I may never meet you personally, do realise that by putting on your inside armour of Light every day you become a child of Light. We all become one family, and will always recognise each other in this world and the next, because it is true what Christ said:

"Let your light shine that men may see your works, and glorify your Father which is in heaven."

Men saw His works, and they recognised His channelhood.

"If", He said, "ye had known me, ye would have known my Father also - for I and my Father are one."

There is our model of perfect channelhood. But listen!

"Greater works than these shall ye do," He said, knowing the capacity of humanity and hoping — still hoping.....

FOUNDATIONS OF THE TECHNIQUE IN LIGHT

In order to get the maximum benefit from the Technique in Light, it is necessary to be very clear about its foundations. Those who practise it need a brief preface describing its purpose and methods, and the results to be expected from its use. Certain ideas underlie every one of the exercises, and though they are not specifically stated in each one, they should be in the background of consciousness all the time.

The general purpose of the Technique is the complete reconstruction of the self, including the actual substance of the physical body. The self, when transformed, becomes a channel for the transmission of new life to all other living creatures, and of new radiations to the very earth itself. Though we speak of it as new, it is actually a return to the state enjoyed by humanity before the Fall. At the Fall man chose to cut his direct link with divine energy, and so to corrupt his own substance, and upset the entire equilibrium of the earth planet. The essence of the redemption which Jesus Christ accomplished for us was the restoration of this link, and His teaching, when fully manifested on this earth, will give us back all the powers we originally had. The Technique is a means of bringing about in Christians this complete manifestation, which has never been demonstrated in full since the days of the early Church. It never can be demonstrated unless, and until, a group of ordinary people like ourselves will make its demonstration their conscious aim. That is what we are doing.

The method of acquiring this new experience is to draw from God, its source, through Christ its only mediator, a new quality of life energy, and each exercise brings some measure of this increased energy to the self. The result, at long last, is a self transmuted, freed from its fears and inhibitions, immune to disease, and able to transmit healing and freedom to those with whom it comes in contact. In the long run, this new humanity is to be delivered also from the power of death, and from all limitations of the material environment.

The activities of the Technique never come entirely from within the self, as do so many present day meditative systems. The physical body can be kept alive from moment to moment only in dependence upon factors from its outer environment, and the whole being of man, from spiritual to physical level, obeys the same law, and can live only by the repeated inbreathing of the life energy of God. Christ never said, "Within you is the power." He Himself always drew upon the Father for power to perform His works, and said very clearly that we must draw from the same source and receive our life energy through His own mediation. Thus the exercises call for a triple consciousness, and three separate yet combined factors are essential to the demonstration of new life powers.

Our first awareness must be of God the Father, the ultimate source of that pure life energy we are being trained to assimilate. This consciousness is given us in the earliest exercise as the Point of Infinite Radiance, and with this we are in explicit or implied touch throughout.

Our second contact is with the mind and person of Jesus Christ. Note that His own words on the necessity for this contact are very emphatic.

♦ "No man cometh unto the Father but by me."
♦ "He that hath the Son hath life, and he that hath not the Son hath not life."
♦ "Except ye eat the flesh and drink the blood of the Son of man ye have no life in you."

These statements puzzle many people but the facts of science show up their truth from a new angle; for it is literally and scientifically true that man, in his present diseased state, could not survive a contact with the naked life essences of God, they would shatter his being. Even the impact of gamma rays is fatal to the human organism; how then could it endure the far more powerful radiations of pure divine force?

It was man's inability to reach up to the powers of the Father that brought the Son of God to this world to make for us a bridge out of His own divine and human substance. Within His body He stepped down the divine radiations, so that man could absorb them without injury. All the exercises, therefore, presuppose the mediation of Christ as the transformer of divine into human energies and powers. In order to accomplish this, and make a safe human-divine radiation always available to us, Christ brought it down literally to earth level. He poured out His blood, wherein it was stored, actually on to the earth's surface when He was crucified, and from that hour to this, the radiations have vibrated here among us and may be picked up today by those who know. This supreme fact is the very starting point of the Technique. The abiding consciousness we are to develop is of a Figure of Light at our feet. We summon the Christ vibration to us at the literal

lowest part of our physical experience, and are remade by it from the feet up. This truth is woven into every part of the training, and the awareness of Christ at earth level, as well as in the transcendental rays which we learn to absorb, keeps us from slipping away into fantastic worlds which have no connection with real life.

The third level of consciousness concerns ourselves. We are the instruments by which this supreme and superb life energy is to be earthed, and transmitted. We are the receptive end of the process, and our function is to receive and transmit the radiant life of God in each sparking moment of which life is composed. By so doing we form within ourselves a new and glorified substance, and in transmitting it we help greatly to uplift and redeem humanity and the world.

The more thoroughly this threefold consciousness is ingrained in those who practise the Technique, the quicker will be the results of the exercises. Notice that each aspect is definitely established in the primary Ritual of Light, before any exercise is given. There is the actual self upon the bed, the contact with the Christ radiation at the feet, and with God the Father in the Point of Infinite Radiance above. This ritual is implicit in all that follows.

Consider next in this training the

function of the mind. Since we are to be receptive to forces outside ourselves our mind will not engage in positive thought. It has, however, to bring these forces into the focus of our consciousness. This is done by visualisation. The mind creates the picture of the forces involved, and watches them at work. The forces are, of course, beyond the range of the normal sense organs, but are none the less completely real. They are invisible ranges of energy akin to light.

The first and basic material which has to be visualised is breath. Breath is not in itself a force, but it is the carrier of both sound and light forces. Within the range of our senses sound must travel upon air, and life energy appears to follow the same principle. The same law holds for transcendental force as it functions on this plane; it must be carried on air or breath. Hence the Technique starts off with visualised Conscious Breathing, thus creating the track between God the Father, Christ the mediator, and the human being who is to receive transcendental life. In the same way each exercise is done on the rhythm of an inbreath and outbreath, and so the medium for light or sound, or for both together, is created.

All exercises consist of the

visualisation of light. It is important to understand that this light is an actual force, and not a symbol. As there are, in the world of matter, many varieties of substance with different uses, so in the world of Light there are many qualities and kinds of light substances, each performing a different function, each, doubtless, of a different wavelength. There is light which cuts away, light which suffuses, light which absorbs impurities, light which quickens the vital functions. Each is a reality, and plays a part in regenerating our actual substance. There is also a connection between light energy and blood. It is very probable that the life energy in the blood, whose precise nature is still unknown to science, is a high-powered ray energy similar to light vibrations. When Christ spoke of the life-giving power of His blood and the need for us to absorb it, He spoke therefore, of this transcendental light which is the life essence of all blood, and in His case was absolutely perfect. This is the perfect energy mediated to us in the Technique. It is an extension in modern terms of the sacramental system on which the Christian Church is founded, and adds much to our understanding of what the central doctrine of the Eucharist means.

Some of the exercises are accompanied by a sound vibration, but many are not. The significance of those sounds has not been made clear, but each is possibly the sound vibration which corresponds to the quality of the light visualised, and perhaps intensifies its effects, as sound and light are correlated in colour music on our ordinary sense plane. Some of the exercises are done to the Name of the Father, and some to the Name of Christ. The full extent of the power of sound waves in the regeneration of the human instrument has yet to be revealed.

It is important that all the exercises should be done in a state of complete relaxation, both physical and mental. While it is good to get as vivid a visualisation of each one as possible, worry and effort should be eliminated. It is better to work with serenity than to strain after visual effects if they are not easily produced. The effects are there, whether they can be clearly pictured or not, and will do the work required. The more quickly an exercise can be flashed through the closer it approaches to reality, since the speed of light and similar vibrations is some 186 thousand miles per second. These activities are self-adjusting and in no way dangerous. The body is so constituted that it absorbs only as much of this high-powered energy as it can safely take: it becomes progressively able to take more. The process is completely voluntary in all its stages. There should be no feeling of compulsion about it. It is offered to each individual as a regenerative gift from God, but is in no way thrust upon him. It is not meant to intensify effort and suffering, but to eliminate it, and in practice it is found that reluctance and resistance, fear and inhibition fall gently and imperceptibly away as the course proceeds.

Finally the exercises should be done daily, thus conforming to the 24 hour rhythm which governs this planet, and applies to spiritual as well as physical growth. The complete self must be built up and kept nourished every day by regular absorption of transcendental life. Results may be neither speedy nor obvious, and will vary in every case, so that nobody need compare himself with others. Perseverance and patience are bound in the long run to bring results to all, since the factors at work, though invisible, are not imaginary, but very real substances governed by certain and immutable laws.

It should be clearly understood that the Technique brings no alien teaching into Christianity, nor does it presume to change or add to those doctrines which the Church has taught throughout its history. It does point out however, that what we now know about light, sound and other radiant forces is in effect a burst of new revelation on old doctrinal teaching. Nineteen hundred years ago, Christ spoke to people who were utterly without scientific background, and only a fraction of His vast message could then be revealed.

Only in this century and for this generation does its scientific content start dimly to dawn. It is not strange therefore, that there should also open up a new technique whereby the newly understood teachings may be more quickly built into the self, and radiated to the world . This however, is the only sense in which the Technique is new. Its foundations are firmly rooted in the Bible. Each fresh revelation opens up ever wider horizons, but the road it travels comes direct from the eternal truths of the Old and New Testaments.

RITUAL OF LIGHT

The development of spiritual consciousness is a process similar to that of physical growth, and is brought about by the training in, and practical application of, the Technique in Light. Its purpose is to expand the capacity of our minds so that they will become able to register instantaneous contact with the Divine Light.

If we want electricity in our house, we have first to get it wired. The Technique corresponds in the body to the wiring process in the house, and enables the body to receive in a flash the divine spark of eternal life energy.

When you wake in the morning, lie relaxed in every joint, especially in the head, and with the palms of the hands facing upwards. Then think a radiant Figure of Light at your feet, with the soles of your feet touching the soles of this figure. This contact with the feet is the necessary earth for divine power to spark through the body. Once you have earthed your Figure of Light, it is there as a light to your path for the rest of the day.

The next second, send your vision soaring upwards until you see above you an Infinite Point of Radiance, which is God. That point is the station from which inspiration and revelation can be flashed into your mind throughout the day, whenever you choose to re-focus your mind upon it.

Having now your earth and your mental focusing point, instantaneously think a flashing circle from the right of your head, round the head of the Figure of Light and back to your own head, thus completing the circle. The radiant image of Christ sanctifies your feet for the day's activity, and your mind is made capable of receiving inspiration. Whether it does so or not depends on you.

This ritual must be a daily renewal of strength, or daily bread of life. Do not let the mind wander, or dwell lingeringly; let it flash, and then finish. This trains our minds to spark, for one cannot meditate on, or contemplate, a flash of lightning.

One must not linger on any part of the Technique in Light: it is a quickening process in every sense of the word, and should be done so quickly that even the busiest people can spare a flashing moment every morning for the reception of their daily bread.

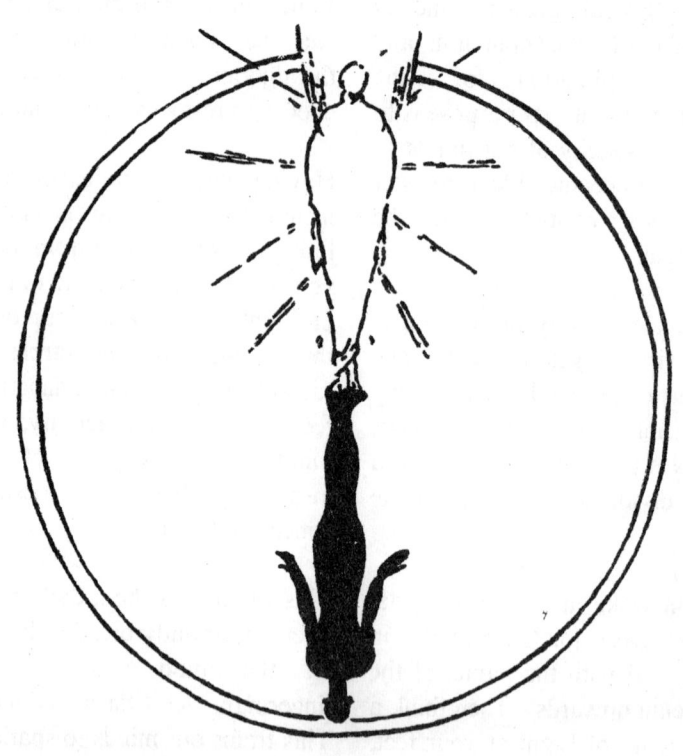

CONSCIOUS BREATHING

Our first understanding of the Christian Initiation comes from our Conscious Breath. Physical breathing, which is the rhythm of our physical life, is largely unconscious; but Conscious Breathing, which will bring into being the rhythm of our eternal life energy, must definitely be visualised, and can never be an automatic or unconscious condition.

In this, and every one of the exercises to follow, remember that when you visualise breath and light you are actually creating them in invisible substance, though they will not become visible to your ordinary sight. You have just carried out the Ritual of Light, so that having visualised your circle and Figure of Light and your Infinite Point of Radiance, they are really there. Continue to lie completely relaxed, the palms of the hands still up, the feet resting against the Figure of Light, and see your Infinite Point of Radiance above you. Then inhale an ordinary physical breath, and at the same time visualise breath going down outside the body from the solar plexus to the feet. Exhale, and visualise breath going straight from the solar plexus to the Infinite Point above you. This completes the process of Conscious Breathing.

Take six Conscious Breaths in this manner every morning, immediately after performing the Ritual of Light. You may do more if you feel that you need them, but do not linger over them and get involved in thought. Let your physical breathing be perfectly normal, and try to do it as rhythmically as possible. The breath which you visualise looks just like ordinary breath, as you see it on a cold morning.

Do not think yourself into any unreal or mystical surrounds, but see yourself lying in bed as you really are. The Christian Initiate must be more sane, more balanced, more real than the average man. He has to attain a plus condition of power and consciousness in the very midst of his ordinary surroundings. Do not, therefore, look for mysterious results or psychic sensations. The results will appear in due course, in the day by day experiences which are provided by our circumstances. They will vary with each person, but will bring to each a knowledge of himself as he really is, and an awareness of his divine capacities. Do not expect the results to be repetitive. The life of the Initiate does not go round in a circle, but in an upward spiral of progressive experience.

This exercise should be done in the morning as a regular routine, but need not be limited to that time of day. Any time during the day when you are worried, uncertain, annoyed, whether you are sitting, standing, or moving, take a few Conscious Breaths, and you will find your equilibrium returning.

You cannot think of anything else when you are visualising the fusing of your breath with the Divine, and you can thus transcend, at least for one brief moment, the pressure of material care. Use it at night also if you are sleepless, and it will help you to sleep without worry or fear.

TALK
The Ritual of Light and Conscious Breathing

You may wonder if it is really necessary to have a new interpretation of the work and teaching of Jesus Christ, but in these days of world chaos, it is of great importance that we should understand it in relation to the capacity of the individual to embody in himself an entirely new quality of life. Christ came for the express purpose of giving this new demonstration of how to live. He did not come to give a mere teaching, but an understanding to human beings of their individual divine capacity, and He came to make that demonstration a universal one, and to tell the world that what He did, was possible for everybody to do.

There are many types of Christians, but none of us really know how to live for a single day as Christ lived, nor can we manifest His powers. The imitation of Christ in paths of self-denial is fairly easy, but few of us have the remotest understanding of what He did in taking on human nature at its lowest condition. Fix your mind, not on doctrine but on what He actually did two thousand years ago, and understand that it is possible for a Christian to do similar works in this twentieth century. It is no good trying to follow in Christ's footsteps unless you understand what He really achieved. We have studied minutely the patterns of His teaching, but the mind has run far ahead of any human performance of His works.

We have today, from the human scientific mind, the formula for splitting the atom, and thereby releasing such destructive energy that the world itself may be destroyed. Two thousand years ago there was a scientist who gave the formula, not for destruction, but for the creation of a new body by the integration of the atom in human flesh and blood.

Christ made His own body into a perfect channel for life energy to be transmitted through the substance of His blood into the bodies of those who were diseased. What they were suffering from was immaterial, for it does not matter to perfect energy what the minus condition of a patient is. The split atom must destroy, but the whole atom must create. Jesus earthed the power to create perfect matter and perfect flesh and blood.

We know enough of science today to realise that one must have the reconciliation of opposite conditions, positive and receptive, to produce perfect results. If you have not got an earth you will not get perfect transmission. We have not had an "earth" for all these two thousand years. We have had a pattern of good life in the head, but we have not had the feet earthed as Christ earthed them for perfect transmission of atomic energy in safety.

The Technique in Light is the Christian Initiation, and it is for the purpose of earthing in the ordinary individual the capacity to receive perfect creative energy into the physical body, and to transmit it unconsciously, not as an induced condition or as a virtue, but as the natural operation of a law. It is the law of being a channel for divine energy. Jesus claimed no inherent power, but said always, "I of myself can do nothing. It is my Father that doeth the works." That is the key to the matter. We can do nothing of ourselves, but everything can be done through us, and if we know this, we have the answer to every world problem.

We have to be willing, as Christ was, to go through ordinary human experience. For thirty-three years He was trained in human emotional reactions, until the supreme crisis was upon Him, and the hostility of His whole world was directed against Him and the Jews demanded His life. They understood only the letter of the law, but He was the living manifestation of truth, and because it threatened their system they wanted Him put to death. Christ put up no self-defence, and met this treatment with no personal reaction, and it was because there was no hatred generated in Him by His human persecutors that the marvellous reconstruction of His humanity could take place. No human individual would have been without resentment in His circumstances, but to harbour resentment means that we injure our receptivity to divine wavelengths, and a destructive condition is set up when the ego offers resistance.

You may say that such a selfless reaction is impossible since we are all human, but it is indeed possible for us to become divine in this way. It cannot however, be done by the exercise of personal effort, but only through our receptivity. We must understand how Christ earthed His divinity in His human body. He received His power from the Father and did not induce it Himself. He received it through the continual focus of His mind on the mind of God. Where your mind is focused there you yourself are identified. If you are afraid, you identify your mind with fear and have the physical manifestation of fear, because your mind is focused on it. If you fall in love, your mind is focused on love, and you expand and radiate and feel everything is worthwhile. So we can begin to understand that a wrong mental focus is the cause of our diseases, frustrations and inhibitions, and even of that supreme condition to which man is subject, the condition of death.

Jesus never imposed death, but incarnated to identify Himself on our behalf with life, for God is life. His death showed the world precisely what death is - the separation of the mind's focus from God. Because Christ died voluntarily, and not in expiation of any personal sin, He was able to reconstruct the atoms of His body, and take it back from this earth to its Creator.

Will you identify God with matter in its visible condition, and not just invisible spirit? The moment we separate ourselves into soul and body, matter and spirit, we are dual personalities. The Christian Initiation is the integration of soul and body into a unit. At present your soul presents itself to the world through your physical body; but presently you will leave the physical part behind and go on into an invisible state. But this separation should not take place, for Christ came to redeem soul and body into one integrated manifestation on the physical plane. This He did in His own case as an example for us to follow, and took His transformed physical self back to the Father. Far from following the pattern we have not even looked into its possibilities, but continue to despise the body and release its disease energy into the world, giving its corruption back to the earth at death. As Christians we should go through the process of reconstructing our atoms while alive, and attain here and now conditions of perfect health.

What are health, life and death? I have not worked out any theories about them, and can only share with you the things that have been revealed to me. What I know, I have received from the Source, and have shared it with anyone who cares to train as I have been trained.

I was shown a long time ago that life is fundamentally the energy of light in the blood. When the quickening of a child takes place, the Light germ is being sparked into its blood. When Light leaves the blood, death takes place. Christ came to earth eternal Light in the substance of human flesh and blood. All instruments connected with light fuse when the current is stronger than they can bear, and when we are asked to receive a voltage of energy greater than our mechanism can stand, life goes out of us, and our blood congeals. But Christ came to establish in the human substance of flesh and blood, divine Light energy of eternal quality.

This earthing was not a mental process. The mental wavelength is generated in the brain and radiates at brain level, but the divine energy comes down from above and forms the perfect light cross. For the cross is formed and earthed by the two processes of receptivity and transmission. The divine wavelength comes direct from God to its human receiving instrument, and only those who believe in Him can receive it. From the Fall, through history, men and women have chosen to insulate themselves in greater or lesser measure from this wavelength, but actually the body as originally constructed, was the most perfect instrument ever made for contact with God, and intercommunication from one world to another.

Blood contacts disease, and our blood we cannot keep to ourselves. Anyone who is in touch with our blood radiation must receive its condition. We have no power over it. This Jesus knew, and He knew that if only one human being could live a life of utter selflessness and of focus on the Father, His blood substance would be changed, and the radiation from this one human body could change the capacity for receptivity of the whole human race. His object in incarnating was to restore to perfection human receptivity by first receiving into His own body a perfect radiation of eternal light energy, and transmitting it, without resistance from the human mental wavelength. If He had doubted His Father's capacity to transmit perfectly through Him, He would have failed; for the moment one doubts, one acts according to the doubt, but the moment one really knows, one is an expert, and acts according to one's certainty. Jesus functioned according to His perfect certainty; we function according to the measure of ours. If we can focus our mind on the Christ, instead of relying on ourselves, we must and shall receive His blood radiation.

Why do you think it was necessary for the disciples that Jesus should leave them? He knew that the longer He remained on earth, the less would they develop their own capacity for receptivity and for demonstrating miraculous works, and He left them in order to establish a line of communication so that He could broadcast into the receptive instruments of all His followers.

The receptive instrument of the human body is the brain, and the pineal gland is the television set. Here Jesus received His patterns of action straight from the Father, and the moment He had identified the law or pattern He was enabled to make the substance necessary to its fulfilment. He was the perfect manifestation of God's mind, and if we can become the perfect manifestation of the mind of Christ, we must again have perfect flesh and blood.

In this generation, because of all the discoveries of the scientists, it is easy to identify eternal energy with the light in the blood. When this first came through I thought that nobody would believe it, but I need not have worried. I went to a lecture and was told the story of a New York surgeon who performed a wonderful brain operation, and in so doing exposed the tip of the pineal gland and there saw a spot of phosphorescent light. He was so startled that he went to the mortuary and did the same operation on a dead man, and there was no light. So what I had been taught was confirmed from a most unexpected source.

This Technique is a very exact knowledge, and each of us must go through some experience by which we know its truth for ourself. Often, I know that what I have received is true because it has been confirmed by the experience of others, as in the case of this brain operation.

Jesus knew that blood which could receive His own condition of light would be able to transmute the disease energy of the body. He was always transmitting the radiation of His life blood, not with any idea of sacrifice, but because He could not keep it to Himself any more than you or I can. What one receives, one unconsciously gives out. We are ashamed when we pass on an infectious disease, but if we change the receptive condition of our blood, we shall no longer radiate disease energy. We shall pass on the perfection which we receive from the exponent of perfect flesh and blood. People do not really understand that Jesus had first-class blood to transmit, and that His blood radiation was a certain cure for all morbid conditions, because it was pure energy and had in it no destructive element of personal emotion. I want you to start on this path of identifying yourself with the perfect blood radiation of Christ. It is not a virtue to do so, but an urgent necessity for the regeneration of the world.

Will you realise that you can train your mind to focus on Light and to spark out Light with no effort? The Technique will train you to keep this focus, and it starts by giving you the Infinite Point of Radiance and the Figure of Light at your feet.

The feet are a most important part of the body because they are your earth. If you get the illumination of your mind without the feet earthing the light, you will get a mental mystical condition, but it will not change the physical state. If Jesus had had only the pattern He could not have healed every form of illness. Do you remember how much He stressed the feet? He did not say, "Understand my mind," but "Follow in my footsteps". Pilate said, "What is truth?" but Jesus could not give a verbal explanation of it. It is a matter of being, and cannot be expounded in words. Truth is a radiation, and we have to learn how to become the very essence both of truth and life.

The first thing we have to learn to do is to relax in head and body. The moment your head says "I cannot," your physical body cannot, and that is why the world is as it is, but you can relax if you assert that you can. Every morning be very real, and do not let your mind wander away from your actual self. To know the law of life, and to become the law, you must know yourself as you really are. When you wake, lie relaxed in your bed and focus your mind on your Figure of Light. It is your guide, and if you watch it, it will teach you. Then think of the Infinite Point of Radiance. Do not meditate, but visualise it in a sparking moment. If you train your mind to spark, your whole body will spark, and when you think light in a flash, it is there.

Breath is very important; it is the track down which physical life and light sparks, and when we cease to breathe, we die. The process of physical breath is automatic, and almost unconscious, but in the Technique in Light we must consciously visualise the breath tracks along which eternal life energy will spark to us. The tracks are outside us, and do not in any way change or interfere with our normal breathing. The reconstruction of the body must be done in harmony with the body as it actually is. Starting from this, we have to make it "like unto His glorious body". There is no strain in thinking breath down. The life force is pouring down into the world, but unless you identify yourself with it, as Christ did, you will not get it. You will get it only by receiving.

"Ye have not, because ye ask not." We have to understand that the technique of asking is to open up our receptivity. He came that we might have life, and have it more abundantly. It is all there for us to receive, but at present we have only the barest minimum.

If you are worrying, take a Conscious Breath and focus your mind on the Point of Radiance, and you will feel calm.

This process is the beginning of our capacity to have truth revealed to us, and to become a channel for its transmission. The ultimate end of it is to become a perfect channel for eternal life and truth as Christ was.

AH MEH — A E OOO

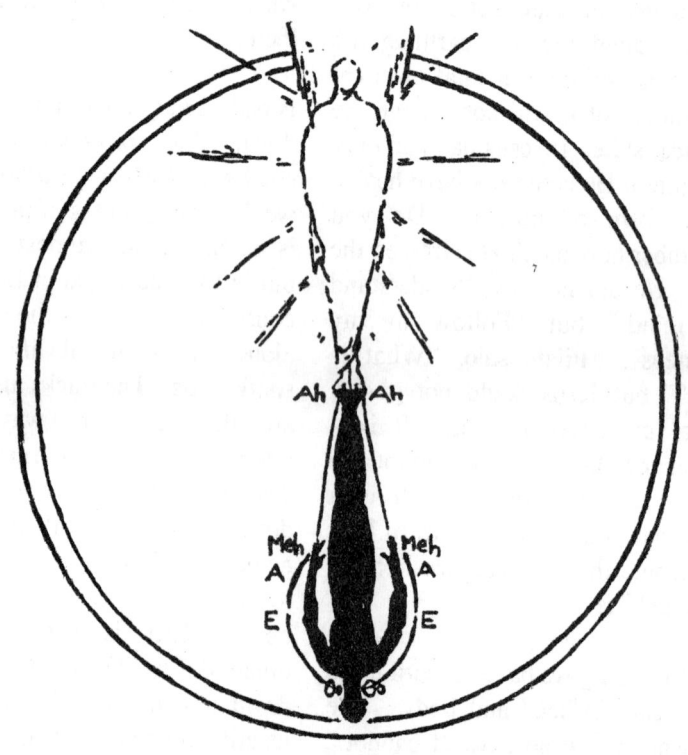

AH MEH — A E OOO

Now comes the first preparation of our bodies to receive in full consciousness the creative force of God.

Look well at the illustration, and you will see that this exercise will bring the light from the feet of the Figure of Light, through the insteps, in a straight line to your hands. The Figure of Light is already there, for you have just visualised it, and made a contact with it and the Infinite Point of Radiance through your conscious breathing.

Now turn your hands, palms down, with elbows slightly bent outwards, and continue to be completely relaxed. On an ordinary inhaling breath, breathe the sound **Ah**, and on that sound visualise yourself drawing from the feet of the Figure of Light, through your own insteps and up to each of your hands, a ribbon of vivid white light. Keep the light in your hands while you breathe out gently on the sound **Meh**. Draw up on **Ah**, retain the light on **Meh**. Do this three times in succession. On the third **Ah**, the light is fully in your hands, and the third **Meh** retains it there finally.

Now draw the light from hands to elbows on the sound **A**; and from elbows to throat on the sound **E**. This is done on one inhaling breath, as quickly or as slowly as you please. From the throat, on the sound **Oooo**, and as long an outbreath as you can, send the light up to your Infinite Point of Radiance. Do this also three times. As it reaches the Infinite Point realise that it fuses instantaneously with the divine Light.

It is the beginning of that oneness in Light of which the Christ spoke when He said, "I and my Father are one". It is the first conscious offering of our spirits, and the first step towards the understanding of, and co-operation with the divine force we call prayer.

Pronounciation

Meh	as in French "d**e**"
A	as in "d**ay**"
E	as in "m**e**"
Ooo	as in "z**oo**"

TALK
Ah Meh — A E Ooo

We have to learn from the beginning to get a condition of reality into our vision; the pattern of what is needed for the reconstruction of the physical body comes onto our television set.

I hope I made it clear last time that this is the Christian Initiation in which we are initiated into the experiences of Christ. He, as an individual, earthed a law, the freedom of the physical body to receive and transmit eternal life. He had to live to demonstrate a universal capacity, and that is the Christian Initiation.

Many minds may wonder why I stress the unique achievement of the Christ. Is it true that He did something which no incarnate soul has ever done? It is true. No master had identified physical substance with God. They had tried to take the human being away from the worldly reality into the mental and mystical realm, so there grew up in the human mind this condition of unreality of religious experience. Everything became mystical and I think that Jesus has been associated more with a mystical condition than any other great prophet. Christian mysticism is a real solace to the human mind and I think it may be very difficult to change that into a conviction, that until you deal with your physical human self, you have not touched the fringe of the real Christian teaching.

It comes down to individual capacity every time, to your hands, feet, eyes, mouth, to your heart and all the organic functions of your body that are to become free. Your soul is free, your body is bound; and whatsoever things are bound on earth are bound in heaven. Do not think that because you leave your body you are not still bound by the ignorance of your earth condition, for you have to come back again. Christ came because of that bondage, to free the world from mental ignorance, for it did not know the law. We have to become the law as He was the law. I want you to go through the experience of knowing your own freedom.

After you have relaxed in the morning and visualised your Figure of Light and Infinite Point of Radiance, and taken six Conscious Breaths, will you turn your hands down so that the magnetic points, the palms, are facing down towards reality, the earth. Your feet are touching the Figure of Light and so you have your earth in Light, and now you have to get the illumination of the hands. They come first because they are a most important part of your body in daily life. You shake hands with people and touch inanimate objects. We get a freedom of touch and the Christ's hands are our first consideration so that we destroy nothing with our hands, but create a new condition of life and happiness.

As you visualise the Figure of Light, I want you to think light up through His feet to your feet and to the palms of your hands on the sound of **Ah**, holding it there on the sound of **Meh**. It is difficult to give an accurate description of how this eternal life or light is drawn to the body. You cannot make yourself understood unless you speak words, and if you want a definite ingredient in a shop you have to ask for it. When you draw light into your body it has got to be a particular sound which separates that ingredient in light from other substances in light, because there are as many activities in light as there are in matter, and we do not use wood instead of chiffon. When you have to transmute your body you need to know the different substances in light which are going to function as you draw them into your body. The light from the insteps to the hands is drawn up on the sound **Ah**.

Then we have to get the illumination of the arms and the magnetic contact of the throat, so run the light along the arms to the throat on the sound of **A E** and on the **Oooo**, it flows back again to the source. We are earthed through the Figure of Light and connected with this life energy back to the source, and we become one in substance with the Father.

Christ knew what He was doing when He made a contact with the energy of the Father. He identified Himself with eternal life and became the transmitter of it. Whatever we identify our minds with, we become. If we identify ourselves with the worry and depression and burden of life we shall become a bore to our friends. We are then part of the universal worry; but what fun when we have the antidote. Whatever people's worry may be we can connect them up with the source, as we connect ourselves. When we are connected with the source of life, we become life and have something to give, and that is why it is so vital.

Do not think that this Christian Initiation is selfish. Christ was never selfish and it is not selfish to try to receive so that others may receive through us. What we are, we give, and if we have nothing better than ourselves, then we only give ourselves. If we have only worry to pass on, then we only give worry, and the pessimism at this moment is enough to change the weather for the next year. I am certain that the moment mental depression occurs in a person, they exteriorise that depression throughout the world. If you realise that life energy can be sparked from here to Australia in a moment, do realise the your depression is exteriorised in the same time. We are responsible for world conditions and contribute to the gloom or radiance according to our receptivity.

It is not will power; do not mistake receptivity for strength of will for that has nothing to do with it. You may hide your depression and think you do not pass it on. Possibly some people may be taken in, but no receptive person is taken in by control. They will get that depression although it is concentrated inside, and it is bound to come out through every pore, however much one may try to control it.

It may seem extraordinary not to advocate control, but what is the good of control when we can receive something better? We can receive radiance which no control of depression can give. Joy of life must be received and cannot be induced. A brave face is only a facade, so do not change your face, but change your whole condition, and then you have something wonderful to give others.

Draw in the **Ah Meh** three times and your finger tips will be sparking. The moment you draw in this condition of life you have got it and nothing can take it away, except your mind. If you say you have not got it, then you have not, but the moment you have got it, nobody can take it away except you yourself.

Run the light up your arms three times. I see a flash as if it has gone back to the source, when my breath is exhausted, and I am linked in my throat with His throat. We are linking up to perfection so that our tongue can be inspired and our throat becomes receptive to true sound; so that we shall not hear ourselves saying an untrue thing but something we did not know until that spark brought it into our understanding.

That is how I have been trained. I do not know a thing but hear myself giving it forth; and that must become universal. The moment your mind is focused on the Infinite Point of Radiance you hear yourself saying that which is right, helpful and comforting. When your mind is only focused on your own troubles and difficulties, you only give them out, but the moment your mind is focused on the Solver of all difficulties, you are free to express the truth. I should not be free to express it if I were concerned with what my own mind knows and directs me to give you, and you would find the lecture dull, with nothing in it that you did not know before.

You will find that there is nothing new which cannot come into your mind, and a new condition of understanding and capacity is essential for all of us for the development of our receptivity. We can only receive something new because He was the only person who dared to say, "Behold I make all things new." We do not understand what that means, we have no conception of anything new. We know repetition and how to make old things look new, or have an appearance of newness, but not how to make all things new. A new individual, new capacities and experiences lie ahead which are available for every person who makes a contact with their Creator.

Do realise that the only person who could demonstrate what the Creator was really like as far as human beings were concerned, was Christ. Other great initiates gave a wonderful pattern, but He gave the substance; a new blood circulation and a new capacity, new hands and feet. He was not concerned with the brain. He knew it must be our receptive instrument; but people's hands, feet and hearts were dying and decaying. Think of the people with whom He had to make a living touch, they were paralysed, leprous, distorted. There was no living radiance in the world two thousand years ago and there is very little today.

Two thousand years ago Christ gave a formula that everybody might have a new capacity for life. He said, "I come that they might have life and have it more abundantly." We must go to the source of life if we want to receive it, and the source of life is Light. He was the Light of the world, and His Father was the Light of Light. We are fools if we do not learn to receive this energy and we must learn to receive it every day anew. It is essential that we do the exercises every morning in a sparking moment. We must not think that if we do them on Monday, it will last until the following Monday, as we think our Sunday observance of Christian ritual should last for a week or a month. We do not understand what contact with Christ every morning could mean to us; strength, health and a capacity for a new experience, prosperity and being in harmony with life, peace of mind and body. Get it every day. Know that when you put your feet against the Figure of Light and make your mind, not blank, but focused on the Infinite Point of Radiance, you are linked with the Light by your mind and feet. You have your earth, and now get the freedom of your hands.

When I was passing on this Technique to my first class, one girl said that she could not get the light further than her feet, and another said that before she had said **Ah Meh**, the light was up to her hands. I tell you this because I want to prove to you that you cannot *make* light function. It is beyond our power to induce a condition of light. Follow the rules, and it functions; whether you see it or not is immaterial. Draw it on breath because breath is the track on which light functions. You have to make the track from your feet to your hands, along your arms to your throat. The light will not function without the breath of the physical body, and so when breath leaves your body, you die, and light has no power to go into your body when your lungs stop breathing. As you visualise breath outside your body you are getting a plus condition of eternal voltage.

You may say that you do not want your mind to be worried by the Technique in Light and cannot do the exercises, but if you can have enough sense to dress yourself and get your breakfast, you have enough sense to be able to visualise this eternal food for the resurrection and reconstruction of your body, by visualising light. It will take a moment, but it is the mind that resists this condition and does not want it and says you are not feeling well and must wait until tomorrow. Do you not suppose that if Christ had forgotten the Father, He could have done so for the rest of His life?

We must establish this eternal sparking

condition with love, light, harmony, peace; but if we allow our minds to dominate us and say that we cannot, we are at the mercy of the bondage we have forged for ourselves in our past lives. We are the expression of our past lives, of the formula of our mental processes. Where we have denied love in our past lives we suffer in our physical body.

We must be able to demonstrate to ourselves the reality of our capacity to love. Love is the essence of life; it is not an emotion, it is life itself and the givingness of life. Jesus was the least emotional person whom we have read about; He was here to give His life to the world. Love is one hundred per cent givingness and not the fifty-fifty which we associate with it saying, "I will love you if you love me, but not if you don't." How many of us live on that basis?

Love is spontaneous combustion of two opposite conditions; you meet your opposite condition and a spark takes place which is the recognition of harmony between two people. We have to get this recognition of ourselves with love. Once we can get love into us, the giving out of love will be an effortless condition, but first we must get our contact with Love.

Do look upon the Infinite Point of

Radiance as the essence of radiant love, and your Figure of Light as the earthing of love; your feet will make a contact with love so that your path is for ever going to be illumined in the service of love, and in that service there is no duty or effort, but a sparking and spontaneous condition of always being ready to give something greater than yourself.

We always recognise what we give when we give ourselves. When we give our time and sympathy we know it and the response to that giving is registered by the human mind and we think we get nothing back. We shall never get anything back when we give ourselves, for that is not appreciated but is thrown back on us. I can only tell you that the things I have done on my own have been taken for granted but when some-thing has come *through* me and been given, I have been thanked for it and it has taken me by surprise because I have known nothing about it.

It is such fun that when one is not concerned with oneself, one is free. Get your contact every morning because of what you will have to give to the people you love and to those you do not know and have not yet seen. I have sympathy with the disciple who said, "Silver and gold have I none, but what I have, I give." It does not matter whether we are poor, if we can give help and peace of mind and comfort, we shall be giving something not to be bought by anyone and we shall never run out of that commodity.

The moment you feel depleted, tune in and take a Conscious Breath and feel renewed at once. Make use of the Technique the moment you feel tired. Visualise the Figure of Light and take a Conscious Breath and you are then a unit of breath and you become divine; your humanity is transmuted into divine capacity. It is at your disposal at any moment of the day, but only do the **Ah Meh** exercise in the morning.

There is no power in the audible sound. Take a deep breath, but the **Ah Meh** — A E Ooo is a sound that travels through us. It can be said aloud but there is no need for this. I want you to be able to do the Technique wherever you are, without drawing attention to yourself. It takes your mind off tiresome conditions because you are opening yourself to receive the unexpected.

SHAFTS OF LIGHT

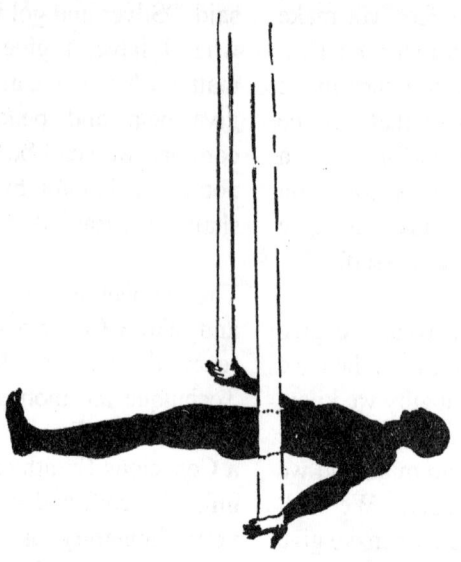

This exercise has a twofold nature. It first eliminates old and undesirable reactions, and having freed you from these, it brings to your hands a very important feeding substance in Light.

After you have drawn the light to your feet, hands, arms and throat in the **Ah Meh** exercise, keep quietly relaxed, holding the feet in the same position, but turn the hands over so that the palms lie upwards. Then as a preparation for what you will receive, eject through your head to your feet, on a short staccato sound of **Ah Oo, Ah Oo**, all the unwanted elements of your being, clearing it as a ramrod clears a gun. Do this emphatically, repeating the sound as often as you need, so that

you feel it travelling through your body and out through both feet into the Figure of Light.

Now visualise two shafts of white light, the ends standing in your hands and the points stretching up to infinity. It is, as it were, the base of a triangle that rests in your hands with the apex outside your range of vision. When you have thought these shafts of brilliant whiteness into your hands, start your Conscious Breathing, seeing your inhaling breath go to your feet, and your exhaling breath rise from your solar plexus between the shafts. As your breath ascends, the softest petals of peach-coloured light come down the shafts into the palms of your hands and are at once absorbed by them. We have to realise the different substances of those two lights; intense shining whiteness, and the softness, like a snowflake, of the peach light. The petals travel down the shafts at varying speeds, slowly with some people, quickly with others. Do not worry if you do not see them at all. Do not concentrate; you cannot make yourself see them. Just know that by consciously thinking, your spirit is working through your mind and receiving its food and strength, and day by day, your awareness will grow and your capacity to receive divine instruction will increase.

Do this exercise as long or as short a time as you wish.

Pronounciation: Oo   as in "z<u>oo</u>"

TALK
Shafts of Light

The Technique has been given to us to enable us to get a new living experience, that we may react to life from a different standpoint. In order to do that and get a new personality, we have to learn to get rid of the old. That is a very difficult thing if we tackle it from the mental point of view. We cannot get rid of our own minds until we have got a different mental inspiration. What is the substance that can change us, and how is this change brought about without mental effort?

Last time you had the **Ah Meh** exercise, drawing in the light to your hands, arms and throat so that the throat, which is a most important part, becomes receptive.

I am going to give an exercise to help you to get rid of that which has accumulated in you day by day and through many lives. We have to start eliminating, right from the top of the head, through the body and out of the feet, because through the feet we can eliminate into the Figure of Light.

The Figure of Light is a universal condition. We can empty ourselves into Light and it is done on a sound. On a staccato sound of **Ah Oo** it is as if we press down from the brain through the body, legs and feet into the Figure of Light, all that which should be discarded in us. It is probably from the

41

subconscious mind. We do not know ourselves at the beginning of the Technique. We know what people have thought of us and what we have thought of ourselves, but we do not know ourselves in relationship to love and life. We may know ourselves in relationship to our family, our friends and our work, but not to the cosmos, to the Father and to the Christ.

When I was given this exercise I saw the inside of a gun through which an instrument has been pushed until it shines. We are not clean inside and we have experiences in life caused by this accumulation of disharmony which has accrued through the years of this life and many others. We have to get rid of it but we do not know in our minds what to get rid of.

This exercise functions on its own law and is not directed by the mind. You cannot make Light do what you want it to do, but it is a happening. Before you learn to receive the wonderful substances in Light, you have to learn to eliminate the unwanted substance inside you. After you have pushed this sound through your body, turn your hands over into a receiving position and visualise two great shafts of white light coming down into your hands, having their tips in infinity, so that your hands are the earthing of them. Take six Conscious Breaths and as the breath goes up there will come down the

shafts into your hands little petals of peach-coloured light which are at once absorbed into your hands.

When this exercise was given I realised that it was the secret bread of life. It is a generating substance, and when we leave our physical body and go into the world of Light, it is the general basic food on which our soul bodies feed. It is the very substance of communal living in both worlds. Thus the substance of our body becomes of the same substance as our eternal soul body. Therefore we are linked with the Christ's resurrection body and with the bodies of all we love on the other side.

Never dissociate your loved ones on the other side from a living vital body. We think of discarnate spirits as being disembodied, but that is a wrong idea, for heaven is filled with radiant bodies. You leave behind your old body like an old suit of clothes, but the bodies on the other side are radiant and as definite as flesh and blood. We have to get our bodies here on earth more like those others so that we shall be able one day to have the same sort of body as Christ had when He reconstructed His dead body into the eternal living substance of light.

Therefore the more light we receive into our body, the more energy we

42

are bound to have, not only mental, but also physical energy. We are trying to get new flesh and blood and we receive every morning a new substance of life changing our mind and body. However old or young we are, the change is bound to take place, and it is not a question of time or condition but merely capacity. It is our mind being open and not closed that enables our body to receive. The moment the mind was closed against the body of the Christ, He could do no good work. The moment we put up a resistance, people cannot come near, and resistance to love shuts us out from life.

The Technique should function effortlessly. I do not want you to concentrate your mind but to relax it. Whether you see light or feel nothing does not matter, for once you have thought it, it is there. Your Infinite Point of Radiance and Figure of Light are there and nothing but your thoughts can take them away. If you think they are not there for you, then they are not, but if you say that you have got your Figure of Light and know it to be a real condition and that your feet make a contact with life energy, and love, every morning when you put your feet against it, then it is a happening and something in you changes when that contact takes place.

I do not mind whether you do the eliminating exercise of the **Ah Oo** quickly or slowly. Be natural about it and do it according to the rhythm of your nature. That which has to be eliminated out of us follows that rhythm of light through the body and goes out. We have so much to get rid of every day, and the fact that things which are easy for some and are difficult for others does not make it comparative. It does not matter that my irritability is different from yours and that the things which irritate me, amuse you. We have to get rid of different things and our difficulties which are perfectly real to us go out on the **Ah Oo**. Do not think about them but only know that you are getting rid of them and becoming ready to receive a marvellous substance of fresh life and a capacity to love.

I know that these petals will give us a warmth inside which will feed our heart and slowly the numbness and hardness goes out. Most of the world is suffering from a numbness or hardness of heart, which has been caused by fear. People are so afraid of what lies ahead of them. Fear is a most important substance of disintegration, so whatever your fears may be, let them go from your mind and body. Your body shows the reaction to your fear and every disease the world can classify comes from fear. You may have an unconscious or conscious fear

43

in your blood.

I started life with very definite conscious fears and only through many long years do I realise that those fears have gone, although I cannot tell you when, but they are not there any longer because when fear goes something else must come in its place. It is no good trying to get rid of fear until you are able to receive confidence to supplant it. I know now that my confidence is greater than my fear, and it is confidence and not fear of which I am aware.

When the petals are coming down into your hands, confidence is coming into your body, into your being, and fear is going out. The race between the emptying and filling will seem almost equal at the beginning of the Technique, but confidence grows and fear is eliminated if we do not feed it. Thoughts are fear food, and the petals are confidence food, so you and I alone know which we are feeding day by day. The more you think of your fears, the stronger your potentiality for disease grows. The more you are certain that these petals come into your hands, the more your confidence grows in the law of life and love; life opens and radiates out.

Fear is introvert but love is extrovert; love is a radiation, fear is an inner tension. Fear is the cause of all those diseases that start and end with growth; nobody could have a growth in them unless they had an introvert mind, and their fears were stronger than their capacity to love. Nobody who loves their neighbour need be afraid of a growth. All those conditions which are hard are caused by a numb or hard heart. When people have used us badly, a hard condition forms in our heart organ which hardens our arteries. This happens easily in old age when the heart gets weakened through difficulties and circumstances, and we cannot love with the warmth we thought we used to. Our heart grows cold, and the moment that coldness comes into a person a hardening of the arteries and capacity for growth of unpleasant conditions are the result.

The Technique in Light can transcend all human conditions and bring about a softening of the arteries, better circulation and an extrovert condition of the mind. You look to see how you can be used in service and not how life is going to hurt. We are so afraid of life hurting us that we put a protection around ourselves. I had to learn that I could no longer protect myself. This is the Christian Initiation and we go through the experiences of Christ in our own life. When I was told that I must not protect myself I had a sensation of my hands being tied behind me. A self-protective movement is to send things away, but I could not send away on the mental or physical plane. I had to learn that as long as I protected myself, I could not be protected. When an individual takes the ruling of their life onto themselves they act without divine protection. When we protect ourselves from pain and suffering, then love, which is the only protection, has to stand on one side until we allow experience to teach us that to be protected is a greater condition than to protect ourselves. I cannot protect myself against tomorrow, or say that I will not have protection tomorrow, but I can have protection for today. Commit tomorrow on the Conscious Breath and you have no further responsibility for it.

Confidence is the experience of faith. You have to have a certain amount of hope in doing the Technique that it is going to function in your particular case. We think others find it easier to do than ourselves, that we have a wandering mind and no capacity for concentration, or that we are not the sort of people to start something new. That is the resistance our mind is bound to put up, so do not pay any attention to it.

The thrill of every day is great because I do not know how much He can reveal today that was not there yesterday, and you will find the same. Something marvellous can come into life as long as we can be open to it.

The early exercises of the Technique in Light are most important, if you can get them into your being without great self-analysis and introvert thinking. Every spark that comes into you must go out. What you have got of your own, and can take about with you all day is the Figure of Light, your earth, and the Infinite Point of Radiance, your source. They are yours, and your source will reveal to you wherever you are and whatever you are doing, a condition of possibility that your insoluble problems will be resolved.

We all have insoluble problems tucked away inside us because we cannot cope. I think the word 'cope' is on everybody's lips at some time during these difficult months. Things are beyond our coping, but be glad you have come to that point of realisation, because you would cope if you could, and then you would not be able to go through the experience of having a thing done for you. All the things I cannot cope with, I commit, and they can be done through me, getting them out of my system and into His. He cannot refuse them, therefore I say that I do not admit responsibility at all. A servant has not the responsibility of the master, and a channel has not the responsibility of the source. I am only a channel and can only put myself in the attitude of receiving with no responsibility for that which comes through me. I have accepted the law and put myself into the position to become the law, but I have no responsibility for the direction of the energy that comes through me. What happens to it is not my affair, therefore results are not our affair. Our responsibility is to make a contact, but the result of that contact is not our concern.

Look at Christ in His life. He did not blame people because of His conditions; He never faltered in His confidence. He knew that He was the representative of the Father, and beyond that He could not go. The moment you put your feet in contact with the Figure of Light you are Christ's representative for that day. You are connected with Him and it is His responsibility when you have made that contact. You must refer your problems to Him and they will be dealt with. You are putting yourself in that position when you take a Conscious Breath. When the petals come into

your hands you have got them for the day but you must do it again tomorrow for you cannot accumulate them. You will have direction and capacity to live for that day and that day only.

Fear is childish and destructive, for it destroys peace of mind. Have peace of mind for today and do not live in fearful anticipation.

Nothing is measured by size or speed in light for there is only the sparking speed. It is the speed of thought, and the moment you have thought light, you are light. When you breathe the petals are bound to come down, and I think you may have a sensation in the palms of your hands, but do not worry if you do not get this. Concentrate on your breath as it goes up and the petals are released to come down. Think only of one thing at a time; first the elimination, then the shafts and the breath, and the petals must come as a condition of reality. The Infinite Point of Radiance always functions for it is an immutable law. When we make a contact with immutable things, the result is inevitable.

GOLD SPIRALS AND BLUE CIRCLES

Our spirits work through our human bodies by day, and through our soul bodies by night.

The next exercise is an evening one, to be done the last thing before you get into bed. If you are accustomed to read yourself to sleep, will you do your reading first and this exercise afterwards, so that your spirit, having made the contact in Light, can tranquillize your human body to sleep and have your light, or soul body, ready and eager for its work, for there is no night in the next world. Our light body does not need sleep to renew its vitality, as does our human body, for in the substance of Light there is no principle of decay.

Gradually one understands that for those who pass into the next phase of existence, death does not separate them from those they love on earth; for in sleep the spirit is free to function in the light body, it can travel on light and it can spend in time, many hours in work and discussion of plans. Alas that we, with our undeveloped consciousness, remain unaware of this freedom! We are often so reluctant to wake and to focus on this world's problems; it often seems as if we had made pleasant contacts and have been so

happy, that life seems a burden that we take up on waking every day. That burden is lifted when we begin to know of our compensating dual existence. The reality of both worlds becomes part of our experience. To achieve this experience we have to cut our dense human substance with light. You will see in the diagram that the spirals start at the nape of the neck, and are drawn over the head from back to front.

Will you stand quite at ease and visualise a long gold thread, like a flexible gold wire, with which you thread yourself through nine times, drawing the thread tight each time, so that each portion of your intersected body is cut with each succeeding spiral? Do each circular cut on an inbreath, drawing it over the head and pushing it through the throat on 1. Then, over the head and through the breast-bone on 2. And so on, until the trunk of the body is completely cut in two down the exact centre, on the ninth spiral.

When you can do it perfectly, cut the nine spirals in one long inhaling breath; but you can practise it for as many weeks or months as you like, taking one breath for each spiral, and gradually increase the number of your spirals in the one breath, as you find you are able to: the breath is not so important as the cutting. It is not an easy exercise to do for often the Light will not cut straight down the centre, but it may dart to either side, and then you will know that, humanly speaking, you are out of the true. The more difficult you find it, the more important it is to do it. When it goes quite easily, then be comforted, for your awareness is becoming part of your natural condition. Then, when we have voluntarily cut our humanity, comes our reward.

Visualise a circle of glorious blue, the glow of a living sapphire, just above your head, wide enough to fall down encircling, but not touching you. On an outbreath, pull the blue ring above your head, down to the one just above your shoulders on (1), and the two rings become one; then pull it down to the next which is on the level of your heart, and the three become one. Continue until you have encircled

yourself nine times and the nine-in-one rings surround your feet, and then vanish.

It is the balm of the Christ's love that encircles us each time that we voluntarily pierce ourselves.

Do this exercise three times, that is the inhaling breath of the gold spirals, and the exhaling breath of the blue rings in succession each time. Then get into bed and visualise yourself as a cross of Light, stretching from your head to your feet, and across your shoulders. Do the Conscious Breathing until you fall asleep. The cross of Light is a protection for your spirit passing through the astral planes.

Thus you consciously provide your spirit with the necessary power to make an instant contact with world of Light and Love.

TALK
The Gold Spirals and the Blue Circles

I am going today to give you a vitally important exercise. We have been drawing the light to our feet, through our hands, along our arms to the throat, but there is a very important part of the body not yet touched by light, and that is the spine.

I want to talk about the spine because it connects with the head and brain, and unless we understand the full mechanism of our physical instrument, and the importance of every part of it, we are not going to understand the Christian Initiation.

48

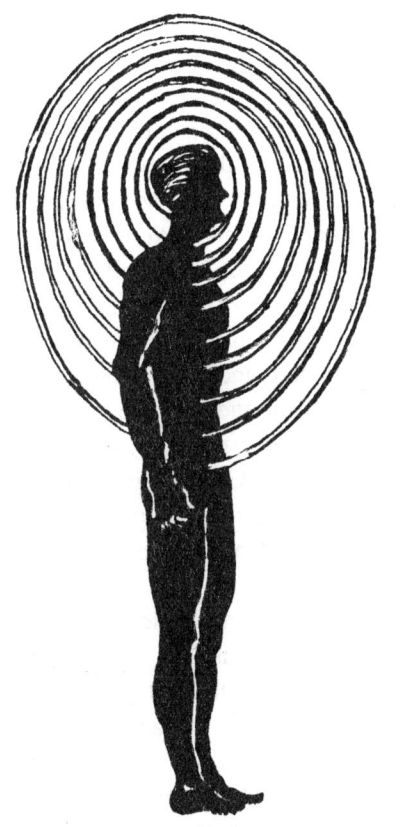 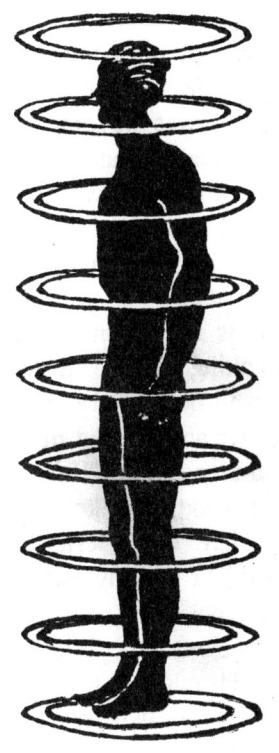

GOLD SPIRALS   **BLUE CIRCLES**

49

Christ came to give humanity a new capacity for living. We live according to the reaction of our mind on our body.

Jesus always made people realise that whatever showed in the body was caused by what is termed sin. It did not matter whether He said to the paralysed person "Take up your bed and walk" or "Your sins are forgiven you," it was the same thing. They were paralysed because they had broken the law of life and when He removed the cause, there was nothing to prevent them from walking.

Sin is in the individual's mind, the breaking of the unity between the human being and the Creator. God is matter and created matter, He is flesh and blood. How could He create flesh and blood if He knew nothing about it and how could Jesus have said to the world "I and my Father are one, if it were not so, I would have told you." Was He a liar? Was God so different that He ought to have said "I am not in any way like my Father, He is wonderful and certainly not of the same substance as I am." Jesus said that there was no difference in substance between Himself and His Father. If that was so, there is no difference in substance between ourselves and God.

It is said that God is a spirit. We do not understand what we are saying when we talk about disembodied spirits, for there are no such things. Do you think that because we leave our body behind in the earth, a formlessness goes back to the Creator? Christ said that He came to show us the way whereby everybody could take their body back again to the Father who created all bodies and is the supreme body of the cosmos. It is time that we made a start in changing our body that it might become more like unto His glorious, or radiant body. If you substitute 'radiant' for glorious, it has a more human touch. We know radiant people and glum people; people who do not radiate love, joy, happiness, but are pessimists, cynics who deny life and God because they think God is spirit and has no connection with them as material beings.

We who are endeavouring to follow in Christ's' footsteps must comprehend what we are doing when we put our feet against the Figure of Light every morning. We are making a contact with His radiant body. He earthed radiance in flesh and blood and knew what He was talking about when He said, "I and my Father are one," because God is radiance. We are not radiant, but God is a radiant being of wonderful flesh and blood past our comprehension. We cannot know the ingredients which make up His body, we only know those making up our body and we have no capacity for touching and handling a substance past our comprehension.

We have the minimum; Christ has the maximum, and we have to change the minimum into the maximum. We can do it if we will make it a daily habit, changing the habit of our mind and our activity. It is not easy because habit of mind is a growth and our thoughts fall back into a groove, until we are able to spark them out of it into this new condition.

The exercise I am going to pass on deals with your receptivity and is the first one we have got which is entirely for the evening. It will eliminate unconscious resistance, and we have all got an unconscious resistance to new conditions. To hold fast is our training life after life, to keep what we have got and continue to accumulate. So we have built up this body of ours on a false foundation, and a renewal and discard must take place every day if we are to have a new condition.

Every night before you get into bed, stand and cut your body through in nine places so that the substance of gold light will go completely through your spine. It goes through the throat, and the throat, tongue and saliva glands need resolving. Gold light is a resolving substance; it

changes and goes through anything and has a capacity for interpenetration. Certain aspects of light would glance off and not be absorbed, but associate this gold light with being able to go completely through you without effort.

I have used the word pierce because it is a piercing through of the subconscious human resistance to love, life and selflessness. Humans are naturally egoistic and concerned with the ego, with self-protection, self-development, self-control. Their own way, opinions and desires are vibrating in the individuals all the time, disintegrating their substance.

This light passes over the head, piercing the trunk from front to back and making a substance of receptivity right through, which will enable our being to receive. We are accustomed only to receive thought, and think that if we get the pattern of life we have got everything. We have to train our bodies as Jesus did to receive the Father in every cell. How can we change if we only change our mind? We have to change the habit of our mind *and* the receptivity of our substance, and these two things are provided for in the Technique in Light without effort. The effort is to live it every day, for that is the test.

You will find it easy to fall away from the Technique. There is a no-man'sland for people who start, in which the old is not so dominant as it was, but the new is not yet integrated into us, and that hiatus depends on our health. If you are feeling tired and nervy you can think that you do not believe the Technique is doing you any good, but perhaps harm, that you had better drop it as the light may attract disaster. Our mind can present anything to us that it wants and will do so, unless we know that our contact with God and the Christ is real to us, and not just the visualising of an unreal condition.

Do not in your mind separate vision from substance, but go through the experience of allowing this substance to pass through you, changing you without your consciousness, and do not consciously direct that change. We are used to changing ourselves through strength of mind.

If you are faithful at the start, you will find how tremendously it pays at the end, and how your freedom will go forward in great strides. Put no limit to your capacity for progress but do not be interested in visionary progress and psychic experiences. Be interested if you can register how Light helps in your domestic problems and your relations with your neighbour. Christ only learnt through human experience. His contact with the Father was absolutely necessary for His mind, but His relationship to the world made it possible for Him to reconstruct His body. If He had led the life of a hermit in the wilderness, always alone praying for the world and not living in it, His humanity would have been in the same state as the humanity of all recluses, dead, sterile, anaemic and not the light of the world. He was not a recluse but a sparking contact with the Father whom He constantly remembered.

The first circle of resolving light comes over the head, passing through the joint where there is a vital fluid to the mechanism of the brain. The second circle is just above the heart and all the important breathing conditions. The next comes between the breasts where is the universal heart. It goes through the spine which should be a very flexible instrument, receptive to life energy. We draw life energy into the spine feeding the marrow of the bones, where rheumatic people suffer from a lack of marrow and oil, and all those substances which harmonise with love.

If you have a resentment with life in your mind, it reacts at once in your spine and you become a dry person and cannot help it. You wither inside because love has failed you. On the human side you wither for lack of contact with love. You have thought that a person on whom your mind and heart have been centred is all that love means to you, and because love is removed for the time being, something in you dies. I know how easy it is to die when that which your heart desires is removed from you, and we individually suffer from that in many forms of chronic conditions. This exercise will give you a capacity but not a certainty. If only I could make it a certainty I would do so, but I can only give you a possibility of renewing your contact with love, because resistance to love will go out of you.

Then we cut ourselves further down where the nerve centres are, and you know how resistance to life reacts on the nervous system. We are not capable of getting mental equilibrium without constant daily help. We must link up all the time so that our contact with love is greater than our resistance and grief. We cannot grieve if we are always in contact with love because then we have confidence. When we are not in contact with love we grieve for the absence of it, for grief is absence from the contact of love.

Our body becomes so vitally important because we love with our body and we have to become love in our body. You may think love is a cerebral condition and that if you mentally understand about love, that is enough. Those of you who have had experience know it is not enough. You have to love in unity of mind and body.

So this is a resolving exercise for the whole of the trunk of the body where all the creative energy, the nervous condition and everything that is you, is contained, and this resolving of the trunk of the body must be voluntary. Do it quickly nine times and that allows the lovely substance to leave a residue. There is a reaction to that light which will be with you all through the night and you will awake with it in the morning.

The second half of the exercise is very lovely. Blue circles of the colour of Christ's love that He earthed are the blessing that encircle us; they fall down from our head to our feet. The amount of His love that you can receive will be the quality of the blueness.

I do not connect love with emotion but I connect love with a warmth and stillness, with happiness, peace of mind, givingness and not receiving. When you have really given, there is a happiness that I think is all blue. You may have given your time to somebody who has asked for it, or you may have given something not because your mind has told you that you must give, but because your heart has wanted to do so. The mind is reluctant but the heart is a giver; the mind will say "For peace

53

and quietness sake I will give," but the heart gives and your mind does not know it. That is what Christ means when He says, "Let not your left hand know what your right hand giveth." The mind always knows, but the heart does not; the heart is such a giver that it does not register and we have to register not what we give, but only what we receive.

You may think that I am optimistic, and perhaps I am, in saying that this exercise will bring about this condition, but it will help and start it. If you do not put a limit to how you can live with an effortless radiation, it can happen, so flash this gold spiral through your body every night and bring down the blue circles and know you are blessed because you have given your body. You are giving your life to Life, and therefore Love encircles you.

We have to understand that Christ gave people the freedom to love, and because He did not condemn certain social acts we are apt to think He condoned them, but He did not. There is a difference between not condemning and condoning; we have to learn in our individual life and it cannot be imposed by one person on another.

We must know ourselves in relationship to love, where we break the law of love and do not break the standards of morality. If we loved our neighbour we could not be immoral, we could not cheat or commercialise love. The method given to us in our generation can accomplish this. We must change if we unite ourselves with the Father and understand the mission of Christ.

THE NEEDS

This next exercise can have no illustration as it is an intimate and personal experience.

After the Shafts exercise and before you sit up, will you extend the arms (still with the palms of the hands up), and let the feet drop gently. Visualise a rushing up of white light from hands and feet, which instantly fuses all round and you find yourself suddenly lying surrounded by walls of light stretching up to infinity, and you are aware of utter privacy and seclusion. Next, visualise a rim of light round your heart and know that a chalice of light lies within it, the rim only being visible.

Now quite clearly and definitely, pray for all your material needs for the day, for the decisions that have to be made, the letters to be dealt with, the interviews and plans for the future, your health, finance and emotional experiences that may or may not materialise. Pray that this day your will may be surrendered to His will; that your decisions be inspired; that your heart may not be hardened in resentment, criticism, fear or self-pity. Pray too for the needs of your family and friends. Put all your needs into the chalice in your heart and on a deep Conscious Breath send the chalice up to the great radiance of the Father, up between the walls of Light where you lie, straight to God, where it is presented and emptied and returned to your heart.

Then, will you pray for all those whom you know and love who have passed on. Pray that their needs may be supplied, that their and your co-operation in love here may become more and more perfect; that your love may be used to help them, and theirs to help you. When you have finished, send the chalice up again on a Conscious Breath.

Then thirdly and lastly, pray for your spiritual needs. That, day by day, you may register all failures and unconscious acts, and pray quite definitely for power to transmute them, including that despondency which comes from loss of equilibrium which is caused so often by such trivialities. Pray too that your desire for oneness with Him may increase day by day, that your spiritual discernment may grow, that all fear may disappear. Then for the last time send up your chalice.

This can only be the barest outline of what the ritual of prayer may develop into for each individual. It is only the instrument (as the telephone is the instrument by which we communicate at a distance with one another) by which we have a *mutual* contact with God. We with Him, and He with us. How far He can reveal Himself to us must of necessity depend on the quality of our desire.

I would like to give this warning. The tendency to wandering thoughts is more clearly revealed by this exercise than by any other, and this makes us understand why prayer is such a weak and inoperative fact in the world.

As we discipline our thoughts, becoming more and more definite in our needs for ourselves and others, so can His power function more and more forcibly through us.

TALK
The Needs

The force that governs the supply and demand of the spiritual world is known to us by the word prayer. It has the same power of exchange as gold in this world.

The greater the wealth here, the larger the purchasing power, and the vaster the capacity for possession. And so it is with prayer. The knowledge that Jesus had of the power and of the source of prayer, and our ignorance of it, is as the knowledge of the greatest financier to that of the most junior of bank clerks.

Prayer is the setting in motion of the line of communication that exists between God and every incarnate spirit. If we look on this wireless communication in Light as a scientific reality, we shall not confuse "much speaking" with power in prayer. Words make a picture of an action, but they are often confused with the action itself. An officer may give the order to shoot; but if his men have no guns, he may put all the emotional desire of his being into the command - but no action takes place.

The repetition of words with no accompanying action, is form without force. The source of the power of prayer lies in God, and God is Light, the Father of Light; and what proceeds from the Source must be of the substance of Light. Therefore to get the full significance of the power of prayer, we must think in terms of Light.

There are different conditions of prayer, as there are different substances of exchange, such as gold, silver, copper, paper and salt etc. People pray to the saints; and invocations to innumerable deities rise daily all over the world to supply the needs of suffering humanity. But we are only concerned to know, as Jesus knew, how to commune direct with the Father.

One thing we have to learn at the outset, namely that when we set in motion an infinite force, we cannot postulate finite results. In other words, that to pray that "*Thy* will be done on earth," is to realise that this involves learning what His will is. Most of us know only too well what our will is, and pray (quite unconsciously) that it may be done; and are most bitterly discouraged when the reverse occurs. It is however, only a matter of experience. When we learn really how to pray, we learn also to register the true results.

The whole object of praying is to have our needs supplied, but we are often very hazy about our needs and have never really examined and classified them. They are not the same as our desires, the fulfilment of which may often do harm. Prayer should state very definitely what we believe our needs to be, but we must accept their fulfilment according to God's pattern of action and not our

own. Since the Technique in Light has been given to me I have understood prayer from a totally different angle. I have understood it as a law of demand and supply, and if I know how to ask, I am bound to receive that for which I have asked, for Jesus said emphatically "Ask and ye shall receive." But we must ask in accordance with the immutable law of receptivity.

This law is connected not with the brain, but with the heart. Cerebral activity is out of touch with God, because it is subject to our fears and lack of confidence. These destroy our power to receive adequate answers to our prayers, but the heart contact is immutable; blood to blood is a law of receptivity and transmission. If your blood calls to that of God, His blood answers yours. It is the asking of the heart, and through that organ you are bound to receive.

The exercise of the Needs is the very law of prayer; it is prayer from your heart to the Infinite Source of supply. If you put into the chalice the material needs of yourself and your family and friends, and breathe them up, they will be supplied. The mind may be afraid to ask because it cannot distinguish between its needs and its desires, but you should not be afraid to state each day what you believe them to be. You must, however, be very clear-cut and definite about them and you will find not only that all your true needs are satisfied, but also that you become increasingly aware of what they really are, and ever more confident of their fulfilment.

You next put into the chalice those who have passed on into the next plane of existence. In this case you cannot know their needs, but you set up, as it were, a communication in Light, and can be their agent for serving such needs as they have left behind them on earth. Some people pass on quickly, with an unfinished life; we cannot know the exact service they need, but we can be at their disposal in case we can in any way help them or their friends. Sometimes people I have not thought of for years flash into my mind, and I breathe them up from my chalice, and ask to be used if necessary. I have had some strange experiences in this way.

The third sending up of the chalice is for our own mental and spiritual needs, and the development of our characters. Through it we can be released from those adverse character conditions which the will is utterly unable to transmute. We become increasingly conscious of the changes we should like to see take place in our own personalities, and we should put them all into the chalice for transmutation.

This chalice is a wonderful comfort. It

is received with the speed of light, but the results in us may be slowed down because of the lack of light in our systems. If a lamp is only partially connected there is poor light, and if the instrument of our body is connected with the Source of energy only intermittently, reconditioning will take a long time. If we can remain connected all the time the change will be very rapid, for the more receptive we become, the more quickly it takes place. The less obedient we are to this technical process, the more we delay our progress and allow it to be held up by mental insulation.

We are confronted with the necessity of knowing ourselves. There is so much of our personality which we cherish and are afraid to lose. I feared for instance, that I would lose my sense of humour in surrendering to this process; but realised later that God would have a better sense of humour than mine, and that I could not lose mine by being connected with Him. We none of us want to become like everybody else, nor does God want us to be standardised. He has made millions of different individuals, no two of whom are exactly alike, and must have a million facets of personality Himself. It is the human mind that tends to standardise, as modern developments show only too clearly. The purpose

58

of God is to individualise, and the nearer we get to Him the more we are fulfilled along our own individual line.

When you lie relaxed and visualise the golden chalice in your heart, be quick in your contact. The mind wanders so easily, and a friend's name is often a jumping off place for a mental voyage of endless length. Do not let this happen. Think of a person and his needs and drop them into your chalice with the speed of light; then pass on to the next. Mental activity is no aid to the transit from your heart to the Source, and the sooner your definite requests go up, the sooner will come the answers.

You should not try to foresee how the answers will function in your life, or those of others. You may be certain they will come but do not predetermine the shape they should take, nor despise them if they do not conform to a pattern of your own making. Nor should you demand the answers within a certain specified time. They will come in the right time for you and your friends. They partly depend on the rhythm of our capacity to receive, as God cannot project them into our lives except in proportion to this capacity. Above all, do not keep problems on your mind. The brain has no capacity for

transmutation, but has a repetitive movement; whereas if you put a request for changed conditions into your heart, it travels straight to the Source.

There is a great difference between an urgent mental prayer and the confidence of the heart. Prayer from the heart is infinitely more powerful because it creates a living substance of connection with God by means of which He can answer. If those you love are worried or ill, or perhaps dying, you are bound to get help for them if you pray in this way. It is best however, to surrender their condition to God in complete confidence that He will do what is best for them, for a tenseness of demand and a strong desire creates a hindrance to His power to act through you as a channel. He cannot work without confidence and receptivity at the human end. We are entitled to ask for healing as urgently as did the centurion, for life and happiness should be the natural lot of all of us, and we ought not to accept death and decay. Nevertheless, people cannot always take in an injection of life energy because of the weakened state of their bodies, and it is then that death occurs. Death is the inability of the organism to take any further spark of life, but if we train the body to receive, with every breath, the transformed life energy which Jesus had in His body, there will be no more disease, for we shall be eternally receiving His health, happiness and vitality.

You have to get your heart working, and allow your brain to be quiescent. Let your brain be clear and serene in the morning when you dedicate your whole self to this great condition of receptivity. Do The Needs exercise every morning for the current day alone, with no looking ahead to the morrow. If you should forget someone or something, and remember later, simply send up the need on your breath, and do not do the exercise again.

When you do the exercise, you are lying in a little cell of light, with walls of light on each side of you, so that you are private.

We often find we want to change the reaction of others to their circumstances, but do not know how to do it. Get them off your mind and into your heart; your mind will cease to revolve in a recurring state of worry and your heart radiation will help their transformation.

Do not tell people that you are praying for them, but let it be a silent service. The desire to change others rather than ourselves is only too natural to all of us, but our own changed self is really the greatest gift that we can give our neighbours.

E.O. LIHUM

This is an exercise which will be very helpful to you, and with which you can help others, especially in all times of mental stress. I was given it at a time when I had a great need. It is done in three parts and on two planes:-

1. For those in this world.
2. For those who have passed on.
3. For oneself.

Do this exercise immediately before or after The Needs.

It is fun to have this in summer, as I was made to take a glass of water and see the colour of light, which is a crystal colour, like water in the sun. It is such a brilliance of light that is in water, for we rarely see pure water. It is not the blueness of stream water, but brilliant white with a shadow, the crystal light. I know that the crystal sea which St. John talked of was this crystal light, always shining round the throne. The purity and the power to still the mind is something that we must experience.

Visualise a streak of light of a pure crystal colour - like water, glinting in the sunlight. Coming into the left ear it passes through the head and out of the right ear, and flashes on through the head or heads of those you want to help. It then circles back in front of your face and spirals swiftly up to the Father. The sound is **E.O. Lihum**, very difficult to express in writing - just a light breath sound. On an inbreath you draw the Light into your head on the sound **E**, and in the same breath, on the sound **O**, it circles through the heads (quickly visualised by you) of your friends. On an outbreath, on the sound **Lihum**, the Light spirals back in front of your face, up in a split second to the Infinite Radiance of the Father. **Lihum** is a gentle breath sound, and the whole exercise is done on the rhythm of a sigh.

The first time you do it for people you want to help in this world, all our muddle-headed friends, all our self-willed, opinionated friends, whom we try to help by talking, which invariably makes matters worse. This exercise must be done silently and selflessly, never telling people we have done it for them, but being content to be the Christ's agent for service to those who cannot make their own contact.

The second time visualise swiftly the faces of those who have passed on, and this time the encircling light unites our minds with theirs, in the unity of the mind of Christ, so that we are for one brief moment of one mind in Him.

The third time visualise the head of Christ in front and above you, and on the **E** the crystal light circles through your head, on **O** it flashes through His head, returns to you in front of you, and spirals up as before. I say do it once, but often I have found myself doing that last encirclement several times, until my mind seems as steady as a rock, and a flash of understanding of oneness of will and desire with Him floods my being.

This marvellous crystal light is of the substance of the eternal waters and washes from our heads, and from the heads of all who receive it, all worry and fret. In return we get a crystal clearness of vision, which is of the substance of the divine being of God. The crystal light is that which St. John saw around the throne.

When you fall back into the old way and find your own mind coming up, send the light through His head and yours. Sometimes I bring it through my head three times before sending it up. You may prefer to do it first through the Christ's head, then through your friends' heads and then end up again through the head of Christ.

TALK
E.O. Lihum

The object of this Technique is self-revelation.

The revelation which comes into our minds on the Technique is for the purpose of knowing ourselves, our soul bodies and our physical bodies, and to understand where the fusion between the soul body and the physical body begins - we have not yet begun to view the end. We must understand that this beginning of the domination of our higher selves, the Christ in us, can function in us as a natural condition with no great stress of personality, and what is more difficult to realise, no virtue.

I had periods of being taught the Technique, and then there were periods in between in which I had to strive to become one with the knowledge which was being taught me. That is why I now keep to school terms; that first we should learn, and then *become* our knowledge. My brother said, "Knowledge *is* over here": and we have only to talk to people to realise that knowledge *is not* in this world.

We wonder whether we know a thing and whether we can do it. We have got to cease from wondering or thinking of ourselves as anything but a vehicle, so when someone asks something of us, we do not feel "I cannot do it", "I am not far enough on." We are so afraid of failing. If we could eliminate fear; it is the condition that makes us fail. We think of ourselves as an individual who can do something: but if we begin to think of ourselves as empty vehicles through which divine power must come if our minds do not set up a self-conscious barrier, we are just inevitable vehicles for healing. We shall never be healers, but through us healing must come, which is a very different thing.

Let us try to get rid of this haunting self-consciousness, this self-importance, this self-depreciation. We nearly always suffer from one condition or another. We often think too little of ourselves, which is a sin. We must only think of ourselves as vehicles through which everything can be done and said which is true, and set no limit to the capacity of the divine power to function through us. The stumbling block is the way of inherited thought. We have been accustomed to think along certain lines, and have only found life possible if we think along those lines. If we visualise the strength of our will we think it will pull us through every catastrophe. I am sorry to shatter that illusion, but your will will not always pull you through. We must see ourselves as vehicles through whom divine will functions in perfect alignment, coming through this glorious soul body of ours.

Light must make contact with Light, and the light in us is the magnet which attracts His will, His energy and His marvellous light. We must concentrate on developing a capacity for seeing ourselves from a different point of view, making not intense, but instantaneous thinking, as an easy habit of thought. If we could contract a different habit of thought we should develop a different outlook.

We have to change the habit of our thought and understand that one knows nothing and can do nothing; so when you find yourself depreciating yourself and thinking "I cannot do it", think of it as an opportunity for Him to manifest through you. Each time we become aware of our inability, it is a supreme opportunity to change our capacity for experience. Every moment of the Technique lays us open to a fresh experience. Nothing recurs in this condition. We have been used the recurrence of an experience, but with the Technique, the moment we have had an experience we are ready for something else. It took me a long time to get the sense of adventure and fulfilment along that line of thought. One is apt to sink back and think one has got over something, and can now think of it and enjoy it, but that is when we are ready to have some sort of experience which is even harder.

I want to talk of our soul body, and how this fusing of soul and body can be a natural condition without any Christian sacrifice. Many of us have looked upon this initiation in the footsteps of Jesus as a thing of sorrow and sacrifice, but I know it to be a thing of light and rejoicing. We have finished with that habit of thought which has nailed us to our pain. People think they have to go on doing that, but He did it for us. He said He died for us. Why was it possible for Him to die for us? All through these two thousand years we have missed the point. He died so that we should produce in happiness this condition of His resurrection while in the flesh.

We must get this body of light as a dominating factor in our lives, building it up and not destroying it, because when you have that condition in you there is no sacrifice. There is no sacrifice in eliminating disease and worry, and there is none in being good.

We have always looked upon the opposite of goodness as sin, whereas it is ignorance. Once we know the law we do not wish to break it. Until we know it, we break it, and we suffer for our stupidity. You must not be stupid socially neither must you be stupid spiritually. Do not look upon anyone as evil or sinful, but only as ignorant, provoking pity and tolerance. Only in our wisdom can we give love, and only when we understand love can we be the vehicle for love.

Everyone is so quick to pick up our ignorance here. As soon as we have learnt, our past ignorance is forgotten. We cannot go back - we always go forward. Whatever the appearance, we do not go backwards. We have different experiences on different levels. It looks as if it were the same level because it is the same circle. It looks like this because it is more difficult to function on a higher spiral, where we have functioned perfectly on the old spiral.

We are more horrified now of any loss of equilibrium. Things are now being done through us, and it is a pleasure to be free of the old bondage and failure.

There is not a single thing we can fail about from now on, if we will believe that all things are possible in Him, and everything is impossible to us. You are right in feeling you cannot do a thing, but wrong in thinking it cannot be done.

Our mentalities need help in attaining a clarifying and calming condition of mind. Often we have tried hard to refuse to function on the old vibration but cannot get a new standard of fulfilment because our minds play us false. This exercise was given to me when I was in great stress of mind. It was given to me as a personal experience, and I was apt to look upon it as only being for one or two, but I know it is one we all need.

If the reader has been consciously undertaking the Exercises, so far they should be practising the following:-

MORNING

Ritual of Light
Conscious Breathing
Ah Mou — A E Ooo
Shafts of Light
The Needs
E. O. Lihum

EVENING

Spirals and Circles

THE TRANSMUTING LIGHT

The great desire of our spirits is to progress and to transmute our human characteristics, and our failure to profit to any perceptible degree by the training in Light, often produces a condition of depression and sometimes of despair. One appears to be unique in the slowness of one's progress. The lack of vision, the uncertainty of contact, and the recurring doubt that after all, this may not be *the way*, at any rate for oneself, is a constant stumbling block. Other people's difficulties, if they are not our own, appear so simple of solution compared to that condition of secret rebellion towards God - fate - or circumstances - that seem interwoven in the very fibres of our mentality.

This next exercise is a very wonderful one, for it does provide the way of escape from this despair, and gives us the knowledge of how to change our humanity. It is done to the sound of the word **Father**.

Visualise two shafts of brilliant white light, coming from infinity on the right and left.

On an inbreath, and on the sound **Fa**, draw down those two shafts simultaneously, and visualise them crossing as they pour into you. The shaft from the right goes into your heart; and the one from the left, into your right breast.

On a deep outbreath, on the sound **ther**, visualise the white light changing to a wonderful deep amethyst inside you, so that the whole of your body from head to feet is filled with an incandescent glow of amethyst light. Thus:-

On **Fa**, draw the white shafts into your breast and heart;

On **ther**, send the light right into your body.

The contact of the white ray with your body and flesh changes the light into amethyst.

It is called the Transmuting Light for it is the condition of light that has power to change instantaneously, and with ever increasing power, the condition of our humanity. If it is done every day it will change our individual rhythm, the rhythm of our flesh, until we become perfect flesh, as was the humanity of Christ. It depends on the quality of our faith, the measure of our desire for perfection, and our co-operation with Him. According to this, so must we

THE TRANSMUTING LIGHT

draw into ourselves the necessary quality of power.

This exercise is done standing, if possible, but no physical posture is essential. It can be done sitting or lying down. If it is done only once a day, do it at midday, before lunch as a regular habit, but you can also do it at any time of the day or night when physical or mental conditions distress you.

What water is to the body, the Transmuting Light is to the mind. Certain substances make indelible stains on our flesh, and it needs much scrubbing, and cleansing solutions, to eradicate them completely; while ordinary dust and grime disappear with one application of soap and hot water. And so it is with our minds. Drawing in the Transmuting Light for a few minutes will always change the surface irritation or despondency, and give fresh hope and vitality. But to change the very fibres of our being needs a continuous condition of contact.

This exercise can be used also to help other people. Draw the Light into yourself first, and then draw it into them in exactly the same way. It is immaterial whether they are in the room or quite far away. In the latter case, visualise them as clearly as possible, and finish by drawing a cross of Light from their head to their feet and across their shoulders. You leave them in His protection and love, not demanding or postulating the result, but giving them all you have to give.

TALK
The Transmuting Light

It is important at this stage of our training to know how to use the Technique in Light. It is a very exact formula in which every step is a preparation for the next one, and has been designed to free some physical condition in the individual. In its entirety it will free the whole of the physical body, and will also co-ordinate it with the soul. The soul has, up to now, lived at a different level from the material self; materially we have one standard of living, and spiritually and mentally another one, so that we have never known what it is to have a co-ordinated human life in which the physical body is dominated by the soul body, or body of light.

We have to go through the experience of learning how to live at this new level, which is one of happiness, health and prosperity. Every step in the Technique helps this process, and before we discuss this new one, I want to stress again the importance of the Figure of Light, the Infinite Point of Radiance, and your breath as essential factors in your development. Breath contains the pure essence of life energy and without it energy could not be earthed in physical substance at all.

The Point of Radiance is your eternal source, and the Figure of Light is not just a symbol, but provides a physical means of elimination. Unless we learn to eliminate into it, we shall never enable our body to receive this greater happiness and health which we were constructed to receive, and which is our normal inheritance. The plus condition we are striving to achieve must function along the threefold path of receiving, absorbing and eliminating, which must go on consciously all the time. In the morning, when you visualise your Figure of Light, know that it is there to receive all of yesterday's exhausted energy, all the turmoil that has been set up in our mind by unforeseen happenings, or the hostile behaviour of other people. Our minds find it impossible to get rid of them, but this is a process by which everybody can eliminate mental stress on the physical wavelength into the Figure of Light.

Your source, the Infinite Point of Radiance, must be the focus of your mind. Realise that you are drawing from God, the Father, and are changing the substance of your body so that it will no longer react unfavourably to all those friction making conditions which are the prime cause of our different diseases.

After you have learned to send up your needs to Him you will find this a wonderful exercise for changing your physical condition, and you will begin to understand how the transmutation of physical substance is brought about. Your breath must make a track for this new substance in Light which is called the Transmuting Light, and is drawn down from infinity into your body, entering at the heart and the right breast.

The body corresponds in every detail to the building of the temple, and is made on that plan and pattern. In the old days the priest was a living part of the temple, representing the inside or soul of it, while the actual building was the outside or body. The breasts were very potent spots, and the Urim and Thummin in the high priest's breast-plate represented the personal and impersonal. In ourselves, the physical body is the outside of the living temple of ourselves, and the soul or light body the inside, and when these two are co-ordinated you get a very magnetic condition. Look upon your heart and right breast into which you draw the Transmuting Light as part of a living temple in which you are your own priest. It was to give to each of us the right and power to officiate as our own high priest within our own temple as a free individual, that Christ incarnated. Whether we do so or not is an entirely voluntary choice. You can officiate in

the mysteries of being to an unlimited degree, if you voluntarily accept the responsibility of being trained to make your body into the living temple of divine energy that it is meant to be.

In these days we are much concerned with atomic energy. If we can form a group of people who know how to earth this new creative energy of which the human body alone is capable, we are going to be instruments for preventing the destruction of the world. Jesus incarnated two thousand years ago to save the world. I believe He incarnated to save us from the split atom, which has already destroyed past civilisations. He came to earth a new radiation or voltage of light into the only instrument capable of receiving it - the human body. Physical flesh and blood is more receptive than any other substance, and contains more light energy. It has a capacity for the conscious reception and transmission of divine energy to which no other creature can aspire, but the capacity remains dormant until we make a voluntary decision to develop it. God will not impose His gifts upon us. If, however, you will make a voluntary choice to undergo the necessary training, you will be helping to save the world from disaster.

You may think that the world can be saved by intellectual formulae, and that the scientific mind will find the way out, but it will not, and cannot do so. Jesus knew that the radiation of His body would provide the way out and not His mind at all. Formulae for colossal destructive energies have been earthed long ago. In places in England I have picked up one that existed in pre-Atlantean days. The formula of creative energy has been perfectly earthed in one body only - that of Christ. Through Him it could be put into operation in a million human bodies but He must have their voluntary co-operation before it can be done.

If Jesus had been able to impose His formula on people a world war could never have happened, but He will not force eternal life on us, and if we prefer to accumulate riches and power we are free to do so. Two great wars have shown us the terrible results of human lust and greed and the appalling destructive power available today, but we have yet to see creative energy in effective action. Two thousand years ago Jesus operated it, and earthed it for all time. His fame has endured down the ages but His work has been neither fully understood, nor fully consummated in any succeeding individual.

If we are going to enter on this training it is necessary that we should say, as Christ did, "Not my will, but Thine be done." How can we bring about in ourselves the transmutation of our will into His will? It is not a matter of the mind, but involves a new physical condition which will change our actual heart action. Given the desire, and the conscious decision to achieve it, the change may be brought about effortlessly by absorbing the different light rays of the Technique. The Transmuting Light of the present exercise is particularly effective for this purpose.

When I was given this exercise, I saw the will of God as a brilliant white ray representing all His attributes, and out of that whiteness, the amethyst ray in particular, will change the atoms in the human body; it is a co-ordinating, transmuting substance, which floods the whole body and blood. As you draw it in, the physical condition changes, becomes less tired and takes on a different quality of life. Do not think, however, that we can accumulate it and store it over a long period of time. We have to take in physical food all the time to maintain physical strength, and we must also take in Light all the time if we are to maintain our equilibrium and the capacity to radiate out.

You can do the Transmuting Light for

others after first doing it for yourself, but it is better not to tell them about it. We should not put people under an obligation for any service we may do them. We have no monopoly of the Light, but simply share it with our neighbour, and in sharing there is no favour. It is definitely an exercise to do on others. You should not try out on anyone else the Figure of Light and Conscious Breathing, which are for your own development, but you can give anyone an injection of Transmuting Light. It has a calming effect on hurried and nervous people, and will help those who are too self-absorbed or too agitated to listen to anything you may say. Their bodies will receive the Light, though they may know nothing about it. You can also use the Light for absent healing. Visualise the pattern into your patients, but again do not let them know; for the mind is apt to become tense or to put up resistance and the light cannot get absorbed. When there is no resistance, it cannot fail to exert a transmuting effect in some measure. If you are suffering pain, you can direct the Transmuting Light locally to the place where the pain is.

Remember that the Transmuting Light works best when you have eliminated your undesirable conditions of fear, worry, etc., and that, for this elimination you should use the Figure of Light. When you do the Conscious Breath know that you breathe down all that you want to get rid of physically. If you make full use of the Figure of Light, you will get free more quickly of any physical disease. We have not learnt to earth our co-ordinated soul and body, or to have the freedom of our feet. Our bad health often goes into our feet, so let us get rid of it into our Figure of Light.

THE NAME

The Name of Jesus is the key which opens the door of life to all who wish to cross the threshold into the kingdom of God. It is the human name of the Word made flesh and so contains the perfect harmony of sound, colour, form and movement. Jesus, the Son of God, brought the cosmic harmony of the heavens into visibility here and transmuted the discord of human flesh and blood into the harmony of the Word. We have to learn how to tune in to the radiation of His Name so that we can become one in substance with Him. That can be brought about only by blood transfusion, and He wants us to learn the laws of the radiation of the blood. He incarnated to teach us how to tune in to His own flesh and blood and so receive His perfection. He knew how to tune in to the perfection of the Father, and to radiate it out in works which were thought to be unique and miraculous, but He said that if we followed in His footsteps, the works that He did we should do also, effortlessly and in certainty.

The human Name of the Word, Jesus, represents the three aspects of perfection necessary to perfect manifestation in this world, namely equilibrium, receptivity and transmission. The Christian or personal name, represents in sound the personality or radiation of the incarnate soul to whom it belongs. To call a person by his Christian name is a sign of intimacy, and all intimacy is a privilege varying in degree in accordance with the receptivity and radiations of the friends concerned. This exercise gives us the privilege of tuning in to the personal Name of the Son of God.

The Name is pronounced **Dyè-Thu-Th** Say it slowly to yourself.

Dy is just the sound of the letter <u>D</u>, and **è** of the word "<u>yea</u>" (French "tr<u>è</u>s") **Thu** is pronounced as in "c<u>oo</u>", and **Th** as in "<u>th</u>-at".

You may ask why **Dyè-Thu-Th** and not Jesus. It came through in these three syllables, but no explanation of its form was given. Years after, one of the members who was a great linguist and knew Aramaic, told me that **Dyè-Thu-Th** is the Aramaic form of the name Jesus.

The first syllable of **Dyè** represents equilibrium in matter, and is in the shape of a triangle of vivid deep blue light. It is flashed down at the back of the head on the right-hand side, starting

73

just above it. It runs along the nape of the neck, and flashed back to the point above the right side of the head. It is brought down on a deep outbreath to the sound of **Dyè-è-è**, forming a right-angled triangle.

The next syllable **Thu** is also in vivid blue light, but the shape is a chalice on the top of the head, starting on the left side, and the base of the cup is the top of the head. The shape of **Thu** represents perfect receptivity. Form the chalice on a deep inbreath, and know that you will receive in Light all that you can.

Th is a very soft breath sound, on an outbreath. It is a flash of light that comes through the head, flashes through the body, and ends in the left side in a spiral movement forwards, and feels like a pulse. It is perfect transmission and givingness.

Thus Jesus represents on earth the radiation of perfect flesh and blood - the Triangle, equilibrium; the Chalice, receptivity; the Spiral, transmission.

Tune in to Him, and become Him, receiving His body and His blood.

Dyè-è-è, on a strong outbreath.
Thu on an inbreath.
Th on a soft outbreath.

The Sound of The Name is:-   **DYÈ-THU-TH**

The Triangle is:-   **DYÈ**   (on an outbreath)

The Chalice is:-   **THU**   (on an inbreath)

The Flash and Spiral is:-**TH**   (on an outbreath)

74

THE NAME

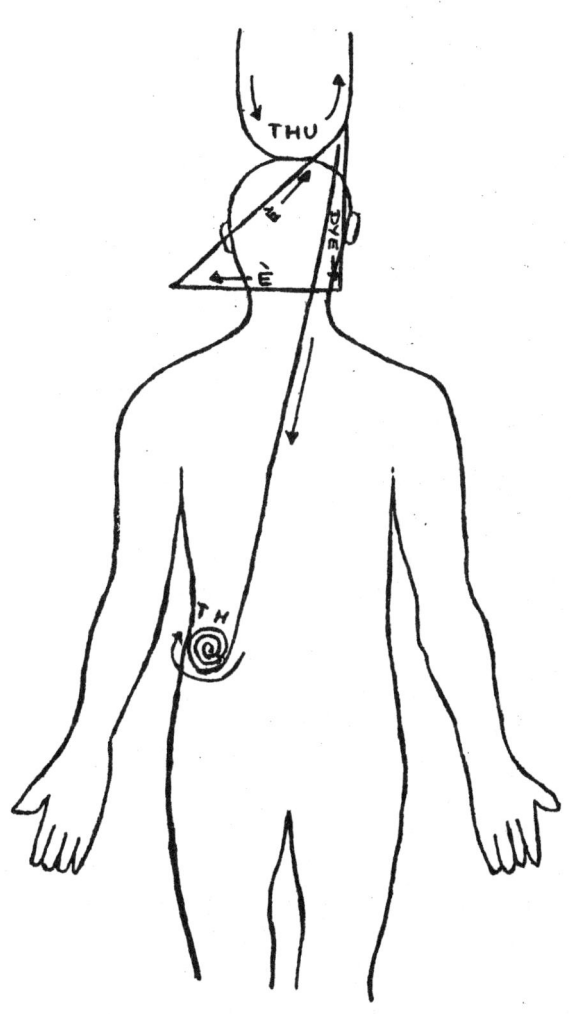

TALK
The Name

You know that this is the Christian Initiation and being initiated into the experiences of Christ necessarily makes us focus our minds on trying to understand what enabled Him to demonstrate a new way of living. Most of us are educated to rely on ourselves, and even if we are told that there is a God who will direct our lives for us, we have not a very great belief in Him as someone who really understands world affairs.

We put God onto a spiritual and mystical plane, and we are quite unable to understand how He functions from a worldly point of view. Through our religious teaching we try to understand the mind of God and how He works in heaven, but we have little or no comprehension of how He works on earth. If wars are the result of God's direction we do not think much of it, yet if they are not ordained by God who is all powerful, what is the use if He cannot prevent man from destroying himself and nations? Where does God stand in relationship to world affairs? Jesus came to demonstrate that to us. He taught that given mental confidence, God can work through the human instrument and bring everything to pass, but He needs the human instrument, and therefore He sent His Son to demonstrate the fact that mutual confidence is necessary to manifest God's will, and how it should work on earth.

I think you will realise that most intelligent people do not believe this to be a working proposition. They think that if you want to do a thing, do it yourself and it is futile to wait for God because you may wait all your life. Yet if we look at the record of the New Testament we realise that Jesus never did anything without the co-operation of the Father. He stressed it again and again that the things He did were done through Him by God, and His Father was able to do exactly the same works through anybody who would give Him their confidence.

This confidence in divine power was a new movement in life, and theologians have found it difficult to reconcile the humanity and divinity of Christ. They thought that either He was a wonderful man with no divine relationship or that He was God come to earth, so that it was ridiculous to think of Him as a normal human being. They were blind to the possibility of co-operation between any individual of the human race and God the Father. So we have to re-focus our minds, and no longer to have any *self-reliance*. We must place our reliance where it belongs, into the power of the Christ to function through us as the Father was able to function through Jesus. The method is the same, and He initiated the disciples into that method, which was recorded as being technical, scientific and unemotional. They were most matter-of-fact ordinary people with nothing particularly psychic or intelligent about them, but normal people whom you could take from every walk of life as He did. There was Matthew from a sedentary occupation, Luke from a more technical side of life, and Peter an ordinary fisherman.

He had to have twelve aspects of human mentality, and to demonstrate through these twelve this method of co-operation; but He did insist on a certain formula for them after He left. He said that they must tune in to Him and that they could not do it in their own strength; they might get swollen headed because the things they did were above the average, and if they wanted to do the things He did they must have the same confidence in Him that He had in His Father. "It is the Father that doeth the works," and if they remembered Christ, He would do the works through them. That was the method. They must focus their minds on Him because He

radiated out harmony of matter. In His flesh and blood He had changed the condition of insulation into receptivity. He received from the Father and He wanted to train the twelve to receive from Him in the same way.

They only had the same as we have, a body to do it through. He never stressed the brain or chose the best brains in the country for His demonstration, as we do. The world worships the brain, but the trouble is that there are not good enough hearts or blood in their veins to be able to make a contact with the body and blood of Christ, because the world does not believe in His power. The world believes in its own strength of mental will.

How do we do it without mental effort or fear of extraordinary results which we are not prepared to face at the moment? It is normal to have a personality and name that will give you confidence and that is why trademarks have been invented to recognise the real from the synthetic. Hatters and costume makers put their own name in their creations and so you know they are responsible for that form and design.

I want to talk this morning about a name. It is of vital importance that we understand the Name of Jesus and what it represents in radiation. We know what electricity represents in radiation but we do not know what it would mean to us if we could contact the body and blood of Jesus in the same way as He contacted the body and blood of God the Father.

Do not think it was only the mental wavelength that enabled Jesus to heal leprosy. The Father had to have Jesus as a physical instrument through whom this voltage of health could be transmitted. God had to have a body on earth through whom perfect health could be transmitted; He had to have somebody who could receive perfect health into His own body. I want you to realise the solid substance of the body of God. Do understand the relationship of He who created matter, with matter. Do not divorce Him from His own substance as so many spiritual minds do, who cannot believe that He is physically substantial. He is not of the visible physical substance such as we are burdened with, but with matter as it was in the beginning, is now and ever shall be. God is radiant matter, the energy that produces form and substance: such form and substance and radiance as our eyes have never seen but which our inner eye does occasionally receive. A pattern of such beauty and potency that Jesus knew well and was familiar with. It was normal to Him to know that He only had to ask the Father for health to pass on to suffering humanity, and He would receive it in a spark.

I am going to pass on to you your capacity to heal suffering humanity as Jesus did, by drawing into you the substance of health, the harmony of perfect flesh and blood. The church was built to preserve a portion of it; we have churches all over the world for different aspects of the same truth, a contact of substance of this world with the next. Bread and wine, flesh and blood; how much do we believe that the bread and wine we take really represents the physical substance of the body of Jesus? Bread and wine are not symbols to us when we are hungry and thirsty, but they have become symbols of mystical unreality.

When I was first given the shape and colour and sound of the Name of Jesus I thought it was a very individual experience, and as it is in human nature to retain and secretly enjoy a wonderful experience it never entered my head I should have to pass on to others something so beautiful. You feel that the moment you pass on something, part of it gets spoilt. Minds spoil beauty quicker than any other method, but when I started sharing this knowledge with anyone who wanted to receive it, I came to a point when I knew I had nothing further to give unless I gave them this. Everything in me shrank from making public something so secretly precious, but I was shown that He had not given it to me as a secret but to pass on as you would pass on to people who needed it, any abundance you had received, and it was everybody's right to make this contact with Him.

The Name of Jesus represents three aspects of God. Perfect equilibrium in matter is in the shape of a right angled triangle of deep blue which is flashed at the back of the head as a protection. Not one of us has perfect equilibrium in material conditions but if we tune in to that condition of earthed humanity, we must receive it. We do not acquire or possess it but we have it radiated into us every time we call upon His Name.

The second syllable is in the shape of a chalice on top of our head which then becomes purely receptive to the will of God. This will is a brilliant white ray pouring down onto the chalice made to receive it, for that blue of perfect humanity attracts God's will. We become one with that condition of receptivity and one with God the Father when we make the chalice on our head.

The third syllable is like a flash of lightning going through our head and body to the left side. When this understanding and diagram in Light

was given to me, I was taken in a flash to the cross and was shown the spear piercing His side. It was at the point where the water and blood were released, the serum in the body and the glandular substances, the white and red corpuscles. It was a transmission of life energy, and it was not just by chance that the soldier pierced His side but a cosmic design. If only the human race can understand that this universal capacity of receptivity and transmission of life is ours for the asking.

So the whole of His Name which has been called **Dyè-Thu-Th** is the blue triangle, the chalice and the flash down to the side with a little spiral that works until it is so established in our body that giving is a radiation of happiness and not a mental thing at all. When we give out at the side neither our right nor our left hand register. That which is given out of the head is registered but what we give out at the side is a radiation of selfless love. It must become a new normality to do everything in His Name. "If ye ask anything in my name ye shall have it," and that is absolutely true. It is equally true that our own brain functions so quickly that we cut our contact almost before we have made it.

In the early days when I gave the **Dyè-Thu-Th** to people they wanted to know why it was called **Dyè-Thu-Th** and I could not tell them. I could only pass on what I had received and knew to be true, not mentally but through my own experience. You can pass on the pattern but not the experience and I could only say that I knew it worked, as they would know if they would try it.

I was always being questioned as to the reality of the sounds that came through to demonstrate the different substances of light. I had accepted for many years that the name of Jesus was **Dyè-Thu-Th** in Light. Later on I was talking to one of the members who was a very great linguist and we were discussing the fact that sound never ceases. At that time there had been a hint of an invention that could pick up sound of many years ago. That led us to wonder whether the voice of Jesus was sounding in Palestine and if it would be distinguishable. We realised that not one of us could speak Aramaic so that we should not know what He was saying. This man went off and started learning Aramaic and came to me in great excitement to tell me that the Aramaic for Jesus is **Dyè-Thu-Th**. If I had demanded confirmation I should not have got it, and I have never demanded confirmation of that which is revealed, but so often it is given to me as a gift.

The sound was confirmed but the understanding that **Dyè** is in the shape of a triangle, flashing at the back of the head is the revelation of the Technique in Light, given for our generation for making the contact with Him that His disciples made, and the works they did should be done as easily through us as long as we do them in His Name.

This is an exercise for us individually, for the changing of our own physical radiation into a harmony of expression, so that the difficulties and disharmonies shall be absorbed in His harmony. That was how His miracles were done, because He radiated natural harmony as well as human harmony. He was one with nature, the elements, human nature and God because of the harmony of His substance.

We do not understand harmony of oneness. We try to match things to get them as much the same as we can, but in reconciling two opposite conditions, oneness is produced. It is not striving to make ourselves into imitation Christs, but trying to become one with Him. When we try to imitate Him we are not finding out what He wants us to do. He did not imitate God and say, "I am a very good imitation of my Father." On the contrary He said, "If ye had known me ye would have known my Father also, I and my Father are one." That is oneness. The sharing of ourselves with Jesus makes us one with Him. We share His Name, His equilibrium, receptivity and givingness, His transmission, and become one in that sharing; one radiation of human achievement, and so the things He did shall be done by us again. Because the problems of our modern life are more complicated than those which confronted Him, those are the more complicated or greater things to be done in our generation. If they are done by the same method we shall be used to resolve them, but we must remember that we can only do it in His strength.

Do the exercise every morning and as often as you can remember during the day. When you have difficult contacts to make, go in His Name, then you are out of the picture and He is the focal point. Most of us try to brace ourselves to meet the emergencies of our daily life. Become so impregnated with equilibrium, receptivity and transmission of love and life that at a moment of crisis you will function spontaneously and not on a preconceived formula.

If I had not been given His Name I could never give a lecture, but I know He can talk and take over as long as my mind is tuned in to His. When we do that, the responsibility is His and not ours, but the moment we go in our own strength we must take what our weakness draws to us. We are not strong and He wants our weakness. His Name glows when our weak vibration is resolved in His. He feeds on our weakness and does not need our strength, for He is strength. All our inability to function is the very substance of His being. It is like feeding any instrument; you have to add oil, wood or coal to make a different energy. There is no heat in coal until the opposite condition is brought into action and then the radiation is heat. When our weakness is brought into contact with His strength, it is life, so never be afraid of using that Name at any time. Nobody need know. I do the Technique with my eyes shut because I can focus better, but if you have to do His Name in a public place your television set can see the blue flash at the back of the head, the chalice, and feel the spark, and it is done in three breaths.

We have to re-focus and realise that when we know we can do nothing, that is the moment when anything can be done through us. As soon as we feel we ourselves are doing it and we are the focal point of the works, we have terrible disillusionment. It is there I think that most organised conditions break down. If any individual makes themselves the focal point of love and life, they are bound to be humiliated, and they deserve it. I think that caused the breakdown of the early church;

when the focus was changed, the works stopped, when the focus goes onto an individual or group of individuals, and not back again to Christ. We could not have so many different aspects of Christ if our minds were focused on Him, but when they drop to bricks and mortar or vestments or ritual, or anything away from Him, then there come these separate points of view, arguments and disharmony. If everybody in every nation in the world could focus their mind and understanding on the method Jesus incarnated to give to the world we could have a renewal of life and energy, and the fear of destructive conditions that might dominate would vanish away. If we can integrate the atom, what does it matter how many people split it?

I think it is very interesting to realise the disharmony of nature at the moment of the crucifixion. The atom was split when He voluntarily separated His atomic energy from the Source, and the whole disharmony of the exteriorization of that scene took place. The moment disharmony is earthed it goes on and on; and the moment harmony is earthed, it too goes on and on. Do not think that disharmony has greater strength than harmony, for that is where fear lies.

Jesus Christ was a very ordinary person like ourselves. He never set out to be extraordinary; right from the beginning He took such care to be ordinary and have nothing more than any other person so that never should anybody suffer from an inferiority complex. The moment you tune into Love and Life, you are love and life. You cannot separate yourself from the focus of your mind. Therefore none of us can ever claim merit for anything we do. If we do, then we must of necessity bring down the whole level of Christian achievement into the dust. That which is done through us is not done by us. We have no responsibility; what is good in us is not us, and that which is not so good is ourselves; that is where we stand.

Do not pass this exercise on to anybody. It is given to us individually and is a very intimate contact which we have no right to pass on to anybody from an interesting point of view. I found in the early days that people used to give their friends certain exercises and talks to try to interest them. Do not do that for if they want the Technique they will do so because of your works and not because they will just be interested on the mental side. We need instruments and people who are willing to empty themselves of themselves, and be filled with Christ's energy. I do not want to stimulate people's intelligence but to train those who want to be trained.

RHYTHM OVER THE HEAD

The next exercise in Light follows the Transmuting Light. Our bodies are outlined in Light, and we have received our daily bread through the exercise of the Shafts; made known our needs and been strengthened internally by the Transmuting Light.

Now sit up with feet crossed and hands, with palms upwards, resting on or just above the knees. In this position we visualise the first definite rhythm in Light; a rhythm which is very important because it brings Light to two most vital parts of the body, the spine and the head.

In the given sitting position and on a long inhaling breath, draw a ribbon of white light from the base of your spine to the nape of your neck in one curved line: in the same breath bring the light over your head in three short curved lines, and on an exhaling breath, pour it into your hands, completely filling them with light. This both vitalises and protects your spine, head and hands. Do this three times.

Then, while your hands are thus filled with light, dedicate them and your feet in the following way. With the tongue, make a cross in each hand, and with the two moistened forefingers, make a similar cross on the sole of each foot.

Thus you start the day outlined, fed and protected in Light, and able to use your hands and feet in creative service throughout the day.

Rhythm over the Head

It is difficult for people when first starting the Technique to realise what is the action of light and breath on the body, how it energises the blood and changes the mental wavelength and ability of the person to receive in a flash the illumination of their mind.

It is not important for us to know how light functions but it is important that we know the reactions of our thoughts on our physical body. The life energy changes our mental radiations; we draw in power, life and as our mind reacts to the energy, so shall we either think in and make ourselves the focus of that energy, or we will radiate out into the world because we want to serve our neighbour and change conditions. Either we want to be the focal point, or the world is the focal point. Whether we are an introvert or an extrovert is discernible by our actions.

We are all educated in our different environments and we function according to our education (I am talking of the way in which life educates us). Our circumstances and environment produce a definite condition of mind in us, and we must have a pattern by which we know ourselves in relationship to truth. We generally know ourselves in relation-ship to somebody else, possibly another member of the family. We may think ourselves to be more or less clever than our family, and we have a comparative condition which gets us nowhere at all, so let us compare ourselves with the mind of Christ which we know was the reflection of the mind of God. Christ brought the mind of God into physical demonstration through His living radiation.

The Technique in Light is to enable us to do two things: to focus our mind on the mind of Christ, and therefore to get the radiations in our body of the physical perfection of the resurrection body of Jesus Christ. These are the two objectives, and we cannot do it without learning to focus our mind.

Some people are so self-centred that you may spend hours with them and never get beyond their ego. There are others in whose company you may spend an equal number of hours and they never talk or think of themselves; they may take you out into the world and seem to encompass the whole world. If we focus on the mind of Christ He is bound to give us a completely cosmic point of view. He was the cosmic mind made visible. He knew the laws that govern nature and identified Himself with them. He knew human nature and He knew it because He loved it. We only know the things we love. We may think we know about the functioning speed of light; we only know by experience how light works on the body and we can only know truth by experience. We have to realise by the demonstration of Jesus Christ that He knew, and through our own demonstration, that we do not know.

Humanity does not know how to live, they do not know the source of life or what happens when life leaves the body; they know nothing of the before and after. Yet all knowledge is available to the person who is trained to receive it, so do realise the simplicity of our training when you think of our great objective, which is the complete physical health and happiness for any individual who can receive it. Do not ever in your mind think that the training for so great an objective is complicated. You may make it complicated and say that other things are more important. You may be prepared to pay vast sums to doctors and nursing homes but not to give a little time to receive into your own body that which you are prepared to pay for. We have always depended on others to do things for us and live for us.

This training is for self-healing, self-revelation and complete independence of everybody else except yourself and the Source of life. We shall of necessity share with our neighbour the good things we receive for we cannot keep them to ourselves, but the whole objective of the training is for self-healing; not that you come here to be healed but that you shall know how to receive your own healing. Everybody who is a channel here has received it in the same way as you are starting to do; it is a universal condition but it all depends on the process of your mind, in fact the whole of the result of the training depends on that.

"Ye have not because ye ask not," and in your heart you want something else. You want mental power and the development of your own mind rather than to receive the mind of Christ because we have not tried to know much about it. We have not looked upon His mind as being the fundamental need of every living soul. We have thought that we must acquire knowledge but not that we must train people to receive true wisdom and learn to absorb it into their being so that they shall be wise.

You cannot be wise until you make a contact with wisdom; and you cannot be fed until you receive food. Our soul bodies are starved until we make a contact with Light, and so we have this very simple process which will provide for everybody the experience of knowing for themselves that they have as great a capacity to receive from Christ as the disciples had two thousand years ago. There are very ordinary people alive today and they were very ordinary people who lived then; we hear their names in churches all over the world - Matthew, Mark, Luke and John, but they were not greater people with a greater capacity than us. They were not great scientists or very intelligent, but their need to make a contact with the mind of Christ, and His need to have minds that would make a contact with His, were so great that the attraction of His heart drew those few into His environment and He shared His mind with them. The moment He did this they became able to demonstrate in the same way as He demonstrated, and so we come down to the need for learning to focus our mind on Him.

The spine is the instrument designed to receive the cosmic rays and the flexible vertebrae should be sparking all the way down the spine. The perfect physical body is a radiation of the cosmic rays and even in your own spine, though you may have a curvature, that part which is not curved, must spark and receive the eternal life rays of cosmic energy.

I am going to give you an exercise to make your spine spark. You receive the blessing into your head and hands and protect yourself against the incoming mental wavelengths of the human mind. Wherever your place of temptation may be during the day, whether in your home or at your work, this exercise is to protect you against malice and uncharitableness and the critical faculty sparking from the human mind, although you may not realise the need for this protection.

I have stressed the importance of your spine and to learn to spark there; it will spark and become alive and change the whole function of the trunk of the body because it is connected with the inner nerves and functions of the body. It is a most important structure because it is so receptive and it depends on the very marrow that lives in your bones. You learn to vitalise the spine, bringing the vitality over your head, pouring it into your hands, making the circle round and allowing the elbows to spark; and this circle will go before you during the rest of your day.

We are so sensitive to the opinions of others about ourselves and we cannot make allowances for their nerves. It is difficult to get up in complete equilibrium in the morning and we have not the outfit to do it, but I hope you will get that outfit when you are doing the Technique in Light in the morning. Think that you are putting on your armour of light, your spine being protected by light, your head having over it a helmet of light, your hands being filled with light and your joints beginning to spark.

As we grow older and our minds get drier and our bones get drier, if we have not got life and energy we must sag and cannot help it, but in this process of taking in every day and changing the condition of our mind, we must get more life every day. If you can only keep that life going and circulating in you, you cannot feel old at the same time, for you are continuing to draw in life and it is a daily service. If it is not a daily service, the mind must dominate this condition of receptivity.

I do not care how receptive your mind is, until you can demonstrate in your physical body, I will not believe that you are really doing the Technique and focusing on the mind of Christ. I will believe that you are drawing on a universal condition, but are you making a contact with the mind of Christ? If you are making a contact with His mind you must take on the body and blood of Christ and the world must know it for you are then a channel; but you are not a channel if you only take on light, you are a conductor.

When you do these exercises in the morning, be real. Realise that you are drawing the light into your hands not mystically but physically. Your arms are absorbing energy, your throat is being vitalised, your mind is learning to focus on the Figure of Light, sparking back to the source of Light. The Figure of Light is your filter through which all the disease energy is going to be breathed down, and through that filter you are going to take all the perfect earth radiations your blood will need.

Do not expect others to do this better than you because they started to do the Technique earlier. You have all benefitted by the years of experience of others, and you can pick it up today exactly as it is being sparked by the group of people who have been learning the truth of this very exact formula.

Visualise to yourself every morning this wonderful condition to illuminate your spine, with the light pouring over your skull. We are getting the condition of the structure of the body in the early exercises and then we are given exercises to get the freedom of the detail of the body.

Do realise the difference between receiving a condition and inducing it. I can only tell you that it is such a spontaneous condition that often it takes me a long time to realise what I have received. That is your safeguard for the mind does not work with the speed of light, so you only have to be faithful each day to allow your body to become spontaneous.

It is not a natural condition in any of us to receive eternal life and focus our mind on the mind of Christ. It is more natural to focus our mind on ourselves, but to get this external condition of focus is the freedom from physical illness.

THE SOUL BODY

The soul is the eternal physical manifestation of the individual ego, and it takes on the substance of its environment. When on earth, flesh and blood; and when in heaven (which is the world of Light) it sheds the denser matter of earth and radiates the substance of its environment.

If we had X-ray eyes we would see the basic form of the soul body. Just as the physical structure has the bones, the spine, skull, pelvis, the skin, ankles, feet, arms and hands, so the basic structure of the soul body has a brilliant white trunk in which every colour known, and at present unknown, is contained.

On the left is a beautiful wing radiation of aquamarine light which is the substance of universal love, as differentiated from personal emotion. On the right is a wing of amber light which is the universal capacity to receive wisdom. At the back from the nape of the neck to the base of the spine, radiates a brilliant ruby coloured wing of light, the organ of direction. Therefore the skeleton of the soul provides the activity of love, wisdom and direction, received and transmitted by the trunk of brilliant white light, the I AM of the ego.

Every soul body is linked in radiation with the body of God. The brain of the individual on earth determines the contact; it can unite with or separate from the Source of Love, Wisdom and Direction at will. It is the mental wavelength that provides the contact. Jesus came to teach people their capacity to unite their eternal bodies with the Creator.

Mind governs the forming of substance; therefore if the mind focuses on life, the body receives it; if on death, life recedes. If our lovely and perfect soul bodies could triumph over the physical encasement we should be able to fuse the substance into the intense radiation of Christ's resurrected body and it would become one with the ether, travelling as He did on the etheric currents out of visibility.

If only we had the mind of Christ! That mind which never turned inwards but always observed the need of the world and so never provided, as we do, the substance of insulation from life.

This is not an exercise. Only experience can cause our wings to shine, our soul body to glow with eternal life. Contemplating or taking thought will add no lustre to our wing of direction. Only focusing our minds on Christ, presenting our needs to Him, sparking our worries away, sharing our laughter with Him, identifying all our homely occupations with His humble experiences can we begin to realise our capacity. When nothing casts us down, when no human mind has domination over us, when we can give thanks for all that happens to us, then and only then, shall we share in His glorious freedom from self.

AH-LAH-HIÈVE

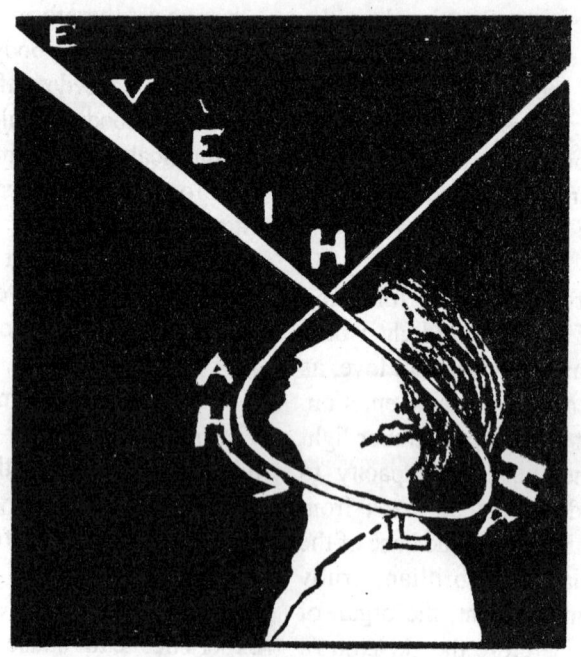

AH-LAH-HIÈVE

Visualise a shaft of white light coming from infinity down in front of the face, piercing the throat and flashing halfway up the back of the head. It rays through the head and out of the middle of the forehead, straight back into the forehead of the Christ.

This exercise is done at night, either standing or sitting, after the Golden Spirals and Blue Circles.

The power of the light pouring through the head washes the mind clean of all dusty thoughts accumulated during the day, and in the morning the mind should awaken cleared of yesterday's failures and frustrated endeavour.

On the sound **Ah-Lah**, on a deep inhaling breath, bring the light down through the throat and up the back of the head.

On the sound **Hiève**, on a forceful outbreath, flash the light through the head and out through the centre of the forehead, back into the visualised radiance of the mind of the Christ.

The head should be tilted upwards and this exercise should be done three times. It can, of course, be done during the day as well - when the need for clear thinking is urgent.

Pronounciation

Hi	**as in "see"**
è	**as in "yea" (French "très")**
ve	**as in French "de"**

91

TALK
Ah-Lah-Hiève

I want to talk about the balance of the physical and spiritual. We have always known that the Christian Initiation is achieving the balance of the Christ's divinity and humanity. It is very difficult for ordinary people to know whether one's material physical life or one's inner spiritual mental life is the more important. Which governs the activity of our life? Is our body the result of our mind, or are we spiritually the result of our physical health? Doctors will say one thing and another, and we think that if only we had better health we should be nicer people; or we cannot understand why, because we are nice, we are not physically stronger.

What does the Technique in Light do to establish the balance of our physical and spiritual life? Why do some people suffer physically, and others suffer mentally and spiritually? What is the right course and how do we change?

Only lately I have understood how accurately the Technique in Light is designed to produce that balance. Every exercise is for the revitalising of a certain part of the body. The cutting exercise at night goes right through the spine and trunk of the body. Is it only a visualisation to concentrate our minds on that gold light, or is it really doing something? What is the reaction of these different substances of light on our physical self? We can only know through our individual experience: I cannot know for you, but only for myself. You know for yourself because the reaction of your personality to your individual life depends firstly on the receptivity of your mind and secondly on the reaction of your body, your nerves and your glands. Therefore we must put first the focus of our mind because we have to change the mind so that the body may change. It is not mind over matter and the development of your mind to govern the physical reaction of the body, but it is the necessity for changing the habit of your thought and eliminating fear out of the mind. Fear of present day conditions is the cause of nearly all the physical ills of present day life.

Fear is a mental condition, a spiritual sin, because fear is lack of confidence in God, in divine direction and in one's ability to receive divine direction. We could not be afraid if we knew always how to turn to the Light, for darkness disappears when we put on the light. Fear must be eliminated when we have confidence in God, but as we do not know God the Christian Initiation is to teach us to know, through experience, the power of Jesus Christ.

God is all power if we are connected up with that power, but He is impotent to heal a disconnected person. When we disconnect the focus of our mind from the mind of Christ, fear is the natural reaction. We are afraid of taking a false step and making a wrong decision, of saying and doing the wrong thing, and we fear the future. The only person who is not afraid of the future is the one who has complete confidence.

Christ was fearless because of His experience - not because of a lack of experience, but because He went through every human experience. He did not try to get over the obstacles presented to Him, nor to get round them, or to retreat, but He went *through* them. I have always told everybody that the Christ dimension is *'throughness'*, through experience into confidence, and that is why we have these difficult experiences.

How should we know that we had confidence if our human mind did not fail us, or if we were self-satisfied people who said, "I always know my own mind, what to say and do, and I am never afraid of speaking my mind." Very few of us are like that

and most of us become exceedingly conscious that we do not know and cannot know until the moment of receptivity is in us, for that moment is the present.

At any moment of the day you can tune in and know, and you will continue to know. You cannot know for tomorrow but you will continue to know for today, which is all that is necessary although you may not think so. You may say that you have to make plans affecting the future and to know what the result of your action is going to be, but that is not true. Nobody knows what the result of any action is going to be when you get divine direction, you simply have to trust. Jesus never knew until the reaction was there, and He could not know because He did things in this world that had never been done before. He was a channel for the Father to demonstrate through Him; the Father had never had a perfect channel through whom He could demonstrate before, therefore there was no precedent known to man as to what the result of Christ's love for humanity was going to be. He tuned in to the Father and the Father told Him what to do and did it through Him, but Jesus did not know the result of that action. We demand to know and want to know what is going to be the result of being obedient.

How can we know the operation of the

fourth dimension in this world? How do we know when we go through an experience what the result is going to be? We do not know. Jesus did not know from moment to moment, and we shall never know the result of this change of mind. We cannot know what the result in ourselves is going to be like, nor the reaction on somebody else. If your individual faith is established so that you are not afraid to own to acting on inspiration and the result, whatever it may be, will be right, that is where fear will be eliminated, when we are not afraid because we know we are acting on the divine direction of our own inspiration. It must function in us every minute of the day.

I want to give you an exercise which revitalises the glands of your head. Most of us are so muddle-minded and disconnected through lack of energy of the pituitary and pineal glands. Our minds do not function quickly enough and we do not know how to spark. We may have been trained along contemplative lines and if given enough time can arrive at a fairly good decision, but we think we must have time. You must not have time for a condition of inspiration. Do not give yourself time, but learn to so spark in the present that time is unnecessary for the true functioning of your mind. The result on your body of this sparking condition of contact would be effortless living, where we are now dying. Some of us have dead eyes, our ears, muscles, nerves or organs are all in a state of disintegration.

You may say that your case is hopeless because you are minus this part or that, and it is too late. From a reasonable point of view I agree with you, but I have changed any reasonable point of view and finished with reason, for I do not need it. I do not know how the Christ can function today through a disintegrating body. He could do it two thousand years ago, and I believe that He could do it today, if He had the channel.

I want you to understand our individual responsibility. The Father could function through the channel of the humanity of Jesus, and He can do it through our humanity. The only thing lacking in your humanity and mine, is the focus of our mind. The mind of Jesus was focused the whole time on the Father, and that sparking condition was continuous in Him so that He never knew fear, therefore He was without sin; it is absolutely simple. It is perfectly possible to be without sin if you are without fear. If you are without fear you are one with Love, because perfect love and the contact with perfect love, casteth out fear. Torment is the reaction of fear and you are tormented in mind and body through a condition of fear.

This exercise is called the **Ah-Lah-Hiève**. It is a very flashing condition of light coming straight down in front of the face, passing through the throat, running halfway up the back of the head, through the brow and into the brow of Christ, so that we are linked mentally with Him and at the same time we are being revitalised in every condition in our head. There should not be a single nerve in our head that is not touched by the **Ah-Lah-Hiève** light, but do not direct it to any particular nerve, for light will always find the minus condition. We have to focus our mind on this radiant bar of light.

When this exercise was shown to me I saw a slat of light. I was told to direct the light through my throat, head and brow and straight to this bar of light where the whole contents of my head would be merged into it. It was a merging of the disease energy, ignorant thoughts and fear, out of my mind into the light. I did that exercise for some time and one evening as I did it, suddenly saw the face of Christ and realised that what I had thought was a bar of light, was His brow. I had been directing the contents of my brow into His, and He was sucking it out of my system into His. That which I gave of the contents of my mind was fused with the brilliance of His.

We have to understand that Christ's mind is one with the mind of God, in which there is all knowledge and love; all caringness for humanity is in the mind of Christ. It is difficult for us to realise that as individuals we are of great importance to Him. He needs our humanity as the Father needed the humanity of Jesus. He needs our humanity to demonstrate again this freedom from fear and there is only one way of getting rid of fear, and that is by offering it to Light. Fear is the very substance of darkness and you can tell by the look in a person's eyes if they are telling a story that has an element of horror in it. People go dark with fear and horror and with all things that are the works of darkness.

There is only one way of getting all conditions of darkness out of our mind and that is by being obedient and sending our darkness into Light. "Lighten our darkness." That refers not to night, but to thoughts, and it is done on the **Ah-Lah-Hiève**. The whole of my mind goes into His on that ray of light, and I am empty of myself. It is the beginning of emptying our mind into His so that in a flash He can spark the inspiration we need because our mind is empty of clutter. It must take place every evening so that we go to bed free of the continual thoughts circling round in our mind, perhaps over domestic worries. When the light is out, how easy it is to remember the things which have been forgotten during the day and those things for tomorrow which an active mind finds it difficult to release.

Do the **Ah-Lah-Hiève**, not lying down but with the head raised and the direction of the mind going upwards. Do not earth it down because you will not get rid of it. We do that and the weight of intellect drags the head down. Old age takes the head downwards but it is a sign of eternal youth if the head is always up and the spine straight. This will be so if it is the habit of your mind always to look up. If you always associate the unity of your mind with the mind of Christ, you cannot look down. I could not give a talk with my head looking down for I could not get my contact and so the habit of my mind has been changed through these technical exercises.

We have looked to the Source of light and found it, and revelation has come into us all because we have been obedient in looking for it, and asking for it, and in trying to get rid of ourselves.

The paradox of being important to God and unimportant to ourselves is true. The world teaches us to be self-important, or we think with false modesty that we are only specks in the universe and that we are not important to God or Christ, and He does not recognise us or know us individually, in spite of the detailed information given to us on that subject. We have been likened unto sparrows, and more so. Even the sparrows are individuals to the Creator, yet we dare to say that we are not important and it does not matter if we live our life according to our will and desire, that it will not have any effect on the divine plan.

More and more in this time of difficulty and chaos do I realise how important we are to Him. If in our lives, difficult as they are, He can be certain of a mind that will react instantly to His voice, so that all our organs will respond to His, once we have given Him our mind do you think He is going to withhold His from us? The object of giving our mind to Him is to get His in exchange. Which of us would rather have our own, if we can have the knowledge of the operation of law which Jesus had?

Will you do the Technique quickly and faithfully sparking. Get rid of yourself and your personality, and then drop off to sleep in the certain knowledge that you will wake up in the morning knowing for your day what is needed of you. Do not send your mind in fear to the future. Live your day, day by day, and see what it can bring forth. Empty your mind

96

at night and walk your way in confidence.

Light is stronger than darkness; life is stronger than death, and if He can get such a magnetic personality earthed so that all the disconnected spirits will be re-connected in their humanity back again to Love, then this appalling separation from Love that we are witnessing in the world today will belong to the old earth.

If you and I cannot do it, why should we think that anybody else will? That is why Jesus incarnated and lived such a drab existence, for nobody had a more restricted life than His, with nothing outside to help. If He could go through drabness into glory, so can we.

Do not be afraid of the restrictions and difficulties which we have to go through here, for the reaction from then will be utterly new. Never before have I been so happy in the utter certainty that this work is coming to complete fulfilment and fruition. I am equally certain that everybody in this room is going to know for themselves, for it depends on everyone here whether that condition is going to become the new earth, the new race, the new heaven that is prophesied. How can the former things pass away unless they are taken away and the new be brought into manifestation?

THE THROAT

In the middle of the human throat lies the magnetic centre of the light body. Its activity corresponds to that of the human brain, for it is the focusing point for all the cosmic rays.

Physical food is taken through the mouth and spiritual food through the throat. To live in this world it is essential to draw air into the lungs and circulate it through the body. To live in the spirit, it is essential to draw light into the soul and circulate it through the light body.

To develop our spiritual brain we must understand its form and its functioning powers. Will you look at the diagram and realise that you have a flower of living Light in the centre of your throat? The nine petals are of intense white light, and the centre is a glowing ruby light which is the magnetic point of power. It draws into itself all attributes of divine power, absorbs and transmits them into the blood, so that in time the very substance and rhythm of our blood changes and we become aware in every fibre of our being of a quickened condition of spiritual awareness. We must learn to draw into our being the very substance of God.

Will you quite simply visualise this lovely flower in your throat and know that when we are spiritually unconscious the nine petals are folded over the ruby centre. We must quite consciously unfold them one by one, rhythmically, until when they are all open the ruby centre receives according to the ego's development, the cosmic rays of creative power, and then instantly closes up again.

This exercise should be done at midday - though any time between 12 noon and 4 o'clock p.m. will do. We need to do it as regularly as we eat our midday meal. It should become as much a habit as washing our hands before we eat. Either stand or sit. Moisten the first finger of the right hand with the saliva in your mouth. Outline the nine petals one by one, starting at the centre, going up the inside of the petal, and ending in the centre. It is done clockwise - that is to say from left to right on the following rhythm — - - - — —, for each petal. Moisten the finger between each petal. Each one stays open until all nine are done - then for a moment in time the ruby centre is fully exposed, draws in all it can receive, and then the petals close instantly and remain closed until the ritual is repeated next day. Every day increases the receptive power.

RHYTHM

♩.	♩♩♩	♩.	♩.
1	2 3 4	5	6

TALK
The Throat

This exercise is one of the most difficult both to explain and to do. I have understood that there has to be a fusion between the soul body and the physical, and that the point of union between the two bodies lies in the throat. There is a receptive point there which is like a battery or, to use another simile, like a sieve through which the energy that is pouring into the soul body passes into the physical body.

99

I was shown this point of fusion in the throat is the shape of a flower with nine petals of a brilliant whiteness, closed over the centre point which is of a marvellous ruby light, and is really the beginning of our wing of direction. In everyone's throat lies this battery, the link between the two bodies. Just as the brain controls the limbs and organs of the body, so is this battery the controlling brain of the energy that comes through from the soul body into the physical. If it is only partially operating only a limited amount of energy passes through. In people whom we are used to think of as young or new souls there is a lack of balance between the two bodies. The centre must be open for this perfect equilibrium.

We are so ignorant of the functioning power of the blood, and the saliva is closely allied to it. It is, after all, the barometer of our emotions and is therefore controlled by the harmony of our blood. The white corpuscles in the blood draw in the forces of Light, and the red corpuscles attract the magnetic forces of the earth. I had a most interesting talk with a biologist who had found what he called the divine substance in the blood. He said that if the component parts of the body were sorted out, you would find that half come from the earth and half from the light forces. This light is transmitted into the human organism through the white corpuscles, and saliva is the essence of that substance of receiving. Therefore when we open these petals we are making a contact between the Light and our physical bodies. I have been asked why there are nine petals instead of eight or sixteen, or any multiple of eight, which is what had been put forward in previous occult teaching. I can only tell you that the ninth petal seems to me to be the petal of revelation - an unknown petal with an unknown result.

The ruby heart of this flower is the central point of the activity of our receptivity, and we will register a different condition of our power to receive revelation when it becomes natural for the petals to be open. We come into this world with the centre protected, and when the soul is ready for the return path or the way of the resurrection body, there must be a conscious opening of the petals. We receive the blood energy of the body of the everlasting cosmic Christ; it is being transmitted into the Christ within each one of us. So few of us realise the capacity we have to draw into us His body and His blood. As we draw it in, we take on also His power of transmission, so that in time we also shall transmit health and harmony.

As you do this exercise, realise that

it does function. Just as water brought to a certain heat must inevitably become steam, so the contact of your saliva with the rhythmic opening of the petals must, just as scientifically, result in the disclosure for one moment, of the centre, which attracts to itself the full charge of the Light which is eternally pouring down.

If we start this Technique on the assumption that it must go along any known line, we shall not get very far. These conditions are unknown and unexpected. We know so little about ourselves and so little about the soul body. Even the terms spirit, soul and body are often confused. I can only pass on to you what I know.

The Spirit is the Eternal Energy.

The Soul is the Individual Eternal Form.

The Body is the Individual Finite Form.

Spirit is the uniting principle running through all form - you never have a fusion of soul, only of spirit. Christ is for ever the Christ in form, and His soul body the most glorious that any incarnate soul will ever behold; but His spirit we can contact and attain to, and become one with it in understanding and power. At death your soul and spirit will throw off your physical body, but your soul will be always the form that will take on different garments on different planes. The spirit will change and progress till we all have the same quality of perfect wisdom and perfect love which we will then transmit through our individual soul bodies.

If we had no separate soul body, we could not express that radiant loveliness of incarnate spirit. People who pass on keep their own individuality, but as they learn, the spirit shines through their soul body. Just as family relationships are a permanent link on this plane, so over there, love is the magnet that draws people together in their soul bodies.

The astral plane is just as much a changing condition as is the earth, of which it is, as it were, a suburb. The soul could not suddenly stand the rarefied atmosphere of the plane of Love, but once one is on the wave-length of Love, one can go straight through to the eternal habitation, here and now. With that contact there could be no fighting on this plane, and no expiation of sin, for the Law cannot be broken.

EQUILIBRIUM OF THE NAME

This exercise should produce the equilibrium of the soul and body. In order to function perfectly on this plane we have to establish a condition of balance in ourselves, between the elements of the earth and the rays that focus in us from the heavens. This can only be accomplished by making of oneself a channel, for until we are empty of ourselves a condition of harmony and equilibrium is not possible. While we do this exercise visualise the Name:-

The blue triangle at the back of the head, the chalice on your head and the line of light flashing into you and curling up on your left side.

Stand with your arms extended in front of you at shoulder level. Let the right palm face down, focusing the earth forces and the left palm face up, focusing the rays from the heavens. The edges of the hands touch, for the little finger of the left hand touches the first finger of the right hand, and the thumb of the right hand points downwards.

On an outbreath, and to the sound of **Dyè, è, è,** move the arms from the shoulders, the left up and the right down. On the sound **Thu**, and with an inbreath, bring them back to the starting position. Now to the sound of **Th** and on an outbreath, slide the right hand slowly over the left with fingers tips towards palms, until the forces concentrated in the palms of your hands have met and can fuse. Then slowly on an inbreath draw them apart back along the same direction, and stand with arms bent at the elbows, elbows into your sides, and palms facing forward.

What you have done is to balance the two forces, visualising the Name as you move your hands. One becomes a channel instantly when one uses the Name, and one takes on His humanity in which is perfect harmony and equilibrium.

Do this as a midday exercise, after you have done the Throat. It is not necessary to do it more than once, nor is it one to repeat during the day.

TALK
Equilibrium of The Name

We must learn together this technique of becoming the Christ - to function here as they function in the Light world, to become all that which is taught in the New Testament as being the Law. What we are learning is experience.

In order to function perfectly on this plane we have to establish a condition of balance in ourselves, between the elements of earth and the rays that focus in us from the heavens. We have to learn to establish the equilibrium of soul and body; to get body, soul and spirit into alignment.

When I was given the Name of Jesus, it was for the purpose of tuning my mind in to His mind. Remember what the Name signifies - in it is all life, all love, all knowledge and all givingness. The sum of these makes up the Life Principle of the whole cosmos, an eternal standard of living. Jesus earthed a perfect equilibrium of life for the human race and when we do the exercise of the Name, for a fraction of time we *become* the Name, taking on His wavelength in the same way that one tunes in to some station on the wireless. We know quite well what it is to tune in to a dominating mind, be it that of a friend, a member of one's family, or someone contacted in one's work - we become subject to their wavelength. Therefore when we tune in to Jesus Christ we *do* become subject to Him, and we become fearless in that contact because we are, for the moment, Him.

When in this new exercise you add the gestures, you are fashioning the instrument for the receptivity of Light in the body.

You remember that brilliant blue triangle at the back of the head, which comes down on the right side, runs along horizontally and flashes back to the starting point, is equilibrium and stability in matter. No material conditions could overwhelm Jesus. He was in unity with all flesh and was the law that could make flesh whole. He was in unity with life; He was life. As you visualise the triangle and turn the left palm upwards, you receive in it the cosmic rays, and in the right hand, palm turned downwards, the earth vibrations; this is the first syllable **Dyè**.

On **Thu** you visualise a chalice on top of the head, the crown of the head forming the base of the chalice; this is perfect receptivity. When we make that shape we become receptive to the will and power of God, we become for that moment that flash, Him, Himself.

On this inbreath of **Thu** your hands go back to the original position. Then on the third syllable **Th**, the light flashes through the head and body, curling round in a pulse on the left side - the side where He was pierced and from whence flowed blood and water to the ground, changing for all time the vibration of this earth. That pulse is perfect givingness, perfect transmission of life.

So the triangle - stability; the chalice - receptivity; and the spiral - transmission or givingness, have now become synchronised with our physical movements. As the Light flashes through the head and body and pulses in the side, the right hand slides over the left, palm to palm, and a sparking comes into them as the contact is made. Then the hands come apart to an upright position with the elbows bent, palms facing forwards, and radiate out into the world at shoulder height. Thus the equilibrium of the world of Light and of the earth is in our hands and goes forth out of our hands into the world.

We have nothing to do with the direction of it because it has been done in His Name and He is the only person who can direct the cosmic and earth forces. Our hands and feet are points which transmit light and life. People give through their hands what they are. In the laying of of hands, the healing touch; in the work of the artist, the musician, the writer, power and creativeness pass through the hands. The feet give to the earth the vibration of our own personalities. That accounts for the sensations of pleasure or discomfort that some places give, it is where some people have trodden and left their vibrations in the earth. I know that if ever I go to Palestine I shall know where His feet have trod; I shall pick up the vibration because it is there for always.

The world is an infinite condition. Because we do not understand the equilibrium of life we have separated it into heaven and earth, but we shall never get an understanding of life on that basis. To get understanding of our own certainty of experience we must go through the technique of the comprehension of the Law. I knew nothing about life until it was revealed to me along this technique. We have always known the truth there but not here, and we have to establish here the truth our souls have always known.

We have to understand that there is no separation between spirit and matter. The red corpuscles in the blood take the earth's energy, and the white corpuscles take from the ether the life principle of Light. At death the red substance of the blood returns to earth and the white returns to Light from whence it came. With birth, when the quickening condition of life occurs something comes into the blood; the earth energy is there but it needs a greater voltage, which comes and fuses with the energy from the earth and becomes one condition of life. At death the quickening condition returns back to the life force and the earth particles to the earth.

We must learn to establish our own equilibrium. It is so difficult to become really stable because of the condition of emotion in all of us; the emotion of fear, of love, of desperate despair. We long for a state of equanimity in which our peace of mind cannot be disturbed by emotions. The only way we can attain that equanimity is to *become* it, not to visualise it as outside and unattainable, but to bring it inside and become it.

That is the great difference between the Christ and us - He is, and we yearn to become: to become love, to know no fear, really to love our neighbour as ourself. We cannot do it until we really are the Law. Mental suffering is the cause of all toxic conditions of the blood. Even after a healing of the toxic condition, if we return to a memory of past mental pain which brings with it a

recurrence of painful emotion, it will react and later manifest in the physical body. So it is important to do this technique quite simply and having been given the wavelength of Jesus, to tune in to Him incessantly. By tuning in to Love one becomes Love and the responsibility of loving is taken from us. We do not love our enemies, but if we tune in to Love, the Love comes through us, and as He has no enemies, so we have no enemies.

When we are our own wavelength we find it hard to forgive and forget. It is so hard not to hold in memory the things that have hurt us, things we have just missed, words we have said and would give everything to recall. The memory is with us. Like a flash I was given the understanding that He does not remember. He only remembers with us the points of our unity with Him, not the things that separate us. If we remember past pain we are hurting ourselves needlessly. When the sudden memory of a hurt occurs, will you instead tune into His Name, and realise that by that experience you are forgetting. Keep *Him* within *your* memory. He is love, fearlessness and power that can re-create all broken conditions.

Wherever we go we give to the world that which we have and are. Mankind was intended to replenish the earth: what have we given up till now in the way of replenishing? Disease and fear! Now things are changing; because we are able to receive we are bound to give. Do not dwell so much on what has happened in the past, but be full of hope for what can happen in the future. Think what an unconscious radiation of the Equilibrium of the Name is going to do to places and people. What we give consciously is of little value compared to what comes through unconsciously. "Let not your right hand know what your left hand giveth." When I speak of giving I am thinking of giving things that matter, such as one's time, one's interest. We fear we shall be bored, but everyone has something to give us, and we and they are both enriched if we can receive from others something that they have never been able to give before. People are shut into themselves because they think they have nothing to give, but they have always something to give us which we need. So I find every contact exciting because it is a joy to give someone freedom and release; when one receives from them it releases their power to give.

Jesus released in everyone with whom He came in contact their power to give. He made a contact with their power to give Him something. I used to wonder why He kept on asking for love. I understand now what a wonderful work He did in asking people to give Him something, since it released in them their power to receive His love.

Once during the day do this exercise and become that vibration. It is co-ordination of mind and action. Be the very gesture and vision of the Christ's equilibrium on earth. There is no diagram for this. You must get your visualisation of the triangle at the same time as the gesture: practise doing the gesture first, feel the hands touching, get the palms together, and then end up with the palms facing outwards - two magnetic points radiating out into the world. The left hand goes high up and the right as low as it can and both come back again on one's own receptivity.

We have to touch this world down to the lowest point of experience. Do not be afraid of experience, nor of touching the earth. We have to touch it. There is no place on earth where He cannot go and feel at home. Only our little minds think that in some places there is less to love. He went most to the uncultured minds, they were more open to Him than the scribes and learned men. He went to the uncritical minds to find love. Do not judge by outside appearances. No matter whether people are rich or poor, clever or not, there is some point of contact, the power to love and be loved. If we keep our contact with love certain we shall not feel the repercussion of points of separation, we shall find love in every other mind, and all other things matter not at all.

We are never saved from difficulties: I had so hoped we would be! I nearly gave up holding the classes at an early stage because I thought, "How can I take people on when I am going through an uncomfortable experience; have I the right to make them uncomfortable?" That was before I knew the end of the road. One's own feet were cut, and one did so want to send others by a smoother path. But now I know the end of the road, and because it is so worthwhile, there is no step I would save you from. Only by going through this condition can we know the certainty of our own truth. We must come to know that there is a point of power that can transcend the reasoning of our brains; there is a way of escape that He has given us and when we find it, every step has been worthwhile because of that way of escape. It is not a question of time. Do not think that because it has taken me a long time that you have to take as long. Remember the parable of the workers in the vineyard, and believe that you will come in the cool of the evening. The reward is the same - happiness and peace of mind.

We cannot impose a time limit on others. There is the accumulated experience at people's disposal to use, and to go so swiftly that the realisation of the truth of the law can be arrived at in a flash. This quickening condition is happening in the world. Some people can arrive at truth in the twinkling of an eye and there is no need to plod if we can arrive in a flash; you must realise that Light is a flash. St. Paul was knocked down by a blinding flash of truth, and in a moment his unbelief was changed into a certainty of experience. This certainty can be ours also. All things that have to be changed can be changed as rapidly as we allow them to be. Length of time does not exist in our minds. We have thought it unfair that people should arrive at a condition of happiness so quickly, but this is the new age, the New Covenant, in which we have all got the right to know Him. We have not got the right to impose our knowledge; everyone will know Him, and no man will teach his brother.

I am not teaching, only sharing the knowledge of a method. Sharing is a voluntary gesture of not withholding. The New Covenant is an instant giving, the quickening process must follow - no heavy plodding, but together, a swift running to achieve peace, happiness and fearlessness.

One question I want to put to yourselves and to answer it also - "How real a condition do you personally think this Technique in Light to be?" You know how real the sensation is when you burn your hand. With this Technique you may get no sensation. We must however have the discernment to receive truth as a mental sensation. It is a shock when someone looks you in the eyes and tells you a lie. It is a mental shock which produces a physical shock. What we have to learn is the reality of mental sensations when we receive truth. I know through experience the sensation of receiving a true impression of an unknown condition. I want every individual to become more aware of recording the truth of the accuracy of shapes in Light and of their effect on mind and body.

Never mind if you do not see or feel anything. It does not matter if you never have sensation, but if you find everyday life becoming a different experience, if you have different energy and integrity, know that the Light is in you. The Technique is for life and living and for the manifestation of those characteristics that up till now have been exclusively the Christ's.

THE INFINITE EIGHT

THE INFINITE EIGHT

The following exercise should be done in the middle of the day.

Stand relaxed, the arms down by the side. Visualise a shaft of white light coming from infinity on the left, striking the ground just in front of the right foot, radiating round the back of the feet, crossing in front, flashing back to infinity on the right, then radiating round the arc of heaven.

The Light thus completes the figure of eight which signifies, as above, so below.

The incarnate soul is the agent through whom the divine radiance can be earthed, so that the will of the Father may be done on earth as it *is* in heaven - that through our radiation of love in the world, the equilibrium of divine power may be earthed.

Bring the light down on an inhaling breath, from infinity on the left, to the ground in front of the right foot. Radiate it round from in front of the right foot, round the back, to the front of the left foot on an outbreath.

On an inhaling breath send the light back to infinity on the right, and watch it radiate round the arc of heaven on an outbreath. Repeat at least three times.

TALK
The Infinite Eight

I want to talk about a condition which is in everybody's mind and that is co-operation. I do not think it is very easy for us to realise what co-operation between God and the ordinary human being really amounts to. How much do we co-operate with divine law and how much is God able to co-operate with man, for unless there is a dovetailing of activity, there is war. There is either peace, which is the harmonising of opposite conditions, or there is friction and war, which is the opposition of two conditions and that state exists in the world today. There is no real understanding as to how we can co-operate.

We know that the Technique in Light is for making the individual a channel and our body a vehicle by which eternal life can come in and out of us. That is the action of receiving and transmitting, but a condition of true co-operation is something of which we are really unaware. Therefore I feel an exercise has been given to us whereby a condition can be obtained with no mental concentration and no possibility of failure. There lurks at the back of our mind the question, "Is one going to make it; is one going to become active as Christ was two thousand years ago; is there a hope of our eliminating ourselves and do we even want it?" We can only know ourselves whether we really want it, but we do want peace of mind and daily direction for service.

I want to give you a lovely exercise called the Infinite Eight. Look at that figure eight, for it is an eternal rhythm with no end or beginning, as above, so below. That is true co-operation.

You may think it impossible that we on earth can function as they do in the next world, the world of Light. Can we possibly continue that rhythm, receiving it as it is transmitted, sending it back, a continuity of activity, world without end? That feeling of eternity, for ever and ever, is so frightening to some people, but it is not frightening if you think of it as a figure. We can make the figure eight without knowing where it started and ended, if it is done in perfect rhythm, and that is eternity with no beginning and no end.

Therefore we have to attract a ray of light down in front of our right foot, visualise it making a circle round our feet, and then going back to infinity and making a circle round the arc of heaven. The physical body is the magnet that draws it down, and the circle round our feet is minute compared with the infinite encirclement of the arc of heaven. That is the comparative condition in true proportion. When I was shown the exercise I watched this current of light go round the throne. There was a group of people around a central figure and the light rippled through them and then flashed down to me. It is the sign of perfect co-operation, that which links our service with theirs and it is a continuity of love.

I find words difficult to give you an adequate feeling of the sensation of that oneness with those who are invisible. I do not mean only those people who have gone on just ahead, but the whole nation that lives in the world of Light, the children of Light. They do not have a comparative condition of time there between a person who comes today and one who has come thousands of years ago. We mark our passage through this world by time, but there, they mark it by service and co-operation.

Jesus said, "I go to prepare a place for

you that where I am, there ye may be also," which I interpret that we may be in the same place doing the same things. He had never found anybody before who could travel to where He lived and He had to go and prepare a place, just as anybody going abroad would prepare it. He went on ahead of them to prepare a place where they could live.

We live perfectly normal lives over there, but our environment is of great importance and we prepare for it here. Jesus knew these things and that because there were those of the disciples who understood what He was talking about, and could co-operate with Him here, it was expedient for Him that He should prepare this basis of co-operation between earth and heaven.

Therefore they have given us the pattern, and this Infinite Eight is the substance which we draw down when we do this exercise and function on that substance. You will get a certainty that what you are doing is smiled on in the world of Light, that you have no friction but will get direction if you do that exercise once a day. It strikes your right positive foot and that is your 'earth'; and you could not do this exercise if you had not visualised the Figure of Light, for you would get a mystical but not a human co-operation.

The world has missed human co-operation with God. I feel that God must be tired of all the visions people have had, of all the thoughts with so little action; it was the activity of the disciples that made their dwelling place with Christ. It was not because they wanted to get something for themselves, but they realised that after He had gone, they must do the works; it is works that matter and not vision!

You may think it odd to stress that when I go on giving you visionary exercises to do, but they are the skeleton. You have to make the substance on that skeleton. I give you the bare bones and you have to clothe them with flesh and blood. Therefore your own foot attracts down this substance of light, of co-operation, and it will find its own way round your feet. It is a halo for the feet and not the head. We have to get the halo, which has been forever surrounding the head, down to our feet. Then we flash back the track to infinity. It is a word but also a sensation. I saw the ray travelling back into Light, and as you see a current in water, I saw this current in Light travel through the domed arc of a crowd of living people. It rippled right through them and I knew I was joined with that ripple and could attract it down and encircle myself in it. I was forever one with them in substance and activity.

I did the exercise faithfully for some time, being very aware of the little circle I was making and of the immense circle which they had made, a living radiation in the world of Light. One day I saw tiny radiations coming out of my circle, which made it a different shape, and then only did I realise what that circle really meant; if I was faithful the radiation from it would have the same dimensions as the circle over there. The radiation would go out into the uttermost parts of the world. We need not travel, but we could let the radiation travel for us.

We could be where we live, but that co-operation, that substance, would ray out in a second to the ends of the earth. I do not say that any of our radiations will get to that size but I know they are an inevitable happening and not a personal thing. It must radiate for it is a universal condition and this exercise entails a world radiation from the feet.

Therefore you see the importance of every step of the Technique in Light. Some people have a facility for vision because in past lives they have had wonderful mystical experiences which have been satisfactory, but in this life it is a way of escape in which we must not indulge. It is not the age of vision but of realism, and unless you get a real condition, you are going to have a sterile time in the next world. You are going to find that mystical experiences over there produce no fruit. They are barren and not a living thing but only the pattern, and we try to give it life. We cannot give it life here, but we do so in the invisible world, and when we get over there we find those things are concrete there which were abstract here.

All our thoughts and mystical contacts with Christ have no real connection with Him for He cannot live in that world. He lives in the world of Light and there is a corridor between through which we have to pierce. Jesus said that: He went through, making a path right through the world of illusion. He established a real contact with His disciples here, and He needed their physical humanity to do so, but He did not need their vision of Him. They had to remember Him as He really was and that is why He stressed food. He wanted them to think of Him as a real man who ate and drank, walked and lived with them. It would have been easy for Him to have built another temple, and there were plenty of them. If He had wanted the disciples to remember Him as a priest, He would have given them the architectural design of a church, but He did not want it that way.

The last meeting was in the upper room of an inn where people went to eat and drink, and so He went to the good man of the inn who was a friend of His. It was a simple affair but terribly real. He gave them a supper to eat and drink, and while they were doing so, He told them of the law that governs two worlds. He took water and washed their feet.

How people have forgotten. He did not say, "Remember me by something wonderful." If He had wanted a Vatican, would He not have built one? He could have built a beautiful place, but He took a towel and told them that if their feet were clean, the whole of them would be clean, they could walk this path for He would show them where to walk.

All through the Technique in Light it will come back to the importance of the feet, of the Figure of Light, of your magnet which will draw heaven to earth. It does not translate you out of your body into heaven, but it brings heaven into manifestation on earth. Therefore you and I, who are normal people, can start manifesting this new normality, being normal in everything and not trying to do unusual things or thinking we are different from our neighbours, for we are not. I hope we are a little happier and healthier, but if not, then we are not different at all.

The peace of mind, which is so important today, can only come about by our sense of security of direction and our sense of co-operation with the will of God. Do not think that the smallest substance of resignation comes into this condition of co-operation. Do not resign yourself to the will of God but just know that this substance of light is that which links us with His will. His will is this eternal Eight always functioning on earth as it is in heaven.

"Thy will be done on earth as it is in heaven." What have we got that is identical on earth and heaven? The substance of light, life, love and bodies, spirits, minds, understanding, eyes, ears. We have everything that they have got and everything God has got in embryo; it only needs this living germ to bring it into manifestation.'

The exercise is done three times and I linger a little on the circle above. If you watch it, I believe you get a sense of place, and it was as if the place revealed itself to me. With my eyes shut I watched the light travel, knowing it would find its own way round the arc of heaven. I believe we could travel on those rays and arrive where there is a unity of substance, place and people. Over there everything is one, and here everything is divided. We look for the division between earth and heaven, but it does not exist, and there is a condition of being able to travel and return, with no distance. There is no distance but the distance of your thought. The moment thought divides, there is division. If thought unites, there is unity. The danger is in our thoughts that there is this separation of the individual from the givingness of God, which keeps us poverty stricken and resigned. Unity is radiant and sparking; resignation is gray and fibrous. So when you think of the will of God, think of it as something that you would give anything to have, so wonderful is it. It is like that with everything, if we had eyes to see. There is not a single condition that lies within our power to receive, which we would not want to receive, if only we could know the happiness and the eternal abundance of it.

I feel this exercise gives you a sense of capacity for achievement. There can be no co-operation with Him unless we actively co-operate for He cannot impose it. He cannot say, "I want to have the co-operation of the British Empire and the understanding of my values which I need; I want them." That may be true, and I think He has chosen groups of every nationality all over the world because of their capacity, but unless an understanding is awakened He may want in vain because He cannot take; He can only receive. When we give Him ourselves, as Jesus gave the Father Himself for a whole experiment, then the unity between ourselves and Him is accomplished.

The moment you do this exercise, you are one. You have nothing else to do and nothing you could leave undone. You have been the magnet which has drawn the Light down, and you have identified yourself with it because it encircles your feet, sending it back again, watching the co-operation and how it works, as it is a continuity.

In the diagram the exercise has been shown in true proportion, with the circle round the feet and an indication of what you will find. But the end of the circle is out of the radius of this world and so we have not attempted to show it.

SAH-VEH

This exercise should be done in the evening after the **Ah-Lah-Hiève**.

Stand relaxed and visualise a golden chalice above the head on the right side, and another chalice of deep blue colour between the feet.

To the sound **Sah** on a deep exhaling breath draw the golden chalice down to the ground, and simultaneously the blue chalice is drawn up through the middle of the body, up through the head, and is then filled with Light.

At the same moment that the golden chalice descends and the blue chalice rises, a shaft of light rays out from the left side.

On an inhaling breath on the sound **Veh**, the gold chalice ascends and the blue descends, and the left side closes. This exercise should be done three times.

The gold chalice is Wisdom.

The blue chalice is Christ Love.

The ray of white light from the left side is the beginning of our power to radiate love and wisdom into the world.

Wisdom is brought down to the earth from on high. The Christ love is sent through the human body and mind to be fused in oneness with the Father.

TALK
Sah-Veh

There is so great a need at the moment for the three qualities included in this exercise. If we can get these three conditions perfectly poised - wisdom, love and givingness - we shall have very few fears left. It is so difficult to be wise. It is quite different from being clever. One is sometimes afraid of clever people, but never of wise ones.

We are told that if any of us lack wisdom we are to ask for it. The need for wisdom is most urgent. If there were no human agents in the world no wisdom could be earthed because it is a condition apart from natural law or nature. The growth of plants and animal life would continue, but wisdom is the mind of God being transmitted into the individualised minds of the human race, and a really wise person must of necessity be exceedingly humble.

The wise men sought the incarnation of wisdom and love. There was at that time a great radiation in the world, but little is known of the receptivity of those men. They got their directions individually and they went humbly to offer their homage and to take a gift. I feel that we as a group have come to the point where we have something to give.

As always in transcendental things, a gift from us to God is always the exact opposite of a gift from God to us. We can only give of our poorness. I was thinking what a tremendous gift it would be if we would present to Him the arrogance of our spirits. If we could make a parcel of all the knowledge and experience of our past lives, and present them, so that under no circumstances could our emotions ever betray us again; His gift to us would be wisdom and humility.

So I think this exercise of the **Sah-Veh** would be enhanced if, when we send back the chalice of wisdom on the sound **Veh**, we could visualise sending it back laden with the vanities of our mind. Let us be definite about what we send back. We are so little aware of the peculiarities and lacks which other people notice in us. There are those

thoughts in our minds which prevent us being wise; those things we say we are nervous of. If we did not think like that, the quietness of the wisdom would give us such a poise and certainty that we should be able to answer all the questions people ask us, for our inadequacy would be filled by His wisdom. Only now do I understand that we are meant to send our inadequacy back in the chalice.

The perfection of His wisdom and the imperfection of our minds, makes a complete whole.

We cannot help being analytical, although this is generally an unproductive thing. Let us use it to help us to get rid of those conditions which are a stumbling block both to ourselves and to other people. We can make a real exchange on the **Sah-Veh** of our mind and His.

Do remember, from the experience of other people, when once you do an exercise and set certain forces in motion, they will continue to function all night and next day.

I want, if I can, to make clear what wisdom is. It is important that the word should mean the same to all of us. It includes right judgement in all things. It is a condition of knowing instantaneously the answer to all immediate problems; not those which should be dealt with in the future. Our wisdom *must* be a continual condition of inspiration. I suppose really that involves never having an answer ready to a question you know you are going to be asked. Know that you cannot know anything before the appointed time.

One is apt to think that time exists only here. I was made to understand that time is a rhythm that functions through every world and plane of existence. We know time as it functions in this world; I learnt that the rhythm of timelessness is as exact as the rhythm of time here. One rhythm is that of the soul, the other is that of the body. The great revolt of the soul is because it finds itself, on incarnation, caught in the rhythm of time and space here. When our souls and our bodies function harmoniously together - when our bodies are dominated by our soul or light body - then shall we know on earth that freedom which the soul experiences when it leaves the body.

When one has knowledge one no longer rebels against conditions which seem blind and difficult, for we realise our capacity to transcend those limitations. The Technique in Light is the method by which those conditions can be transcended. Life can then become the most marvellous adventure; every incident in it, whatever appearance of catastrophe it may present, can only be the widening of the door through which we are going to walk into our freedom: we walk into it with no more preparation than when we faint. It is a supercharged consciousness, when we shall be so aware of this great incoming of wisdom that we shall function quite naturally in peace and harmony and certainty; and the old conditions will be as quickly forgotten as our loss of consciousness when we faint.

So will you look upon every step in this Technique as the most tremendous opportunity for happiness, the passing away of the old conditions with no clinging to them? Nothing can pass out of our lives if our souls have not really finished with it. Old emotions have to be discarded to make way for a much happier, greater condition.

I understand a little this method of reconstruction, which is not to demolish the entire fabric of our humanity. It is as if the old bricks were removed one at a time, to make place for the new ones. The process is painful because the bricks have become ingrown through the years. Bit by bit the old bricks are taken out and the new ones put in. It is the very thing we have prayed for, but we never associate our prayers with the shape of the answer.

We pray for wisdom and love, but when any illusion of love is destroyed, we rarely see it as the answer to our prayer. We have to learn urgently, the substance of illusions.

Some of us, when we are offered a good solid brick, throw it away and put something more illusionary in its place. Do know this that when the time for giving up an illusion comes, it is only because we are ready. We could welcome it as an opportunity for completely new construction.

Nearly every morning I hear the words, "Fear not, fear not." Anything that happens in our lives is by our own choice and it is never imposed on us. If we could realise this we have made our agreement with God, and whatever we need we shall receive. All the old fears and old antagonisms to providence would go if we could see that every sorrow in life is a promotion, that courage is a recognition of answered prayer.

The **Sah-Veh** is a short cut and will save all of us an immense amount of unnecessary suffering. Bring down wisdom, send through us that quality of the Christ love that we have earthed, and begin our contact through the world of the love and wisdom to the human race. Do you not see how this must draw to us friends and comrades? It makes a long chain of contacts and must mean ever increasing companionship in this world.

THE RHYTHM OF THE NAME

This is a most wonderful exercise. It is the cosmic vibration of the name of Jesus, which is the vibration of world harmony, the equilibrium of all life in all matter. It is an exercise that must not be done for oneself alone, for it can include all souls and all conditions.

Visualise a silver chalice of infinite dimensions, small enough to contain two people, or large enough to contain a building or continent. In it you are standing with some other person or group of persons, and it is of a most lovely silver light which must not be confused with white or crystal. We must know the different substances in Light, and silver light is the substance of perfect containment, so if you are within you are contained in it, and nothing that impinges can come through it. It is of the same condition in Light as a non-porous substance so no light oozes away. It contains the will of God outside us, and yet in our own dimensions. It brings diffused light into form. As you stand in it, however wide it is, the sides seem to come up about as high as your temples.

Next visualise the brilliant blue triangle to the sound **Dyè-è-è**, as you did in The Name, but this time bring it down on your right side from an Infinite Point of Radiance to your feet. Let it run behind your feet and go up again on your left side to the Infinite Point of Radiance. You cannot see the point where the two sides meet at the top; it is as if you were a figure standing at the base of an infinitely tall triangle whose sides seem to make a doorway. Draw this blue triangle down and across on an outbreath, and return it on the left side on an inbreath. The **Dyè** is a doorway, and the old masonic rites have been based on this great triangle of cosmic light. Draw it down three times until you are framed in a marvellous blueness.

The **Thu** is made up of two arcs of brilliant white light, which cross over the head. One starts from the left side, arches over your head and goes down on the right. The other starts behind you, goes over the head, curving over the first one, and goes down to the ground in front of you. Each one travels to a beat of eight on the sound **Thu**, thus:-

Thu - oo - oo - oo - oo - oo - oo - oo.

Do the first arc on an inbreath and the other on an outbreath. It is important that you should *always* start the arc on your left side and go over to your right; and then start

120

behind you and go over to the front. You go on doing it, getting quieter and quieter, until it stops by itself. After the first arc, it is not necessary to sound the **Th** of the **Thu**. Let it pulse across quite rhythmically to the sound **oo - oo - oo** etc. The breath is like two great sighs, two great currents in Light.

Go on doing the **Thu** until you find you no longer need to do it.

The **Th** sound of The Name we cannot do. It happens by itself. When you have done the **Thu** till you are so quiet it stops of its own accord, then you have made the cosmic chalice, and the **Th** is given us in an ecstasy of stillness. At the moment when the beat of the **Thu** is finished, the spirit is poured down on all flesh.

One can do this Rhythm of the Name for a person, a group, a house or a country. Either bring them in thought into the room where you are, and do it over them there; or, in the case of a conference or a country, do it over them where they are as if you yourself were not there. Visualise a country as part of the map if you like. Let the walls of your chalice extend as wide as the thing you wish to enclose. When you have done the chalice forget about it and go on with the visualisation of His Name. The chalice is, as it were, the scaffolding on which the whole is built, and it disappears. So do not worry where the arcs of light start in relation to the chalice. There could be no difficulty about the impact of one substance in Light on another; but actually the chalice goes by the time the arcs are made.

Do this exercise at least once in the day, as a midday exercise; but it can and should be done any time of the day or night, whenever you want to bring the vibration of His Name over any particular person or circumstance. Do it also in bed at night over a house or person you want to protect. To do a house, visualise yourself facing it and then bring the triangle down on your right side: send the arcs playing right over the house, from left to right and from behind you to the far side.

The exercise of The Name has been given to us for our personal condition of receptivity; but when we use the Rhythm of the Name we are identifying ourselves with His power to function in the world, which is different. It is like knowing Him personally, and then also sharing in His public life, one of service to humanity. So we cannot use the Rhythm too often or too trivially, for there is no condition of human life which is too trivial to be included in the perfection of harmony and love.

This exercise is to be used for other people, and in the service of the world. It is primarily one of protection and can be used against all conditions of disharmony. We all need protection against the world's many destructive conditions. How can we get it ourselves and secure it for others? The answer to darkness is light; and to destruction, creative energy. Christ incarnated to earth a creative force that should be stronger than destruction. How can it also be earthed in us, so that we can be the instruments and transmitters of God's perfect protective power to the world?

Of ourselves we can indeed, do nothing; but there is nothing that cannot be done through us. The whole Technique in Light is designed to change the impotent self into a channel of the power of Christ. In the Name of Jesus there is perfect equilibrium, perfect receptivity and perfect transmission, and if we are willing to be used in His Name on behalf of others, we can earth protection for them, and as a member of our community promote world equilibrium, world receptivity to true law, and world transmission of harmony.

In the first exercise of The Name, you received it for your personal equilibrium at the back of your head: in the Rhythm of the Name it comes right down to your feet, and it is not only a personal but a cosmic condition, to be used in world service. It protects, not only flesh and blood, but all substances on this earth and concerns all the elements. It is a protection against fire, and all destructive conditions whatsoever that may harm human beings. There is nothing that cannot be held within its harmony and equilibrium. All of us here know from our experience during the war that it is a sure protection against all forms of destructive energy, and if you learn to be the agent for it, you can protect every person you care for.

As you flash down the blue **Dyè-è-è**, you make a doorway, and it is the threshold of a new condition of protective service earthed through you. The inverted arcs of white light sent on the sound **Thu-oo-oo** from left (heartside) to right, and from back to front, are flashed on that rhythm of eight, which is the Christ number, and signifies an endless flow of energy from heaven to earth, and earth to heaven. Everything under that protecting arc will have the protection of His Name, because you have earthed it for Him on a cosmic wavelength. His own feet earthed it two thousand years ago, and He sent His disciples out to earth it in every part of the world. Today it is more necessary than ever that He should have human agents for the same purpose.

The Rhythm of the Name can be used against disharmony and disruption in two different ways.

It may be used personally to resolve our disharmonies with our friends, families, neighbours and enemies. In this case it is important to visualise clearly the silver chalice. This chalice has the texture in Light of hand-beaten silver, and it is a resolving substance. In it we may put, along with and facing ourselves, any person or group of persons with whom we are at variance, especially those whose mental radiation is opposed to our own. There is a love of the heart which transcends and is not changed by mental opposition in the loved one, but the condition causes much unnecessary friction, which we can eliminate by this exercise.

Everybody has a right to his or her point of view, and we do not necessarily change this in others; we can give them mental freedom without adverse reaction on our own part, and we do also help to resolve what is prejudiced and intolerant in their outlook. We may by the same means resolve differences with definite enemies, and with all people whom we find difficult. Use this exercise too for committees and conferences. It will help to make all the minds concerned receptive and harmonious. The Rhythm is also a gift for universal use in creating world harmony. Do remember how desperately harmony is needed today, both in world conditions and in human affairs. But it cannot be had apart from the Name of Jesus. Only He is harmonised with all substances under heaven, and therefore can resolve all disharmonies, including those of the human mind. He has the key to every individual mind throughout the world, and what cannot be done by any amount of human argument, can be done through us by the creative power of Christ.

Seeing that He came precisely to "make all things new," why should the human mind and human nature be left outside this transmuting process? Unless we give our time to do this Rhythm of His Name the world will not be changed. Jesus gave thirty-three years to perfecting the process of harmonising human substance; surely we can give five minutes of our day to our exercises. Do it in the morning that you may actually be throughout the day, a living radiation of His Name, not a Christian but a Christ, having His equilibrium, His receptivity, His power of transmission. Bring the power down to earth and earth it in your feet; do not let it be merely a mystical, an occult, or an intellectual proceeding. You can use it in your own environment, or at any distance for public purposes where men and women are conferring on important affairs.

The second way of using the Rhythm of the Name is for protection against physical disharmony and destruction. You can protect with it, not only people, but buildings and places. If you are throwing protection over a house you may, if you like, lie in bed and visualise the blue triangle coming down on your right, running under the foundations, and going up on the left side. Then throw the white light over the roof from left to right, and back to front, making over the house a complete protection of light. I have done it over buses, trains, ships, aeroplanes. It is a condition of protection which nothing can deflect.

Do not think there is any substance whatsoever which cannot come within its scope, and do not have any fear. We fear because we have very little understanding of love, for "Perfect love casteth out fear."

When I first did this exercise I had the sensation of having my hands tied behind my back so that I could not protect myself by my own power. I had it for a long time until I learned by experience that through the Rhythm, danger passed me by every time, and now I have a profound certainty of His protection in all circumstances. I know that no disharmony can touch me if I am tuned in to this Rhythm. His Name is perfect protection, but do not fear and doubt, because doubting mental radiation cuts off and insulates you from the love which protects.

Often we do not have the protection we might because we forget to ask for it. Every day must have its own quota of light and energy, life, health and protection. If you do it today, you must do it again tomorrow. We can all have protection and health every day if we ask for it every day. Our health deteriorates because we do not get it afresh every day. The Technique in Light has been given to us for that very purpose; to get fresh experience each day, and to renew daily our health, our vitality, and our protection. If we thus reconstruct ourselves as a daily process, we cannot decay and grow old. If we are faithful to it, there comes a time when the old self passes away, and the new self becomes integrated in this new experience.

Do the protective Rhythm of the Name mostly at night over your friends and the places where they live. When you do it for a place at a distance, visualise the place, not going there yourself, but thinking of yourself as the transmitter, as an instrument sending out wavelengths. Thus He can send out through a person who cares enough to do this service a profound condition of protection for all in need. It is a secret service of love.

If the reader has been consciously undertaking the Exercises, so far they should be practising the following:-

MORNING	MIDDAY	EVENING
Ritual of Light	Transmuting Light	Spirals and Circles
Conscious Breath	The Throat	Ah-Lah-Hiève
Ah Meh — A E Ooo	Equilibrium of the Name	Sah-Veh
The Needs	The Infinite Eight	
E.O. Lihum	Rhythm of the Name	
The Name		
Rhythm over the Head		

HI-YOU-MEH

Visualise a ray of brilliant white light above the head. Place yourself directly under it. It is the will of God and is composed of all the myriad colours which go to make up the white ray. You now stand in complete alignment with the light of His will. When, from your own head the rays coincide with the rays of the Divine will, then you will be able to do the will of God.

Hold the hands up, with palms facing outwards, and arms bent at the elbows.

Visualise in front of you a knife edge of pale gold light. This edge stretches to infinity above you, below you, and away from you; its near edge is, say, about two feet in front of you.

On the quick inbreath sound of **Hi-You**, draw this edge of light towards you so that it will cut you on the medial line. On the sound of **Hi**, the light cuts upwards, and on the sound of **You**, it cuts through the body. It is so quick that the two movements are almost simultaneous. Then on the outbreath **Meh**, a suffusing glow of the transmuting amethyst light pours through the body from head to foot. Do this three times.

Then stretch out the arms sideways, palms down, forming the cross. The exercise is repeated three times on the same sounds, but now on the **Hi-You** sound of the inbreath, the pale gold light, as it cuts up and through the body, pours into the ruby wing of direction.

On the **Meh** sound of the outbreath visualise:-
(i) your breath running along the outer surface of both extended arms, outwards towards the finger tips.
(ii) on the same sound, visualise the light doing the same thing.
(iii) on the same sound, visualise both breath and light doing this, but breath on the inner surface and light on the outer.

Note that on breaths 4,5,6 there is no suffusion of the whole body as in 1,2,3.

This is the crucifixion in Light. The Christ did it on the cross, and died to do it. We live to do it. It is the very essence of the resurrection body. It brings about the change of the rhythm of the human body. It is the soul or light body dominating the vibrations of the material body. The breath down the arms is a preparation for the incoming power of the breath ray - "the breath of God" - the essence of power.

H<u>i</u>	as in "m<u>y</u>"
<u>You</u>	as in "<u>you</u>"
M<u>eh</u>	as in French "d<u>e</u>"

TALK
Hi-You-Meh

I am going to give you an exercise which has to do with the synchronising of time because when you visualise light it has got to be a quick thought. Perhaps you can meditate on light and take a long time, but you cannot meditate on the speed with which light functions. Light is the life germ in the blood and therefore it is a quickener. When light comes into the blood it quickens, speeds up and makes motion. Death has also got the same quickness, the quickness of a breath; one moment you are alive and breathing and the next moment in time your breath stops and you have passed over.

Everything to do with life, with divine substance, is spontaneous and has no time in it at all. Therefore time is a factor that human nature has created for its own convenience. God never created the time hiatus, the lag in time between thought and accomplishment, for with Him it is spontaneous.

"Let there be light and there was light." With us there is an enormous interval between thinking about a thing and doing it. We can put off the activity of doing what we would like to do for a whole lifetime and for many lifetimes. How many of us have not in some life wanted to make good and have a life of service, to love our neighbour? Yet somehow or other so many things have intervened and we have put it off to another time. We have indulged ourselves and thought that when we have got what we wanted we have something to give our neighbour, and until we are really established, what have we got to give?

We are getting an understanding of the quickening process of light. How quick it is! 'The quick and the dead' is a most wonderful expression; those who are in movement, quick, spontaneous; and those who have no movement, for movement is the difference between life and death.

This exercise of the **Hi-You-Meh** is for

the coordination in our mind of thought and activity. It is an instantaneous visualising and activity of light. Up to now we have had time to think about drawing the light through our feet to our hands, of taking our breath and the petals coming down. When we have done the exercise of The Name we have had time to think about the blue triangle at the back of our head, the chalice and the spiral in our side. This is the only exercise that has to be done in a flash. When it first came through they made me see two actions in light done simultaneously. Here we have no simultaneous movement or sound, yet with my ears and eyes I was shown these two conditions being one.

Perhaps you will be able to get your own inspiration of this quickening process of thought and action. I saw a knife edge of gold light going up to infinity and down through the earth and stretching backwards. It was the edge of a ray which would move on a sound, cutting up and through me simultaneously. In Light, up and through is one movement, but in matter I had to separate it into cutting up and then passing through; and the reaction to this was a suffusion of the Transmuting Light right through my body. If we had not done the evening exercise and prepared our body by the cutting spiral the **Hi-You-Meh** would pass us by, being unable to come through because we should still be full of resistances. The evening exercise is for gradually reducing resistance until we are open to the Light, and having done the cutting spiral we are in a position to magnetise this condition of light up and through us.

I want to talk about the condition of simultaneousness because it is utterly foreign to our nature. We are not often people who get inspiration in a flash and can register true understanding; and we may never have come to the point of contact with truth. Truth is a substance of such beauty and of texture that the human eye has never seen it nor human hands ever touched it; yet it is a condition of reality which when your mind registers it, you live truth in your body. That truth means true reaction to experience and it is the thing Jesus established in His body but nobody else established in their body. To most people truth is a mental apprehension and not substance or reality. Therefore when He stood before Pilate, Jesus had established it in His body and He was the Law.

When with our minds we make a real contact with the Infinite Point of Radiance, with the Father and with the mind of God, we must in a flash get something, but we lose it again almost immediately. Often we identify ourselves with the mind of somebody else, with the written or spoken word or with the radiation of a human being whom we love or admire, and we take on that radiation of thought because it is nearest to our heart. The nearest to our heart is the nearest to truth that we can get, and we cannot get nearer to truth than our heartbeat. When Jesus' heart beat in oneness with God, He was truth. If our heart beats with His, we too can know what truth is and we shall become the very substance of truth.

The Law of the New Covenant was that He would write His law, the law of truth in our inward parts, and in our hearts He would write it. However true we are outside in sound and however hard we may find it to prevaricate with our mouth, I do not think one of us can say that every part of our body has true reaction to life and love, because part of our body manifests the fear of imperfect love. In the love of Jesus for the Father there was no fear, therefore there was no substance in His contact that was not true. Fear makes us say and do untrue things in self-protection, and we should not be untrue if we were not afraid of public or private opinion. If we had confidence that we were the expression of His will and heart we should never say or do an untrue thing.

Therefore the **Hi-You-Meh** is to bring about this individual freedom. You cannot do it on anybody else and should not try. The exercise is for the cutting up and through of the individual body, this temple that can hold the substance of truth. Therefore if we will do it on our body we need not worry about insincerity in others because when we are sincere we must release sincerity in others. Many of us are devoted to truth but not entirely sincere, and we are subject to illusions about ourselves and others. Illusion is a step away from truth. There is this gossamer condition of illusion about a fact, and when it is dressed up in the tinsel of our desire and hope, it is not the substance. We think that if we take away the tinsel of illusion we shall find something drab underneath, but the reverse is the truth. The substance of truth is the most beautiful colour and texture, beyond any adjectives to express. It is something your inner eye can see but not classify, a colour not yet earthed so you will not see it objectively but the radiation of it is unmistakable. When a person tells you the truth, when the sound is there you know it and something registers in you.

Truth is often not understandable and is beyond human reasoning. The mind cannot deduce it but it is a flash like a quickening process. Truth is not thinking about a thing. We shall never be able to think truth into substance, we shall only be able to receive it, and the exercise of the **Hi-You-Meh** is preparing our body to receive this substance of truth. It gets earthed through your Figure of Light and does not descend on your head like a dove. It comes through your feet and if they are properly earthed through the Figure of Light, and only through the Figure of Light, it can flash up and through and identify you with your divinity. It will be the most divine substance in you, flashing from the eternal radiation of the body of God. You cannot impose truth on anybody else, you can only receive it yourself, and as you receive it you are bound to transmit it. You cannot keep truth as a possession, it is a radiation, and if we were receiving this lovely substance all the time it would come out of us as a natural radiation of our being which would result in the elimination of fear. You cannot have fear and truth at the same time.

On **Hi** the light cuts up the middle of your body and head and on **You** it pours through into your wing of direction, vitalising it, and going infinitely back. This is most important for if your wing of direction is vitalised every day you cannot take a wrong turning. You may think that circumstances will be too strong and overwhelming if you have a difficult time ahead, but do your **Hi-You-Meh** so that your wing of direction will be in full activity and you will not need to depend on your common sense or reasonable mind. I have learnt that the things I did on my own were hardly worth doing, but the moment I ask Him I know the answer is almost immediate. One is afraid of being let down by expecting a thing to function too quickly. It is through that fear of hoping too much that this expedient way of thought has developed and so resignation and other drab conditions come into our mind as a consolation. We feel that perhaps we should not have expected Him to answer so quickly, but with God everything must function spontaneously and cannot do otherwise. There is no time lag between request and answer, and the reason why the answer does not come at once is because He does not get the request.

The thing I have to look at for myself is, what is it in my own mental condition that provides the insulating substance, because I know that when I ask He must answer at once. He cannot fail any more than there can be any time lag between the striking of a match and the flame. Light must function with the speed of light and you cannot do the **Hi-You-Meh** leisurely for then you will not do it at all. Therefore it is the beginning of spontaneous action of our mind and body. As we think the sound, it is up, and before the sound is out of our mouth, it will be up and through us. I wish I could demonstrate the quickness with which I saw it function when it was first presented. I feel that my speech is like a stammer compared with the swiftness of that up and through of the light, the speed with which His mind and body functions. If we as human beings can eliminate this time lag out of our mind and expect Him to answer as quickly as we ask, we must receive it.

The substance of our body is so resisting that the doubt and uncertainty of our mind makes us unable to register the answering contact. It is like a bell which is out of order and will not ring; it is pressed but there is no answering ring because of the slackness of the line of communication. The line of communication between His body and ours, and His mind and ours, is so slack that although He will instantly answer, we are unable to receive. As we quicken up, so must the answer to our contact with His body become quicker and quicker, until like the body of Jesus it becomes simultaneous. He asked the Father and the answer was instantaneous in His patient. We know in our active group here that this condition is being understood by us and that the time factor is of vital importance.

I am beginning to realise that the synchronisation of thought and action is the answer. We have not been able to think and act in one, but have thought a thing well over before we decide to take action. We have spent weeks in thinking something over and have wondered why at the end we are not very successful, and we then feel we have not given it enough thought. How foolish we are, for it is the amount of thought given to the thing that has spoilt it and prevented His instantaneous ability to function. I know it will get quicker as we get freer from our apprehension and uncertainty.

Do this exercise whenever you can. You will become conscious of the freedom of your spine and this brilliant ruby organ, the wing of direction, can be used by Him almost like a speaking tube. Sound goes forth and direction comes in, and one is stabilised.

We are learning more and more in our work that we know things to be true through our own experience, but although we know a thing we cannot tell how we know it. If you work out a problem you can put it down on paper and know the process of how your brain worked and can come to a certain conclusion, but when you have spontaneous action there is no sequence. Until there is spontaneous action, sequence is a necessity created by the human mind and not by the mind of God. He has no sequence, He *is*. When we become that instantaneous representation of Him we shall find that we do not have to work up to an end, it *is*. It is a quickening we shall experience and know to be true.

Do realise that Jesus never used His experience for doing miracles and could not have done so. A miracle is a spontaneous happening according to the need of the moment, so what is the good of past experience? If we have to demonstrate something new, our body could not have new experience proceeding out of an old experience, for it would only be a renewal of an old experience and therefore not new. The capacity to understand anything new is beyond us, and all that we can do is to make the instrument become capable of receiving a new pattern, experience, substance and reaction. When we are able to do that we are free of karma and the old condition of fear, and we are the substance of truth.

This exercise is the co-ordination of mind and body. It goes right through the trunk of the body, the head, brain and skull, and then cuts back through the spine. It is a substance that goes eternally on and I never see the end of the light. Do not watch what it does at the back but be aware of your reaction of the Transmuting Light, and the whole of the trunk of the body is filled with that light.

THE CROSS OF BREATH

Stand relaxed with your arms outstretched, thus forming the cross.

Visualise the Infinite Radiance (which is the Father) and draw, on a deep inbreath, His breath, His love through your head and body so that you are empty of all but breath, like an empty vase which is full of the invisible air. Then exhale through your arms and hands, radiating your emptiness and His fullness to the world.

Will you visualise one or many friends or patients on your right and on your left, so that what you receive in utter selflessness can go straight through you to them; thus they must receive *Him*.

This exercise may be done frequently during the day, so that selflessness may become a habit of our minds.

TALK
The Cross of Breath

The shape of the cross is of pre-Christian origin. The form was used in the very early days of civilisation to receive and give out energy, and for this it is a perfect formation. The force comes down to earth in the vertical plane and is thus literally earthed; it is transmitted horizontally through the arms of the cross. Put the two together and you have a perfect instrument for reception and transmission of force. Jesus wanted to teach the world that the most perfect instrument of all for receiving and transmitting the life and love energy of the Creator was the human body, which was originally created for this purpose. To make clear this teaching, He consented to take on a human body Himself, thus demonstrating this truth in living form on the physical plane.

Breath is impersonal life force; the breath of God. Through it we can receive and transmit the love of God in the form of a cross in this exercise. The world believed that God was power, but Jesus came to show in physical form that He is both power and love. "The Father is in me, and I in Him," He said, and His life on this earth was the full expression of true form, love, life and law. In this exercise we too may learn to express true form and law.

The substance of breath is taken by us all completely for granted, and we do not stop to consider how very potent it really is. It is the substance in this world down which comes the spark of physical life. Without it no baby can begin to live, and when it ceases to function, life is extinguished. Breath also has other qualities not known to the uninitiated. It can eliminate thought and produce a condition of emptiness. We badly need to be emptied of our worrying, restless selves, but it is a state which cannot be produced by mental activity; it must come right down into the body and make mind and body into one.

As we see ourselves empty of all but breath we create a dynamic condition in ourselves in which divine power can function. We cannot grasp what a great effect this will have. It will take away all undesirable personal radiations, freeing us from those nervous physical reactions which are the result of mental and emotional tension. In most of us the mind has the body in complete subjection through its power to create undesirable mental pictures which react harmfully on the physical self.

This exercise will empty us of these destructive conditions, and fill us instead with divine serenity and power. It is a watching exercise. Be still, see yourself filled with breath, and you will feel its buoyancy, and receive a plus condition which is more powerful than thought. It enhances the capacity for unity with divine substance. It is a track down which the Spirit can spark, filling us with divine wisdom and love, and emptying us without effort, of selfish and harmful reactions.

Emptiness of self is not an easy condition to attain, but only because we go about it in the wrong way. It cannot be done by the mind or conscious will. We all have an overdose of personal endeavour to attain personal satisfaction, and it leads only to friction and indecision. We need to know our self as we really are, and then to get rid of the undesirable elements. Put away comparative thought. Do not compare yourself with Christ, who is too far ahead of us, nor with your neighbours, whose progress and experiences are quite different from your own. It is breath which can make the self empty and give a plus condition of divine power, so that our emptiness becomes a supreme gift to the world.

We should do this exercise once a day; preferably in the middle of the day, so that, for one breath at least, the normal restless rhythm of one's personality is stilled, and our waste thoughts and emotions are eliminated. The exercise promotes a capacity to receive a new quality of health and energy. Do not think about the ingredients to be emptied away. All will go, and serenity will take their place.

Do not separate in your thought the material and the spiritual. Become material-minded in order to make matter divine and transmute mundane and sordid activities. This exercise is to bring about the complete co-ordination of the physical and spiritual self, so that we are fully integrated at least for one moment of the day. The serenity and gaiety of Christ and His understanding of our need are always there but we cannot reach them until we are rid of our own picture of our needs and personality. We shall never know what adverse conditions the "I" creates in this world through its preoccupation with the self, nor do we realise what it is creating in the world beyond.

My brother told me of the way in which prayer operates in the next plane. The activities of our minds become visible substance over there, and every thought is substantiated. If we are egoists here, we must meet our egoism, in visible substance, in the next world, and that will be our judgement. Jesus undertook the enormous task of presenting to us this law, and showing us the necessity of reconstructing the individual here on earth. That which is still bound on earth is bound in heaven and we cannot be freed there from conditions we have created here.

This exercise is of great importance in beginning to free us here and now. By the exercises of the Technique this freedom can be achieved without mental effort. It has been made possible by the resurrection of Christ, who took His body back to the next plane that He might broadcast to us from there. We can put on His body in all its parts and activities and function freely as He did when we are empty of ourselves. Inhale, and see yourself filled with breath, and the result is inevitable.

AH-MOU

This exercise follows the Crosses on Hands and Feet and is the last of the morning exercises.

Visualise in front of you the undefined radiant head of Christ. Your hands are still full of the light which you brought over your head in the Rhythm over the Head exercise. Stretch them out sideways, palms facing upwards, and on an inbreath and to the sound **Ah**, there goes a brilliant line of light straight from the right hand into the mind of the Christ.

Sweep your right arm forward and up until your hand is pointing directly towards His head.

Still holding this vision in your mind and allowing no thought of your own to impinge upon it, on an outbreath and to the sound **Mou**, sweep the left hand forward and up in the same way, and let the left wrist lie over the right wrist, with the palms facing down. Then turn both hands inwards and upwards so that the palms are towards your face, and uncross them.

There is a radiance in the left hand and this crosses the line of light coming from your right hand.

Then listen, and into your mind will be dropped the message for the day.

Sometimes this message takes the form of a text, or sometimes there come words of encouragement or help. Sometimes it is even a warning, which if you have disregarded or forgotten, you will realise by night-time that if only you had not done so, you would not have stumbled or acted wrongly during the day.

TALK
Ah-Mou

I want to talk this morning about channelhood because our revelation is increasing; fresh things are coming through all the time and we have been too concerned with results. Since we found healing was one of the results of channelhood we have been concentrating very much on our capacity to heal.

None of us know what it is like to have the capacity of a Christ. We have looked at His healing and His miracles and have known that the same results should come through the ordinary individual which came through Him, if the law is understood in our humanity. I stress that it is not to understand it with our mental processes because Jesus had nothing new to give to the mind of the human race. The pattern of the law was mentally understood by the Jews and that is why He had to come to them, but where the Jews failed was in understanding the law in their humanity. We have only to look at the humanity of Christ to see the perfectly balanced condition.

It was not enough for Christ to understand the pattern of the law; He had to go through the training of becoming a perfect channel. His ministry was the manifestation of His channelhood, and what the Father needed of the Christ is not necessarily the same as the Father needs now. The needs of two thousand years ago were supplied by Christ, but the needs of today are different, and there is this utter necessity for the Father and the Christ to have instruments through whom to work and who will get inspiration over the everyday things of life. Christ was an ordinary living person of His day. His concern was to make it understood that a person like Nicodemus, if he would follow the formula could have as great results as He Himself.

Therefore we must look to our channelhood, to our capacity for being used as Christ was used, for the needs of the world of today. We have to be accurate in our service. Our tendency is to conserve worn out needs, without understanding that it is our capacity to provide a new model, a new manifestation of life, when we get a group of people who live their ideal. Our service to our neighbour is our ideal, but the difference between having an ideal and being the manifestation of it, is very great, and we cannot do it through our mental processes.

The keynote of the Christ is direct

simplicity of language, form and manifestation. Many people think that the Technique is a difficult and complicated system - they try to understand it and never will - certainly I never have. I have only understood through the experience resulting from the Technique. If you will do the Technique perfectly simply, your reaction and results and revelation will also be simple. If you make of it a complicated system, your understanding will be complicated. There will be no direct understanding between the mind that finds Light complicated and the mind that is Light and radiates Light.

That is why the initiation of Jesus is unique, for nobody had gone through the manifestation of bringing the law into the organic functions of the body. Sin is the crux of the manifestation of the law of love. Wherever we have failed in the law of love we shall get a lack of manifestation and a condition of our body that we shall have to recognise sooner or later. Because of the Technique in Light it becomes possible that our reaction to the breaking of the law is so instantaneous that we do not fail a second time in the same spiral. The slow progress of the spiral of experience is going on in us.

I have had an understanding that is helping me to realise that this Christian Initiation is the freeing of the individual on earth from all the consequences of his past lives, so that he goes on free from all the things which have bound him in the past. The driving force of the ego's own will is always providing the ego with sins of omission which are as great as sins of commission and more subtle, for we never recognise the things we might have done because there is no reaction from another person to show us the truth.

I wondered what I could do, for the people I have hurt are dead and I cannot make amends now. I recognise the truth, and the recognition of the truth of one's condition is the substance of that forgiveness which is the marvellous radiation of the Christ. When one does not excuse oneself one gets into touch with people who have passed over, and the forgiveness and unity of heart to heart is accomplished.

Then I remembered that when my brother went over he came back and told me that he had had a capacity for understanding spiritual things and had not used it. I knew his warm-hearted life and compassion and love for humanity had been very great, and I tried to show him that he need not worry about the things he had not done, but rather remember the things he had done. But no! he said that he had had the capacity and had not

138

used it and nothing could excuse him.

We of this Christian Initiation are given the chance to loose here on earth that which is bound in heaven, for that which is bound on earth is bound in heaven. I want everybody to realise that in the perfection of our channelhood this condition of freedom is inevitable. We shall all be shown what we are, not by friends but direct by Him, and the whole object of the Technique in Light is that we receive direct our contact with the Christ's mind, and we are going through this process.

Therefore I want you to concentrate on your capacity for this condition of channelhood which is the Christ. It is having the Christ body, not only earthing in our minds the wisdom of Christ, but earthing in ourselves the capacity to manifest His wisdom in our own bodies. Because He is the model of resurrection, we have to go through this experience while still alive, for there is no resurrection on earth until we are free, until we have died to ourselves. I believe that this death is what we are all going through, we are all dying to ourselves. All this is finished and to some people it is very grievous. We have been so concerned with the results, and I get letters from people who ask what is wrong because they felt the exercises should prevent these difficulties in their lives and they think they cannot be doing them rightly. They are doing them rightly, for these difficult times are but our own destiny and we have drawn them to ourselves. If we did not have them here we should postpone the condition until another life, so in this accumulation of difficulties we are going through let us know it is the last trump, the last condition before the freedom and resurrection.

Do not think of yourself as being wafted up in the resurrection. Remember the body of Jesus after the resurrection when He walked the earth as an ordinary human being. Do not expect a marvellous expression on people's faces but a marvellous radiation of creative energy that will be going out to everyone and they will not know it. It is not a visible resurrection, but the essence of creative energy expressed in beauty. Wherever beauty is to be manifested we must manifest it. Nothing that is hurtful, self-important, egocentric or making an individual a person to be envied, but building a person to whom everybody will go in love and in the certainty of the solving of their problems. There will be created a radiation of great happiness, and that is a very rare substance.

How frightened people have been of happiness and felt it too good to last! He has promised us that the fear of unhappiness and the shedding of tears is a condition that shall end. Imagine if the world were like that, with no power to impose pain on any living person. That is heaven and a state of heavenly exhilaration, a state we can arrive at if we die to ourselves.

This substance of light illuminating us inside and out is the only energy that will provide us with a new and living instrument to manifest that happiness, and no other substance on earth can do it. It cannot be done by taking thought. This "I" always functions - safety first. People say "I must be safe and think it over." They cannot accept it until they have done something about it and watered it down until they have presented it to themselves in a form they can accept.

If we are to be perfect channels we have to accept things we do not understand, and have never experienced before, things we cannot relate to anything else, and above all which we cannot relate to the past. That is what is needed in everybody - a new experience every day that is unrelated. Christ never went through anything twice. Every step in the Christian Initiation is something new starting in our physical selves. There is no limit to the energy He can pour through us nor to the change that can take place in us and to the texture of our flesh and blood. There is a new

human substance that cannot be brought into manifestation until we have died to the old pattern altogether.

The formula for doing it has to be accurately applied. If I leave off doing the Technique and am cloudy in my mind and do not seek revelation or continue to make a contact with His mind, though the desire of my heart is to ask Him to teach me something new, I shall not get it. It will not come, I can only bring it in at the moment and not because of past virtue. I have never done anything in the past that can guarantee the present: the present is my only guarantee, as I think, so I am at the moment. That is channelhood, and the result of that channelhood must be healing and all creative conditions of beauty and a wonderful manifestation. Do not let us look at results but at capacity. Do not let us have to go on the other side and look back and say: "I had the capacity, why did I not use it? Was I too lazy or too busy?"

When He invited the people to the feast they said they were too busy, and their reasons were varied. We have to get our revelation about that. When He asks us to do a job He will find time for the things that need to be done. It is always His concern to fit in needs, so do not let us worry because He will put first things first. Get into the habit of receiving direction and knowing that it grows through experience. We shall never know if we do not give Him the chance to give us that experience, and we cannot do it by much thinking, but let us say "Shall I, or shall I not? Direct me." In that quick sparking moment you will and must get your direction, if your brain is not quicker. It is the quickness of your brain that sparks in and insulates His direction.

In the **Ah-Mou** exercise this direction of our mind onto the radiant head of Christ as a physical gesture is a most important power in us to focus. I cannot do a single thing until I have got the note for my day. If you draw the light over your head and into your hands and anoint yourself with the oil of light, then after your hands have travelled up on the sound of **Ah**, while you listen, with your eyes on the bowl of light, the sound of His direction will come down the rays. I do it again and again during the day when I need direction and contact with His mind for service, but never for my own personal life. Often when we do not know what He wants of us, He gives perhaps one word. It was on this exercise that I got the understanding of my sins of omission.

I think the **Ah-Mou** is important because of our mental capacity for confusing the issue and not learning to receive direction from a definite sparking point. We know we can receive direction when we least expect it, but when you want it and ask for it, the focusing of your eye and ear must be a unity. If we focus on light, that contact of our mind with His mind sends a reaction of sound to us, and unless we focus on the Infinite Point we cannot expect or receive.

It is a law that if we shoot our mind up to His without wandering, we get it. As your eye travels through the mental plane which the human mind has created, as this diffusion of thought strikes diffusion, it will wander unless it strikes a point. If you get something you cannot comprehend, be glad, for it will be a new experience of accepting something incomprehensible. Those of us who are very concerned with channelhood know we are given much that is quite beyond our comprehension, and it is exhilarating because our mind will, at a given moment, be able to contain that which it was unable to when it first comes through.

THE

ARMOUR OF LIGHT

PART I

VOLUME II

This volume is a compilation of additional talks presented
by Olive C.B. Pixley, as they were revealed through her.

While all the explanations on how to perform each exercise remain
consistently the same, Olive Pixley did give a considerable number
of talks relating to each one.

The following are talks and correspondence course notes,
gathered and presented here as
Volume II
of this new revised edition of
The Armour of Light
Part I
with the specific aim of providing the reader with an
enhanced depth of understanding of each of the exercises.

INTRODUCTORY LETTER

This letter was sent to readers who expressed an interest in undertaking the training of the technique of The Armour of Light, by correspondence course.

I am anxious to give as simple an explanation as possible of the training in Light which has been given through revelation. The manner in which it was first revealed has been fully described in *"The Trail"*, and therefore need not be discussed here.

The training is a method of spiritual exercises for developing the capacity for spiritual awareness which is latent in every human being. At first the Technique was passed on only to a few intimate friends, and in those days it seemed inconceivable that it could ever have a wider application. But those few proved for themselves the power of the exercises to train and develop their individual capacity to receive revelation direct, and to know for themselves what co-operation with the will of God can mean.

From that small beginning the work has spread and spread, until today it has been proved, beyond all possibility of doubt, that the Technique can train the individual to tune in to the mind of Christ. Of ourselves we know that we can do nothing, but to Him, working through us, all things are possible.

From the very beginning I want to make it quite clear that no one who starts this training must necessarily expect sensational happenings. This is the way of living experience, and the effect of the exercises is slowly to expand our understanding so that the things that were dark and obscure become crystal clear; the errors of thought and judgement fall away; the wrappings of self-esteem, egotism, hardness of heart, pre-conceived ideas, all the self-created things that blind our vision, are done away; and we begin to know ourselves, not as we have dressed ourselves up, but as we really are.

To some there may be suffering in this beginning of self-knowledge, and all will need courage and utter integrity of mind to face the truth. But, with self-knowledge comes also an ever increasing knowledge of God, and slowly the picture in the frame of our humanity is changed. Where before we had only ourselves to look at, our own fears, hopes, worries, anxieties, griefs and pain, there is now the living Christ, with whom we can work in utter confidence and trust, knowing that He can never fail us, and that He has not only the will but the power to lead us, here and now, out of uncertainty and doubt into Light and Love and Life.

Before beginning the training I must explain that we have been taught that the soul is in reality a body of light, as real and as much a substance as are our physical bodies; and that the light body, which is the container of our spirit, needs food as do our physical bodies: that in the majority of people it is starved and incapable of functioning as the dominating factor. When this is the case it is the physical body, with its attributes untransmuted, is an insulating substance through which the light and love of God can hardly penetrate. We have been taught that Light is a real substance, the substance of God, the food for our souls; and that by means of the Technique in Light, we can draw this substance into our soul bodies, thus making them the dominating factor.

It has been written, "Men shall see the Light, walk in the Light, and *be* the Light; and man shall again be at one with God." These are the steps; to learn to see the light with the inner eye of the soul; then to walk in the light as He, Jesus, walked in the Light of God; then, to *be* the light, as at the Transfiguration the disciples saw that Jesus *was* the Light. These are the steps of the Christian Initiation, steps which the training in Light will enable us all to take one by one.

In order to pass on this training to the many who are now asking for it, there are free classes held at ...., in which are grouped individuals in the same stage of learning in Light; and they are taken on step by step, as we have been taken on ourselves. For those who cannot come to the classes there is a correspondence course. The instructions as to how the exercises are done have been printed and the various steps are sent to each individual as he is ready for them. There is no charge except the postage and 3d. per leaflet to cover the printing expenses.

I enclose for you (1) The Ritual of Light, which is explanatory, (2) The Conscious Breathing, which is the first step of the training. Will you follow the directions as given in these two and practise the Conscious Breathing daily? Realise that this is not physical breathing. Your physical breath is to be done ordinarily and normally and is in no way altered. The Conscious Breath is the breath of your light body, which you are being told to visualise with your human brain; and even as breathing is the first act of the child when it is born into this world, so breathing is the first act of the soul at the beginning of its conscious life.

146

RITUAL OF LIGHT AND CONSCIOUS BREATH

Correspondence Course Notes

The Technique in Light is a process whereby every individual who desires it may become a channel for the Holy Spirit to pour through and manifest in healing, teaching and living, as was demonstrated by Jesus Christ two thousand years ago. He had to make God the Father a living reality - not a remote Jehovah. We have to make Jesus Christ a living reality through the medium of flesh and blood, and not be content with an imitation of a mystical figure - crucified, dead and buried. We must learn through reality of individual experience that the resurrection body of Jesus was a true scientific demonstration of "a new and living way - through the veil - that is to say the flesh." We have to learn how to transmute our crucified bodies into free, reconstructed vehicles for the divine power to pour through in acts of service and reconstruction.

Never has Christ needed His friends so greatly as He does today to let their light shine. If the lamp of our body is choked with egoistic substance only a fitful glimmer can occasionally be seen. The Technique eliminates all insulating substance. It teaches us how to receive the radiations direct from the eternal body and blood of Jesus into our own bodies so that we may become like the hem of His garment, giving out health. What we receive from Him, we must give out normally. We give our own radiations of irritation, fear, gaiety or sympathy, according to our capacity, but when we learn to tune in to the mind of Christ and not depend on our own limited understanding, we find He can flash truth into our minds, and truth acting on our bodies frees us from disharmony and all its attendant diseases.

So try to do the Technique simply as children do it - realising that the Figure of Light at your feet is the Holy Ghost - that radiant emanation of perfect flesh and blood that was earthed for us two thousand years ago. It is significant that we make our contact first with Him with our feet, for our feet must earth the Light and regenerate the earth. It was for that reason only that we were created - to be channels, to receive and to give, and to withhold nothing of Life. Only our minds have power to withhold, to judge and to criticise; our hearts can never withhold, therefore we must learn how to receive the Light of Love into our veins - not as as symbol but as the experience of a "new and living way."

147

INTRODUCTION
New Class - Autumn Term 1937

This Technique in Light was given to me 11 years ago. I did not understand it - it was not a product of my own mind, and I am not responsible for it. I had no knowledge that it would ever have to be taught to other people. I do not know the needs of everyone here today, and if I tried to help with that end in view, I should fail. I can only pass on the Technique as it was given to me, and the understanding of it has grown gradually.

The Technique in Light is a way of revelation and experience. It is a way that brings its own experience and through which can come one's own certainty. At first, what I received seemed personal teaching in answer to one's own need. Had I had an inkling of what the future was to bring, I think I should have thrown my hand in then and there.

I have come to understand that the only thing we have to learn is how to receive the Holy Spirit. It is not a mental process, having the quality of one's mind. It does not matter how unintelligent a person is, so long as they have a longing desire outside of their minds. A child can tune in on a wireless and this knowledge deals, as it were, with the infinite end of a wireless. This Technique in Light is the Christian Initiation containing all knowledge and all love. Nothing we can conceive of with our brains comes anywhere near it. The mind is not asked to store a great deal of knowledge; in the moment of our need, knowledge is wirelessed through us instantly. Our foundation is the human experience of Jesus and His twelve disciples.

No two of the miracles were ever performed in exactly the same way. The inspiration came through from the Father. We do not have to learn to develop our minds, but to empty them. Spiritual power demands a condition of receptivity. When we are as receptive as little children the kingdom of heaven is revealed to us. We do nothing of ourselves.

We long to do something to help the world, and are overcome by a feeling of helplessness. We are surrounded by people who need help and courage and we are unable to do anything for them. But *through* us can come the inspiration to help everyone, for in Light there is no insoluble problem.

The substance of Light is a completely real thing. Just as there are octaves of sound and colour beyond the range of our ordinary senses, so there are octaves of Light. The third eye of occultism - the pineal gland - is situated in the middle of our brain. A New York surgeon, during an operation he had never before attempted, uncovered the tip of the pineal gland and to his amazement found it phosphorescent. He immediately went down to the mortuary and performed the same operation - but there was no life, there was no Light.

We are being taught that Light is a substance of the blood. The blood of Jesus was different from any other blood there had ever been, not because His human vehicle was different from ours, but because He knew how to draw into His blood the creative forces of the Father.

Just as there are sounds too high for us to hear, so it is with Light; there are octaves which cannot be registered by our eyes but which come into the realm of vision. That is where the third eye comes in. When you are asked to think of what you saw at the Coronation, clear pictures come into your minds of the crowds, the decorations etc. This is a quality of seeingness which is completely objective; although you cannot touch the things you are seeing. We need to develop that quality of inner sight which is our vision, for down those rays of Light which are not visible to the physical eye will come those things we need to learn. This is a transcendental condition right outside our human powers, and can neither be imagined or controlled. The Technique has always been beyond my power of imagining, for always the unexpected happens.

We have to remember we are dealing with Infinite Law with its infinite manifestations. It is human nature to expect finite results. We all know so well what our neighbour should do, but revelation of ourselves to ourselves is always painful, and so very unexpected. We are not concerned with what others think of us - that does not matter - but we do know that those of us who put our hands to the plough *will* find it difficult. We are always sensitive when we get a clear picture of ourselves; but the Light does the job of clearing away debris and dark places for us.

Do not fear that one will be asked to give up this or that. We have always set up a standard of conduct, a code, which is expected of us, and we try to conform to it. When this divine energy flows into us we find something quite different, which is instantaneous from moment to moment.

All the chaos in the world is the result of man being disconnected from the mind of God. If mankind were to tune in to Him and put the responsibility on to Him, there would be no problems.

When you start the exercises, just flop - be so comfortable that you entirely forget yourself. Relax all over, particularly in your head. Do not drift into any unreal condition. Be aware of your own room, your own bed. Feel the contact made by the head with the circle, which is Life. Of our own free will we can place our feet where we will, but the conscious soul places his feet in the centre of the circle against the feet of the Figure of Light. So many people cannot bear the thought of the Figure at their feet. But how can we follow Christ, who showed us the way, if we have not learned to bring down the Light into living experience, down to our feet so that it is earthed and we walk on an illumined path?

It was not for nothing that Jesus washed the disciples' feet, and the moment we touch the feet of the Figure of Light we have a real experience. The circle of light looks like one of those liquid lights that run round in a motor shop. Remember, visualising and thinking are exactly the same thing. There is no form until we think it.

We do well to realise that every form of suffering comes through our minds; so also can happiness. The brain is an instrument and your mind cannot be emptied except through an agency that far transcends anything we can do for ourselves.

The Conscious Breath is the beginning of the giving of ourselves. We make a spiritually conscious effort. Our first act in the world, and the last, is breath. Physical breathing is automatic, but conscious breathing never can be because it is always a conscious act of the will. There is a breath ray that pours down on this world, and the first conscious act of the initiate is to fuse his breath with this ray.

This condition must be entirely voluntary. If you think of a corked bottle - no liquid, however precious, could be poured in - it would go past on the outside, and so it is with us.

When you lie in the circle, turn your palms upwards. There are two positions of the hands, of power. One, with the palms down, drawing up the earth forces; and the other, palms up, receiving the spiritual vibrations.

As the Light gradually replaces the lower particles in our bodies we shall gradually be made whole, and the cobwebs will be brushed away. This is why Jesus incarnated in a human body - to demonstrate the possibility of perfect flesh. The divine cosmic

Christ is outside the body, and not in it. But the spark is within, and the two can ignite like inflammable substance.

Do not fear that you cannot do the Conscious Breathing because you have asthma or any other physical condition which makes it difficult. There is no virtue in the length of time you hold it, and you cannot breathe quicker than your thought.

Do not brace yourself to bear pain. Relax and receive. *Always* relax when you are in pain.

Our revelation can only come through experience. Our aim is to become one with the Christ and to achieve the substance of His flesh. We cannot do this of ourselves. We have to learn how to receive the knowledge. We have only to be empty and receive, and the Technique shows us how. No one of us can be greater than another, because the greatest would only be the emptiest. Therefore do no even have an inferiority complex, it is an unreal condition.

At night, blot yourself out with a cross of Light. It is a protection and a direct passport to the world of Light, with no halt, in your dreams, at wayside stations of nightmares and unreal conditions.

Thus we begin to learn how to be children of Light.

RECEPTIVITY
14th October 1937

I want to make it clear that the important thing is to *do* the Technique, whether we understand it or not. Receptivity is not a question of mental understanding. The human instrument can neither register nor understand the Divine as a whole; it can only transmit the individual amount.

This autumn we have to understand our capacity for manifestation of the Holy Spirit. Through the Technique we are earthing in our bodies the great cosmic rays and in our lives the world should see the divine radiation earthed. We have been prepared, and now we are called on, to manifest the Light.

What we have hitherto looked upon as circumstances of which we were the victims, we now see as an agency for self-revelation. Each of us has drawn to ourself those circumstances which show us up that we may know ourselves. This process becomes accelerated when we start on the Technique; but the path leads us, when we have transmuted our reactions to those circumstances, towards the manifestation of perfect health and complete freedom. Remember perfect health is contagious, just as illness is. Each of us has come into this world with some physical disability which may be visible to everyone, or known only to ourselves. We have come here together to be made whole.

We are following His footsteps in the pathway of Light. The Technique is given to develop our power to receive, to make a fusion of wholeness between our souls and the human vehicle.

We must learn how to receive perfectly, and then we shall give, without any knowledge of the giving. In true giving, nothing of ourselves goes out. The weary and sick tuned in to Jesus and took from Him life, health and harmony. In our emptiness, everything can be given to the sick and sorry; it is a question of *being* rather than of *doing*. The law is a human one - the loving of our neighbours, according to the standard set up when we do the Technique every day. Remember we are not the same person when we do the Technique in the morning as we were yesterday. Follow nobody's example; have your own experience. Do not rely on your old mind and your old mental capacity to control your thoughts; do not trust the old crutches. The contact made when you put your feet to the feet of the Figure has to be photographed on to the eye in your head. Unless you receive and register it in your head, though the Light is at your feet, it remains as it were, inactive. Properly made, the contact with the feet sets in motion power in the spiritual spheres.

Jesus set us a standard in His capacity for receptivity.

We cannot hope as yet to understand the mechanism by which we can tune in to the Energy and be made whole, but the Technique is the method by which every individual can learn how to become a transformer, and every soul tuning in to a transformer will be relayed on to God.

There must be a complete surrender and an understanding that the greatest among us must be least, and an emptying of all personality, of our "little selves". The Technique will enable each of us to be an empty channel. It puts into operation the Divine energy which supersedes the mind. It is a curious fact that when you *cut* the physical body with Light, you *unite* with the light body.

We are stepping on to a rung of knowledge that none of us have been before - one of complete freedom.

The Ritual is the key which unlocks the door, but each person must step out their own individual action.

THE RITUAL OF LIGHT
Correspondence Course Notes

The development of spiritual consciousness is a similar process to that of physical growth, and the individual is equally responsible for both processes.

When I was first initiated into this training I was given, through my mind, a drawing in light and was told to visualise it every morning. My mind was, as it were, the black-board on which the spiritual teacher flashed the lesson to be learnt; and this Technique in Light is for the purpose of so developing the capacity of our minds that they can register instantaneous contact with the divine Light.

If we want electricity in our house we have first to get it wired, so that when we put a plug in the wall, radiation takes place and our lamp is lit. This Technique corresponds to the wiring of the house, so that when we are able to make a contact with the "Very Light of Very Light," and being then "of one substance with the Father," the power of radiation functions in us, and we *know*. So will you, every morning on waking

up, and before you get up (not so early that you go to sleep again, and not so late that you do not give yourself time) visualise a horizontal circle of living white light, which is the circle of life? Within that circle our free will can place our bodies at any angle we please, but the conscious soul will voluntarily place his feet in the centre of the circle, and there he will instantly make a contact with the feet of the Figure of Light, whose head is also attached to the circle exactly opposite his own.

In this first illustration you will see the position of the human and the Light Figure. I do not want you to visualise the diagram, but I do want you to see yourself lying in your own bed, so relaxed and comfortable that your body does not in anyway impede your visualising power. And it is very important that the head should be relaxed. We often think that if our hands are supple we are entirely relaxed; but often in my own experience, there has been a tight, tense, concentrated feeling in the head of which we are unaware until we make the effort to relax our whole being.

Then quietly and gently, think the whole circle round - know that your head is touching it - know that the Figure lies opposite to you, and place your feet so that the soles of your feet rest against the feet of Light. Let the arms lie loosely by your side, palms up in the receiving position.

In that position we make our first conscious contact with the Father, and that is by our breath. "In the beginning was the Word, and the Word was with God, and the Word was God." So says St. John - and St. John *knew*. A word has shape, sound, breath and rhythm.

CONSCIOUS BREATHING
Correspondence Course Notes

Our first understanding of the Word comes on our Conscious Breath. Physical breath is the unconscious rhythm of our life. By its rhythm we can tell when a person is ill, in distress, or asleep; and when it stops we know that life has left the material encasement. Conscious Breath is the visualising of the rhythm of life, continuous or eternal life, and can never be an automatic condition, for when we cease to visualise we drift back to our unconscious, automatic physical breathing.

To visualise is an act, an accomplishment; once having done it, it is. So now, having visualised your circle of light and your Figure of Light, they are there. Continue to lie completely relaxed, the palms of the hands still up, the feet resting against the Feet. Now try and visualise a point in infinity, which is God. Personally I always see my point of light as a break in the sky when light shines through a grey cloud. Eliminate the ceiling and see your Infinite Point of Radiance, and then inhale and visualise your breath going from your solar plexus to your feet. Exhale, and see your breath go straight from your solar plexus to your Infinite Point of Radiance. Do not worry about your breath returning from your feet - it is there to be sent up as you exhale. Always start by inhaling.

You will see from illustration II* the direction of the Conscious Breath, and you will realise that you are doing something completely contrary to the usual automatic physical action. It is both the first stretch of your mind and your first conscious sending of yourself, your breath, your being, your very life, to God. In that first voluntary giving of yourself you have placed your feet on the first step of the Christian Initiate's path, and that path leads you into the intimacy of the companionship of the

Christ Himself.

The Conscious Breathing is in no way a physical action and bears no resemblance to the yoga methods. It is not important how long your breath is. If you suffer from asthma, or a cold, or heart trouble, if you can breathe at all you can visualise the direction of that breath. If you can breathe normally, then try and do it as rhythmically as possible, and visualise your breath as one sees it in cold weather (the one time we can see our own breath). Do not even visualise yourself in any other surroundings but your own. For we, who are striving to attain full consciousness, must be more sane, more balanced, more real, than the average man. Our consciousness is a plus condition, the developing of our "within-ness." Do not attempt to focus exteriorly, do not look for results or for psychic sensations when doing the exercises. Our experiences come day by day, and are provided by our circumstances. They will vary in detail, but correspond in general with this process of our self-revelation.

Our condition is never static, therefore do not look for a repetition of experience. The conscious life is a spiral, and each spiral is a different level of experience; so the sameness of the spiral and the difference of the level will be repeated in our lives, so much the same and yet so different.

The breathing should be done in the morning, for as long or as short a time as you feel you need. But it need not be limited to the early morning. Any time during the day that you are worried, uncertain, annoyed - and it does not matter whether you are sitting, standing, or moving - take a few Conscious Breaths, and you will find your equilibrium returning. For you cannot think of anything else whilst you are visualising the fusing of your breath with the Divine; then the awareness of the real values of life steals into our being, and we are able to transcend for one brief moment the pressure of material care.

At night, if you are sleepless, try the Conscious Breathing, and that perhaps more than anything will develop your power of visualising, for at night, when physically tired, or even in pain, if you can train your mind to make this contact, power comes into you. The rhythm of the Conscious Breath is the rhythm of sleep, when our spirits are free of the earth plane's limitations, and are able to function in their natural sphere. By breathing consciously during the day you make a definite contact with the limitless conditions of the spiritual world.

CONSCIOUS BREATHING

Experience of the Technique in Light is called, and really is, the true Christian Initiation. Initiation is a very simple term - it means 'being taught.' You know how a tiny child can, by turning a knob, get in touch with Paris, Berlin - wherever he tunes in. He does not tune into Paris and get America: it is so simple and easy even for the little child. Well, we must learn to be as little children, in Light, tuning in to Christ's infinite wavelength.

After today, I want you to re-read in the New Testament those terms concerning Light. We have understood them as being symbolic, but it has become clear to me that they were never symbolic but scientifically *real*. Christ *was* the Light of the world, and this will soon be proved scientifically as a fact. If you understand these terms in which He became the saviour of the world, you will realise that it was through His blood. The old-fashioned terms of evangelical teaching concerning the blood of Jesus often repelled. Now the scientific knowledge teaches the understanding of the Light in the blood of Jesus, and Light is the life germ. Even those who cannot yet believe in the continuity of existence will in time come to apprehend what all must inevitably accept, this truth concerning the incarnation of Christ.

One cannot impose this teaching on anyone; the truth must come to each one of us for ourselves. This Technique of Light will give you the truth for yourself, and when that is achieved the exhilaration is indescribable. When you know the truth for yourselves, it does not matter what the world thinks.

I had thought at first that my experience was unique, but I soon grew to know through others that it was really universal. I, a very ordinary person, found that I was chosen to be a "loudspeaker", showing that this new normality was to be demonstrated by a common-place normal person, and that it should be the level for all ordinary human beings. As a demonstration to you of the tuning in to divine wisdom, of this technique of revelation, I will tell you that I am never allowed to prepare what I have to say to you. I do not know beforehand what it is that has to be said. The process that you will all learn will show you that nothing in the Technique of Light comes from my *own* mind - I am not in the least responsible for it.

The Technique of Light is learning to tune in to the mind of Jesus Christ who is *all* knowledge. You may ask, "Why do you say to the mind of Christ - why not to God Himself?" Because Christ was the only incarnate soul who consciously asserted His contact with God. In the beginning there *was* contact between the human race and God. We read in Genesis that "Adam walked and talked with God" - then fear came, and was the cause of the insulation of man's mind from God. Then Adam and his seed had to leave that place of divine contact until such time as it was refound.

I venture to say that in this generation, Christians will again find that contact with the mind of God through the mind of Christ. This would have been impossible unless His great soul had been willing to take upon Himself our garment of flesh and blood to remake this contact which fear has broken. Fear is original sin - there was no sin until fear came and insulated us from God. In God there is no fear. All of us have fears, private and corporate fears.

You will find new truth in the New Testament a fresh understanding of its teaching. Do not let your minds compare the Technique of Light with any other method of spiritual teaching or you will fail in receiving revelation. Revelation is not reasonable as we do not know what it *should* be like in our minds. There is no excuse for anyone who is willing to take another person's knowledge for themselves; each of us must find the truth for ourselves. We have the right to know: do not let the teachings of past generations be all our guide, it is not enough today. Not even what our parents know, that is not enough for a child of Light today - not in *opposition* to them and their teaching, but in co-operation with all truth. It does not matter along what branch you have studied hitherto; that does not interfere with revelation. The only exception to this is anyone who studies along mediumistic waves - they lay themselves open to many contacts with any minds on any planes and this is not for any of us.

I do not want you to indulge in much meditation as we must learn to receive our contact wherever we are and whatever we are doing. Learning to receive this divine contact is not a question of virtue or of brain. Indeed, the more intellectual you are the more difficult it is to stop using your *own* mind, and to receive instead. We are so busy working our brains and find it difficult to learn the difference between receiving and acquiring. For example, if you clutch on to anything you want to grasp, your hand is clenched; if you ask to receive a thing, your hand is out-stretched. You cannot receive a thing if your hand is clenched. So with your minds, they too must be open and ready to receive - to receive that knowledge which will flash into your minds as lightning flashes.

This teaching in Light is for our physical bodies. Our souls are *radiant* bodies, but this physical container is at variance with the rhythm of our souls, and there is a fight between the lack of harmony in our physical bodies and the harmony of our souls. One reason for the incarnation of Jesus was to perfect the flesh, to bring that knowledge of harmony between body and soul into a perfect radiation of love. He demonstrated the loveliness of perfect harmony which should be ours - that harmony of existence without fear, friction or hate. Perfect love, as He showed the world, is a complete link, we are eternally linked in love, it is the Eternal Principle. Therefore Christ incarnated to make this fact manifest, and to achieve it He had to go through death to demonstrate resurrection because the human race had taken on death, which is separation. He said that He had done it once, for all, for us all.

The technique of resurrection, or re-construction is this learning to receive the divine Light and Love so that our humanity becomes fused and our bodies are in manifestation with our souls. This reconstruction needs self-knowledge, and self-revelation is apt to become a painful process. We have such a different picture of ourselves than the one we present to others. We try to impose the self which we should *like* to be, on other people, and are surprised and sometimes hurt when they see faults and failings. We know within ourselves that our souls are really lovely, but our humanity interferes, and we cannot get the soul side, as it were, 'over' however much we try. The Technique of Light will 'get this over' as it is a process by which we become *one* inwardly and outwardly, and the radiations from us will come from the light within, and that is what people will then contact, and not those conditions which we are trying to change. Christ was whole in His perfect harmony, and only thus could He make us whole. How can we look for peace for this world when there is none for ourselves?

We have to learn to relax very completely before we can receive this Light; if you tighten yourselves up you cannot receive. You must not let your minds get into any psychic state, but must be very quiet and practical. We are here to be useful and not to indulge in flights on to other planes. If Christ had stayed upon His plane, He would never have made this contact for us on earth. We have to bring the Light down here, as He did, when He walked on this earth changing its substance by the contact of His feet, and when His blood was shed, giving an energy to the earth which it had never had before. Love includes emotion, but there is no *knowledge* through emotion. We must achieve quietness and stillness; we cannot obtain complete contact when we are upset or overwrought or nervy, nor must we think about ourselves. This Light helps us to know ourselves, but not to become self-analytical. Draw the Light into yourselves, receive it into your minds and know the truth of the Eternal Principle of Love.

The first step in this Technique is the development of your pineal gland, which is your television set. This has now been proved scientifically, long after it was given to me. I had felt that no-one would believe that this 'receiving set' was there, when to my great joy I heard a lecture which told of the experience of an eminent New York surgeon. He had done a marvellous operation on the brain and had exposed for the first time in his life's experience the pineal gland. He found a phosphorescent light at the tip of the gland, and was so amazed and interested that as soon as possible he went to the hospital mortuary and did a similar operation on a dead man, and found that the light was not visible as in the living person. Here was the confirmation of this living light - our television set. We begin to realise from whence genius and invention comes.

This Technique in Light is quite impersonal; I know personally what it has done and what it can do, but there is no personality in it. If personality comes into it, then it is being wrongly understood. When we have learnt how to receive, then we shall be able to give. We come here to learn because we want to give: very few come for themselves alone. We cannot give ourselves, but we can learn how to receive, how to become empty, and thus become channels for the Light to come *through* us, not *by* us. We must become, as it were, the hem of His garment and learn how to become whole first ourselves before we can transmit His perfect radiations. Do not be distressed when you realise that your old self is going to fight these new conditions. Our minds inflict so much suffering on ourselves, indeed all pain is self-inflicted did we but realise it. We are so apt to put it down to others and not realise it is our own fault. The Light will show us where our errors lie.

THE RITUAL OF LIGHT AND CONSCIOUS BREATHING

Talk given to a class 12th October 1939

The first thing which I must explain (for none of you here know more than others about this work) is that this method which has come through me, and is for anyone who wants it, has nothing to do with me. I am merely a loud-speaker, chosen undoubtedly for these reasons, that because of my utter normality what has been transmitted through me can be transmitted through everybody.

I was made to understand right from the beginning that this is the Christian Initiation. The understanding of the Christian teaching has been so distorted that it is difficult to understand that it is possible to become a Christ. This is the understanding of the scientific achievement of the incarnation and resurrection.

People of different kinds come here, some are occultists, and some are simple-minded people. One thing must be understood - that everything that happened in the New Testament is *absolutely* true. Miracles are a new normality. If individuals can understand that the Christ was a channel, the necessity for us to become channels can be easily understood.

There can be no peace in the world until it is centred in the individual. The peace conferences are made up of people who are themselves a mass of disharmony. Peace is not an imposition by God but a radiation through humanity. He is the Light of the world, Light is a life principle. All the references to the blood of Jesus is because His flesh and blood was of a different voltage. People have tuned in to *minds* ever since the Fall.

I have understood that original sin is fear. Jesus was without original sin because He was without fear. Separation between God and humanity came about through fear. People say, "How is it God allows such conditions to exist?" He does not allow them; this separation has brought them about. War is the expression of individual greed and fear. As a community we cannot learn to eliminate fear except by drawing in a condition of fearlessness. Nothing is withheld from us. People say, "That must be sent." Nothing is sent as a punishment. We draw to ourselves the experiences we must go through.

Love is not an emotional condition, it is creative energy. We cannot keep scarlet fever to ourselves, nor our worries. Others tune in though nothing has been said. Contact exists between members of the human race and between the human race and God. We have become so self-conscious; we must lose this self-consciousness in a greater consciousness in learning how to be a Christ.

There is no arrogance in this for no one is greater or less than another. We learn to become a channel, an empty bottle as it were, and there are no degrees of emptiness. But it must be empty of the old wine for the new to be poured in. There can be no hiatus; get rid of one bit of egotism and you are at once filled by power. All the healing that is done here, all the understanding, has nothing to do with what we think.

The greater condition is receiving truth and tuning in to wisdom. It is a sparking condition and it is not the way of meditation. The minute you try to apply your mind to anything it often becomes an obsession, and few know how to empty their minds unless it is filled with a greater condition. The only thing I have to pass on to you is this law of life, if you will do the Technique simply as a child, not comparing it with old methods. Some people start comparing it, but these exercises in

Light are methods by which our vision is developed, and every time it is developed we go through a human experience. It is the Technique of experiences. I do not care how many people have vision, but it is how that vision is translated into fact that is of great importance. We have registered in our lives the truth we know.

I do not know if you have read *"Listening In"* which is a personal experience in which my brother told me that over there, knowledge *is* - you do not wonder, you know. Every one of the conditions you experience there, I understand we should experience here.

There is no division in life except the lack of experience. There is no separation of knowledge. It is wrong to pry into anything; but it is not wrong to receive knowledge. There is nothing that we cannot know, for that is a product of our receptivity and this is the Technique of receptivity.

The first necessity is a complete physical relaxation. Some say that they cannot relax, others say that they are relaxed but their neck and head are not. Only in a relaxed condition can we receive, and you know that the clenched hand is the opposite position to receiving, for when your fist is clenched you can receive nothing. The human race is like a row of bottles with stoppers in. Knowledge is pouring down into our minds, but they are silted up with old prejudices and fears, mostly of ourselves.

People say, "How can I know? I think it is my imagination," and they fear their imagination. In the Technique you find your imagination can play no part. It is not our imagination any more than when a doctor writes a prescription and the words on paper can be translated into definite substances. The transmutation from prescription into the tonic is a very definite condition, and what we have to know is this law of the transmutation of substance, and that is the understanding of the resurrection. Christ transmuted the atoms of His body into His resurrection body. No other incarnate being had ever done it.

I went through the old initiations and I did not understand why until I was led on into the understanding of this Christian Initiation. I went to a person who had written many books on gnostic teachings and I said that it was the Christian Initiation. I knew in consciousness that there had never been a resurrection and ascension before and that was why I had had to go through the old initiations. Jesus had to go through the process of death. It was said that He died once and for all, for everybody, and I understand that He had to go through the experience of the human race in this separation from the Creator, in order to demonstrate to the world while in the world, His resurrection body, and to impress that it was not necessary for the human race to die to get a resurrection body. We have to do it while still in the flesh.

Many who have not had a love of life have wished to pass on, but now they have begun to understand what fun it is to live, and until we have a readiness to live here, we are not ready to die. We have to get this condition of life in our consciousness here, and not wait to come back again to learn how to love. The only reason we are in the world is to learn how to love; not to give an emotional condition but to understand what love is. The world did not understand that He manifested Love. They saw Him preaching and healing but did not understand that it was Love.

To make a person whole is not an emotional process. We have to be the hem of His garment which was infected with the radiance of life. Because of our disharmony we take in the disharmony of the world. Once we are free we can only give out the harmony we receive, if we have the desire, for it has to be voluntary.

If peace and love could have been an

imposition of the Christ mind, do you not think He would have imposed them? Because He has got to wait until we understand our birthright and capacity, He cannot impose it on us. This radiation of truth can be an epidemic and that is how I see the world changing. If we can give out cholera, do you not think this epidemic of peace and radiance and health is as dynamic a condition as disease?

Will you do the exercise early in the morning before you get up? I do not want it to be a long affair, for light is a sparking and functions with such speed that we have to learn to receive in the flash of a second. As the lightning flashes from the east to the west, so shall the coming of the Son of Man be.

Relaxing to receive is the first essential. Visualise the Figure of Light at your feet and when we think in Light, it is. Thought in Light is a definite condition. Think a Figure of Light at the feet which are gently raised to contact with the soles of the feet of the Figure in Light. The only virtue in this is simple obedience. Visualise the Figure and then do not go on thinking about it but flash the circle of light from your head round it.

We all incarnate into Light when our heads are in that circle. We can put our feet where we like but the dedicated soul will put their feet into the centre of the circle and make a contact with the Figure. Will you do it with your eyes shut? We have a periscope at the tip of the pineal gland with which we can receive the realities of this world of Light.

When I was being taught of this condition of the blood and that Light was the life germ of the blood, I went to a lecture and there it was said that they were in touch with the New York surgeons, one of the best known of whom had done an operation on the brain which he had never performed before, and had exposed the tip of the pineal gland and found a spark of phosphorescent light. He did the same to the brain of a dead man and there was no light.

When it was said that Jesus was the Light of the world, it is a scientific fact. He had more light in His blood than any other incarnate soul. We have to learn how to draw in the voltage of light. When He said, "Greater things than these shall ye do because I go unto my Father," He knew that having achieved His ascension body, He was able to make perfect contact with the human race. He had to have the twelve left behind for they had been taught by Him how to receive so He was able to broadcast into them the truth. He said,

"It is expedient for you that I go away," so that there should be this broadcasting system.

You will realise the extraordinary achievements of the twelve after He went. When He was in the same type of body as theirs they were full of fear, but after He had walked and taught them at Emmaus they learnt to receive truth. If only the Church had learnt that every person has a right to know, if only they would prepare their bodies, for Jesus came to prepare bodies and not to save souls.

We all have soul bodies but our physical bodies are below the average and we have to bring them into an eternal condition of reconstruction. There should be no illness or old age. We accept this, but we should learn day by day to know our strength so that no decay should take place in the human body. This law of the transmutation is only a condition; that we take up our life and lay it down in service. Where we can best serve we shall always be, and we experience more and more the ecstasy of service. Where one starts with reluctance, one ends up with joy and fun and adventure. There is no virtue or merit in this way, and you cannot talk about these things, you can only *be* them. If a person knows more they have more to give, and it will never be an imposition of power. We can receive more love, and love is a creative energy.

We have put our feet in the centre of the circle and made contact with the Figure of Light, which is life and energy that have got to come through the feet. In the old days the mystic retired to a lovely world in which mystical experiences were not real. In the medieval days people retired from the world to have spiritual experiences, but in this century we have to go out into the world to get them. It is no good trying to do the Technique and keep yourself to yourself. My brother found that he could not keep himself to himself. However much we think we can do so, none of us ever do, and if we only give out what we receive, the world will quickly become a very different place.

The next exercise will start changing our thoughts and is called the Conscious Breath. Many people think I have a system of yoga breathing, but this has nothing to do with holding the breath or with normal physical breath. It is the breath of our soul body. Our soul is the eternal vehicle through which our spirit operates. The soul body must take on the substance of its environment, and on earth it has an earth body to manifest through. Because of the discrepancy of the soul and the physical bodies, we have to bring about a union, and therefore the Technique was given.

First visualise a Point of Infinite Radiance. I get it as a brilliant break in a cloudy sky, although a boy wrote to me and said that he got it as a star. Do not think you have to puff your breath up to the Point of Radiance. Realise the fusion of the breath ray that is poured down onto the world the whole time and we do not know about it. As it is necessary for people to breathe, so this conscious contact of breath is contact of the Holy Spirit. You may think that breath is the emanation of our lungs, but it is a real condition of life power. There is more energy in breath than there is in light.

If you are feeling tired or worried, make that contact of the Conscious Breath, which is the breath of your body fusing with the divine breath, and it must be an individual experience. After you visualise the circle then start breathing, and if you do it every morning you allow yourself to receive all one is capable of receiving. Relax and think of your breath down to the Figure at the feet. You cannot do it automatically. The Conscious Breath is the fusion of your consciousness with the substance of our receptivity.

As I go on giving you these steps our condition of receptivity functions in us in spite of ourselves. Nothing I have received has been demanded or expected, but everything has taken me by surprise. The understanding has come slowly; and the understanding of our problems may not come in the morning but be flashed into our consciousness at a most busy moment. I have found that every time I am busy, I have received the greatest revelation. You cannot work light - it works you - and I only pass it on to you as it was given to me.

In the law of life it is the perfect opposite which makes the perfect whole. As you breathe in and visualise the breath going out, peace comes, and you cannot pick up the vibration of your last thought. It must calm you. It does not matter what our interest in life is, whatever we do or however we express ourselves, when the Technique is part of our being that expression must increase a thousand-fold.

Do not think it is a way of sacrifice for you will discard everything that is your disharmony. We must receive our standard afresh every day. This is the Technique of the resurrection and if people bring the past into the present, they must suffer and all suffering is self-induced, and we need suffer nothing but what our minds take in. If we did not mind a snub we should not suffer, and it would be negative.

Nobody has the power to inflict suffering if we do not take it in. We are the sum total of all our lives.

How can we avoid this senseless suffering? Mentally you cannot impose it, but I can only tell you that along this way, one is given the understanding of how to change the quality of our minds so that we have no destructive condition, and we shall hear ourselves say the right thing, instead of the wrong. So many sentences start with the words, "I am so afraid."

Worry and fear along every line of human experience is the natural condition. People have thought that if you do not worry, you do not do your duty; but we must have an impersonal point of view instead of a personal one and it is the most constructive condition. We have got to understand the Law and find our capacity for constructive work. The Technique in Light makes our mind receptive to a condition of knowledge which hitherto we have not experienced.

Talk given 27th May 1938

I have been given the understanding for some time that the whole of the earth as we know it, the whole of dense matter, is being raised in vibration gradually and slowly. There is, and has been, a greater outpouring of cosmic rays of positive charged electrons.

It is a scientific fact that when a high vibration impinges on a low vibration, it raises the rate of vibration of the low and smoothes out any irregularities. This is the understanding that has been given me, that these cosmic rays, these

light rays, or rays of divine love that are impinging on the earth now are raising the rate of vibration of the whole of matter, and as these rays penetrate the atoms of matter the irregularities and discords are forced into areas - or are forced to the surface, and are gradually being disintegrated.

But there will come a time when these rays of light will have penetrated the greater proportion of matter, and when this moment arrives the dense atoms will not be able to contain the Light and so it will flash out, or fuse, and matter will be instantly raised to a corresponding higher rate of vibration. Those areas of the earth where discord is still untransmuted will be disintegrated and the earth will be functioning in the fourth dimension, or raised vibration.

When a Leyden Jar, or condenser, is charged to the full by an electric current it cannot contain any more and so sparks across; and this is the understanding that is given me, a similar occurrence will take place. There will be a wonderful electric discharge and owing to the raised vibrations those who have made the effort to prepare themselves will see and hear in these vibrations, or fourth dimension.

Thousands are being prepared consciously and unconsciously for this time, and the understanding has been given to me this morning to expect this physical manifestation of Light now, as it will be seen and felt by all incarnated souls. "Those who have eyes to see and ears to hear will see and understand."

I have been impressed that we must all stand on our own - we must not lean on others - we must stand firm as light-houses, radiating out light, love, harmony, peace and calmness; that we must keep perfectly balanced, tuning in continually to Christ. This message came to me this morning:

"Expect! Expect! Expect! - Tell all!
Stand upright in your body of Light.
Know that I am God - I am eternal love
within thee, and within all."

THE RITUAL OF LIGHT AND CONSCIOUS BREATHING

This talk is recorded on cassette tape

The Technique in Light offers a new understanding of the person and work of Jesus Christ, and of its immense significance for our individual lives, and for the world in general. New political, social and economic experiments will never bring us out of our present chaos; what will do so, is a new quality of living developed and demonstrated in individual human lives. Of this quality of life there is one source only, Jesus Christ. He alone has ever known its secret, or practised the art of effortless and perfect living, and He came to give, not merely verbal teaching, but a literal and living demonstration of how human life should really function.

It is of vital importance to this baffled generation that we should each understand how to follow Christ, and radiate His powers. The works that He did two thousand years ago, we must learn to do again now, and without delay. Because we have not understood the law by which He worked we have been powerless to bring it into operation in our daily lives. He is linked in our thought with theology, a church system, a social ethic, a spiritual and moral kingdom, and Christians all down the ages have done their best to follow Him in these realms, but that they ought to demonstrate His perfect health of mind and body, and carry on His miracles, has hardly entered their conception. Nevertheless it is a true conception, and the authentic way of salvation for the human race. Modern man can split the atom and spill on the earth a torrent of destructive force; creative force he has not yet begun to master, nor will he do so until he turns to study Jesus Christ. Christ, and only Christ, has ever earthed in this world the necessary energy to live without disease, and after death, reconstitute the atoms of the living cell. Not only was He personally perfect in form and function, but He transmitted His wholeness to all diseased persons, raised the dead to life, resisted decay in His own being, and reintegrated His own substance into a form that was imperishable.

Christ demonstrated this law of perfect integration in earthly matter, not as a unique phenomenon, but to offer the process to all who would believe Him and receive it. The Technique is the Christian Initiation into this process, and will progressively teach us how to earth in ourselves the capacity to receive perfect creative energy at all times, and let it go out to others without conscious registration. Let us try to understand how Christ Himself achieved it. It is a matter not of willed effort to do and feel this and that, but of receptivity. Christ Himself stressed the fact that He was only the instrument of the Father. "It is my Father that doeth the works; of myself I can do nothing." That is the key to the secret. If we know that all things can be done, not by us, but through us, we have the answer to every world problem. Therefore we should drop self-registration, and self-imposed effort, and learn to function in receptivity. The Technique in Light will progressively show us how.

The path is neither mystical nor psychic; it must operate in the midst of our daily cares, as it did in the case of Christ. Among sordid scenes of every sort, and in the face of intense personal opposition, Christ demonstrated His utter stability at all times, and proved that nothing can destroy a mind and a body perfectly receptive to the wavelength of God. It is because we are not thus receptive that life has so much power to upset us, and we cannot rise above the frictions and frustrations of our lot. The defence reactions they set up in us of fear, anger and resentment, are our own undoing.

They block receptivity, cut us adrift from our source of creative power and show up, at long last, in definite physical disease.

It is essential, therefore, to understand the law of receptivity as exemplified in Christ. Study His life, and you will see that it is a question of focus. Whatever the conditions of the environment, He had His mind steadily focused on the Father, thus keeping unbroken contact with love, serenity, peace and power. Against this constructive contact, no destructive energy could function, and if we could attain it, we too, should be immune. It is our lowered focus which has brought the human race universal disease and physical death. Jesus never bowed to the principle of death. He underwent it in voluntary identification with our humanity, but it could not disrupt the cells of His body, and in three days they rose to new life.

I was shown, a long time ago, that life is Light energy. When quickening takes place in a child, the Light germ is sparked into the blood. When Light leaves the blood, death takes place. Christ came to restore to human flesh and blood the perfect life energy which it had before the Fall, but we have never understood this, except in the early ages of the church, and so have never become receptive to it.

Note that the energy called life is

closely connected both with Light and with the bloodstream. When the life spark goes, blood congeals. When the blood has disease germs in it, they are spread from one person to another. We have no power over the radiation of our own blood, and anyone in harmony with its wavelength must automatically receive its conditions. This Jesus knew, and He came to the world with a perfect blood radiation to teach His disciples the law by which all who wished might get from Him a perfect bloodstream, and pass it on by effortless radiation to all with whom He came in contact. If we can change the conditions of our blood by receiving from Him a plus condition of light, we too must be able to transmute disease energy in our own and other physical bodies.

If we are to make normal and continuous contact with the light energy in the blood of Christ we must return to the idea of focus. Christ maintained His perfect bloodstream by His unbroken focus on the Father. We might call it the wavelength on which He functioned. The wavelength on which we function is all important. We commonly settle our affairs on a reasoning basis, and the mental wavelength we then use is dependent on the brain. This works horizontally, at the human level only, and has no upward contact. But the wavelength of divine receptivity, on which we are really

designed to function, brings radiation to us from the vertical direction and makes of our bodies the perfect formation of a cross of Light. The human body is planned as a perfect instrument for receptivity and transmission and we should receive our life, health and energy vertically from the Source beyond the world of visible matter and transmit the energy thus absorbed into us along our own human levels. All those who believe in God have the vertical contact in some measure, but unbelievers have cut themselves adrift from their divine source.

Our receptive instrument is the brain, and the pineal gland is like a television screen on which we see the pattern. Jesus received the pattern straight from the Father, and was able to make the substance needed to put it into operation. He was the manifestation in human substance of the mind of God, and we in our turn, can so develop our receptivity and focusing power that we become in substance and capacity the expression of the mind of Christ. In so far as we can do this, we shall again have perfect flesh and blood. If we focus our mind on Him, we are certain to receive His blood radiation. Try to realise that it is an actuality that you can train your mind to focus on Christ, and to absorb and spark out the light of His blood radiation with no strain. The Technique will teach you to do this by training you first to focus on the Figure of Light at your feet, and the Point of Radiance above you.

The feet are a most important part of your body, because they are your earth. If you get the illumination of your mind without the feet earthing the light, you will get a mental, mystical condition, but it will not change your physical condition, nor that of anyone you may wish to help. If Jesus had merely had the pattern in His head, He could not have healed illness. Do you remember how much He stressed the feet saying, not "Follow my mind and meditate on truth," but "Follow in my footsteps." Pilate said: "What is truth?" but he could not get a merely verbal explanation, for truth is a radiation right down into and out of the physical being, and when you get it, you cannot put it into words.

The first thing we have to learn is to relax our head and body. Every morning be very real; relax just as you are in your bed, and do not let your mind drift away from your actual self. Focus your mind on your Figure of Light, which is your guide; if you watch it, it will teach you. Then see your Point of Radiance, not with deep concentration, but in a sparking moment. If your mind sparks, your body will spark too.

Breath is important because it is the track down which light or life sparks. Our lungs provide the track for normal physical life, but we have to make a conscious track of breath down which will come a condition of very much increased life energy. It has to be outside us, and does not in any way change or interfere with our normal breathing. There is no strain in visualising this track of breath down. The life force is pouring down into the world, but only those who identify themselves with it can receive it. "Ye have not, because ye ask not." He came "that we might have life, and have it more abundantly," but until we identify ourselves with it we receive only the minimum.

If you are worried take a Conscious Breath at any time. Use it also if you cannot sleep.

This first exercise is the beginning of our capacity to have truth revealed to us, to attain our own health and freedom, and to become a channel of these good things to others. Ultimately we should become as perfect an expression of humanity as Christ, as we become progressively more perfect channels of His divine life.

AH MEH — A E OOO

This Technique is for our spiritual development. It is a Christian Initiation (initiation is a voluntary teaching) by which we are brought into an intimate contact with the mind of Christ, which contains all wisdom and all love.

Love is an energy, the life force which pours down on this world, and in this Technique we learn to receive spiritually. It is a condition which functions through us but not through our minds, the results of which are manifested when we do it faithfully, although we may not understand it.

Last time I gave the first and second steps in this ritual, the developing of our vision and the relaxation of our physical bodies. We must relax if we are going to receive any revelation. We do not have to acquire wisdom, but learn through these exercises to tune into it.

The process is very simple, any child can learn it, and the only thing that can stop it happening is our own mind, if it is the type of mind that shuts doors. Those of us who learn to develop our spiritual qualities have got to be very normal, very sane. We have got to know how to get this trinity of body, soul and spirit functioning with perfect equilibrium. We must have no imagination when we are doing the Technique, neither must we strain and struggle. Screwing up the eyes will not make us see things more easily, nor a desperate concentration produce a picture. It is only when we are completely relaxed that things will be flashed into our vision.

It does not in the least matter if we are interrupted while we are doing the exercises. Our minds have got to learn to return quite easily to the world of Light, so that we can always pick up again at the point of interruption. We must be able to make and break a contact in Light and make and break it again without losing our equilibrium.

Light functions very quickly but in a different condition to that which we are accustomed. When we visualise it, it is. When for instance we visualise the Figure of Light at our feet, it is a reality; when we draw the light up into our hands, it is there for the day. We may see or feel nothing, that does not matter. What we have gradually to learn is to wire our bodies in every part to receive the different conditions of radiation.

We shall not always find that the

exercises work perfectly, they will only work according to our capacities in allowing them to function. There is no particular standard in them, we cannot do them well or badly, the only thing we can register is a wandering mind. One thing suggests another, and in one second our minds have travelled away from what we are doing and on to something else. It is very difficult to be absolutely one-pointed. If we let our minds be dominated by the atmospheres of other people's minds we are going to make it very difficult for ourselves.

When we do the Conscious Breathing no outside condition can touch us. At that moment we are fused with the mind of God and no other condition can upset us. We cannot have petty thoughts and worries when we are doing it.

Conscious and Unconscious Minds

This Christian Initiation is self-knowledge. We have got to know ourselves as we are, not as others see us, or as we would like them to see us. The Technique is to make us an empty channel, and we are not going to be great in the generally accepted sense of the term but we are going to have great things done through us.

In other lives we may have possibly set a value on what we could store in our minds, now we shall find a value in emptying them. By doing this, the truth will be flashed into them and we shall hear ourselves talking truth, serving in any profession or branch of life as a perfect agent, and instead of feeling the old pride which we used to have in our achievements, it will induce in us a great humility of spirit. Only when we know that we are nothing can we be used, and when we are used we shall have a great happiness.

Every day those who do the Technique are given help for the day, but we cannot store up this help, and we shall never be given enough for two days. We must therefore be very particular in doing the Technique every day afresh. We should not dream of eating two breakfasts in one day, so that we need not eat one on the morrow, and it is the same with the exercises.

The Technique is also a secret service; it is the process of *becoming* and when you are anything, you do not talk about it.

It is an instinct in human nature to cling to things because of that fear which is always at the back of our minds. The fear of old age, for instance, of ill health or the loss of possessions. It is very rare to find anyone who is not afraid of anything.

In this Technique our fears gradually drop from us. We learn to discard, not by a method of self-sacrifice, but by a voluntary casting off of those things for which we no longer have any use. Though we may realise this necessity for discarding, we must not try to impose on other people's minds the need for them to discard those same things which we have found we do not now require.

We only discard to be given something in exchange, and in this Technique we learn to understand the ever increasing knowledge of the givingness of God. God is love, and those of us who have any conception of love know that love is always a condition of giving.

We alone are responsible for the circumstances in which we find ourselves. We have drawn to ourselves everything good or bad in our lives. We have asked, and we have received.

It is the very essence of the being of God to give and the world is not the radiant place it should be, because we do not know how to ask or how to receive.

One person may find one or other of the exercises easier than another will find them. This is due to the different condition of insulation in us and our different lines of thought.

Our minds have got to be dealt with individually. The Light brings all hidden things in us into the open. Sometimes when we have a little illumination we think it would be good for others to have it too, but we can only give the light according to our capacity to receive it and transmit it to them.

If we cannot understand the exercises at first, we must not let it worry us. Little by little our minds expand until at last they are able to contain a fragment of the mind of God.

Every substance on earth has a name. The particular substance in Light in this exercise has the sound **Ah Meh — A E Ooo**.

In the first step in Light the circle starting and ending at the head is important, because it means that we are walking about all day with the Light at our head and our feet. In the next step we outline our bodies.

At night, make a cross of Light down the body and across the heart. By this means we earth in our physical bodies that condition of Light and love which is God. It is also an 'express' by which the soul can travel into the world of Light, escaping the influence of the lower planes. Do this also for others whom you love and wish to help. It is like

174

giving them a present in Light, a present of receptivity by which they can receive those things they would not otherwise receive. We have got to be channels before we can give anything to anyone. The only form of unselfishness is selflessness, and that we cannot do through our own minds, only through becoming empty.

If we learn to receive, it means we can give in a second. When we are love, we give it; when we are health, we pass it on to others. We cannot transmit what we have not got. People tune in to the vibrations we are, they cannot help it. This is the beginning of a really wonderful vista when we shall have, and at the same time give out, health and happiness.

SHAFTS OF LIGHT
This talk is recorded on cassette tape

In this next exercise we begin to see the power of prayer in operation, and with it comes an understanding of the functioning power of Light. If we study the action of light on matter, from a superficial angle, we see its capacity for instantaneous destruction when a person or a building is struck by lightning. We can watch the process of disease being arrested and cured by the action on the flesh of different rays of light.

As our awareness develops, we notice the different quality of power that can radiate through the human eyes. The eyes are the barometer of the spirit. There are the lifeless, cold eyes, or the glowing, radiant eyes and between these two lies an octave of expressions which vary with every emotion. Man can control his words, can speak or act a lie, but he cannot radiate a lie. No human being can radiate love and gentleness through his eyes if there is rage and hate in his heart. He can control his rage, he can profess love with this lips, he can deceive by his manner his unsuspecting victim, but there will be no light in his eyes.

Conditions in this world are the reflection, as it were, of the conditions in the world of Light. Bodies there are made of light. Degrees of vitality are expressed by degrees of radiating power. There God, the Christ, the great masters of Light, are distinguished by the quality of their brilliance. Their soul, or light bodies, radiate their complete ego.

The great mysteries in this world are the kindergarten knowledge in the next, through which every soul graduates. The Christ came to give us the power to develop our light bodies here, and in this exercise we have our first fragment of food for our spirits, our "daily bread" of life.

After having outlined your body in light three times, keep quietly relaxed, holding the feet in the same position, but turn the hands over, so that the palms lie upwards. Then, as a preparation to what you are about to receive, eject from your head to your feet, on a short staccato sound of **Ah Oo, Ah Oo, Ah Oo** all transitory thoughts, clearing your being, as a ramrod cleans the barrel of a gun. Do this emphatically, repeating the sound as often as you need, so that you feel the sound travelling through your body and out through both feet into the Figure of Light.

Then visualise two shafts of white

176

light, the ends standing in your hands, the points stretching up to infinity. It is, as it were, the base of a triangle that rests in your hands, and whose apex is outside your range of vision.

When you have thought these shafts of brilliant whiteness into your hands, start your Conscious Breathing, seeing your inhaling breath go to your feet and your exhaling breath rise from your solar plexus between the shafts. *Know* that, as your breath ascends, so instantly the softest round petals of peach-coloured light come down the shafts into the palms of your hands, and are at once absorbed by them. I want you to realise the different substances of those two lights, the intense shining whiteness, and the softness, like a snowflake, of the peach-coloured light. There is no mingling of the white and the peach light. The petals travel down the shafts at varying speeds, slowly with some people, quickly with others. Do not worry if you do not see them at all. Do not concentrate; you cannot make yourself see them. Just know that by consciously thinking, your spirit is working through your mind, and receiving its food and strength; and, day by day, your awareness will grow and your capacity for direct divine instruction increase. Do this exercise for as long

or as short a time as you wish.

Learn not to get into a state of mind. I do not want any of you to think it is necessary to be psychic or to lose the sense of where you are. It is essential that all of us should be more sane and more practical than others. This is the Christian Initiation, and is the one and only way in which we will be enabled to make this fusion of our divinity with our humanity in our human bodies. It is the one way to make perfect flesh. It is not the only way to make contact with Christ - there are many ways of doing that, but for us we have to earth that condition in complete consciousness. It is the difference between losing consciousness and making a plus condition of consciousness. I do not wish to stress the scientific and esoteric sides of this knowledge. It is the essence of receptivity; it is being able to receive the Christ into yourself; it is being able to live in a state of new normality, the world up to now being definitely sub-normal.

Most of us here are worldly people who have a just appreciation of worldly conditions, and do not think that to be spiritually minded should entail cutting oneself off from domestic life. This Technique will give us a greater knowledge of how to live. Youth — middle-age — senility - so mankind has divided it, but if you understand a rhythm of life flowing in, you cannot so divide it. Over there, on the other side, people are at a certain age of life - the prime of life. It ought to be so here, but we have allowed our minds to absorb conditions of disharmony, which poison our bloodstream; we ourselves have brought it on ourselves. Do not think that these things are sent by God - if it were possible to superimpose health and well-being on us, it would have been done. It is because we now have to learn to receive. It has taken the world two thousand years to begin to learn how to receive.

The people of the twentieth century are capable of constructing a resurrection body in the flesh, not waiting to get to the other side, but bringing that marvellous condition here. We are going to be initiated and to learn how to become a perfect vehicle. Our soul is a perfect vehicle but our body is not. Jesus took on human flesh for the purpose of making our bodies perfect vehicles.

We worry ourselves with problems we cannot solve. They fill us with despair as we look around and only see greater problems, more horrors, fears, cruelties. If you will be faithful and do the Technique simply, without allowing your mind to make devastating comparisons, you will learn to receive the answer to every single insoluble problem. This is the

way of truth, of love and of peace. There are so many good people who are striving to bring about peace in the world, who have not the remotest idea of living in peace, even with their own families and relations! We cannot hope to bring about peace until we ourselves are at peace in every single relationship, until we learn how to live peace, until we learn to receive it.

Giving and receiving are one action. This is drastic. My mind was my pride, and I was proud of quick understanding; but now, if it were possible to feel pride in this training, the only thing I should be proud of would be my mindlessness. Christ wants to give and if we can become selfless receiving sets, then we shall know such an ecstacy of happiness. We are so conscious of other people's mind; we want to help a person or a group, and the only way is to become ourselves, this vibration of wisdom and knowledge.

Disease is a manifestation of the separation of the soul and body; we have to face up to ourselves and find out where the disharmony lies. You may control your infirmities, but there will always come the breaking point - control, in the long run, is no use - the only thing is transmutation. The only thing that can change us is this condition of Light and life. The

Christ knew how to draw down this rhythm of peace, and if your bloodstream is in rhythm with the Father, you will become this radiation of love, not as an emotion, but as an energy, a oneness of substance with the Divinity.

I do not know what I shall do or what I shall need tomorrow. I only want to prepare myself day by day for what is required for today. The circumstances of our life are different today from yesterday, or tomorrow, so we must get the strength and inspiration of how to act just for today, get our spiritual food for today's needs.

If our feet are illuminated they will take us with no reluctance to where we should go. We shall walk a dedicated path. Once you have the Light at your feet you do not have to direct them by your mind, your feet will follow the Light without the stress and fear of your mind. That contact with the Figure of Light is of the utmost importance in helping us not to function in fear and duality. The Conscious Breath is the fusion of our whole being with the being of God. These conditions of breath and light are real, just as food or medicine, you do not see them but you get the result. You do not see the process of a morphia injection, but you get the result. In the Technique you will get the result though you cannot hope to follow the process. Something is happening, something is changing, and although you cannot follow the process you will reach the result.

You will believe all this when the scientists classify it as they have classified infra-red rays etc. A quite different octave of cosmic rays will be made manifest. Each of our individual bodies has exactly the same capacity for drawing the cosmic rays and absorbing them. Flesh and blood is the greatest magnet there is for drawing the cosmic rays.

Our hands are of vital importance as transmitters - hands are of service for creating, for beauty, and for service. In the Church, the laying on of hands is a consecrated action, and if all hands were consecrated we should have none of these conditions of cruelty and horror that are in the world. Your hands must be consecrated so that something of transcendental capacity will come through them. You will find that you can use them with effortless perfection, that you can use them more easily, and you will have a new natural condition of functioning, not a super-normal one.

We are only beginning to understand how we can function on a new normal condition of equilibrium. I do know that not one of us who will follow the Technique to the end will leave this world in bondage; we shall leave it in freedom.

Light is a spiral; it will not save us from experiences but will save us from our reactions. Disagreeable things will not be removed from our lives, but we shall act differently in the face of them and they will not frighten us. Be glad when disagreeable things happen, they give us our opportunity to co-operate with Christ in eliminating them out of our lives altogether - out of our karma.

THE GOLD SPIRALS AND BLUE CIRCLES
This talk is recorded on cassette tape

We cannot keep apart in our spiritual knowledge from the things happening in the world today. We must learn to make this mental contact with the spirit of truth as quickly as possible. When we have got our contact, we have got to hold it and not let it be interrupted by the impingement of other minds. There is an utter necessity to have a group of minds today who are invulnerable against the multitudinous thoughts of agitation and fear for the future, which at the moment are being poured out upon everyone.

We talk about mass hysteria, mass production, but if only we could have a Christian 'mass', the results would be simply stupendous! It could be simple as it does not depend upon political or national ideals or ambitions, but upon the desire for receiving that power which will transcend fear, "..... ye shall hear of wars and rumours of wars: see that ye be not troubled."

We have got the Conscious Breathing and have learnt to tune into our Infinite Point of Radiance. We know what it is to tune into another person's mind, to someone upon whom we can rely. Their advice however, is not always right; whereas if we can get this perfect contact, we need never fear we shall receive a wrong direction.

I want to stress that our power of receiving does not necessarily include a sending out to other people but, by holding stability and freedom from fear in our minds, we give them a different voltage to tune into. It must not be a conscious influencing, but the power to make a contact to receive true knowledge. If we bring it down to the level of our conscious thinking, it will then become no more than the working of our intelligence.

We must acquire the ability to be silent and not to give a hasty reply, nor to use our own judgement. We must not even have a national sense, but remember that we are all citizens of the world. The only thing we must hope for is that God's will may be done throughout the world, and we must pray that we can be used to help in His pattern.

The cutting exercise bears on the situation most acutely, for it is a preparation for receptivity. The quality of the Blue Circles is like balm.

I must try and explain the process of Light penetrating the flesh and what it does to the human body. I have been shown the shape of the soul body. Its construction is the basic construction of the eternal form which we all have in common with one another, just as our physical bodies all have the same skeleton structure.

The soul body glows with radiant colours, but even as you can have a sick physical body, so you can have an anaemic soul body. The soul is ours for eternity, for it is the body in which we function on all the planes.

For all time we are individuals, but spirit, or energy, is that which we share with the Father and the cosmic Christ. This same spirit will transform the form of our soul, and as the energy is increased, so do we become more standardised in beauty.

Gradually we shall have a unity of spirit, but never a unity of soul. We unite with Him in our capacities to create when we understand how to draw this energy of light into our physical body. It is the soul linking up with the physical body.

We have to discard our physical form because we do not know how to unite it with the Father. It is as though it was starved, cut off, which is a condition that was never meant to be.

If we could earth in our bodies this divine energy and truth, they would never suffer from any disease or process of decay, and we shall be able to do it, though it will not be done by conscious thinking.

The old mystery schools withheld so much of their knowledge, but Jesus never withheld anything from anyone. "He that hath ears to hear, let him hear."

The path of the initiate is just one footstep wide, and when we have put our feet at those of the Figure of Light, we have put them on that path and we must not stray from it.

Christ's life was a continual condition of receiving, of telepathy. From moment to moment He received divine direction. He had to establish this telepathy with His twelve disciples, and He had to go to the world of Light in order to make a contact from over there with them, with their minds - "I go to prepare a place for you." Those who were in the world at that time made a contact with His human body, but we can receive the whole truth by making a contact with His ascended body.

Though it may be interesting to receive information from other planes, if we really want the truth of the Law, we must go to headquarters for it and be content with nothing less. That we can

make this divine contact has been proved by myself and by others who are also doing the Technique.

Christ carried all the old mysteries onto a universal contact. He excluded no one. "Other sheep I have which are not of this fold." We have to concern ourselves with this law of the redemption of matter. The physical body has got to be redeemed, and it can only be done through the soul body. We have got to prepare our body and the Technique does it for us.

The following example is a child's registration of the complete accuracy of detail in the exercises. The little daughter of someone who is doing the Technique, saw the light of the evening cutting exercise operating through and through her mother, twelve hours after the exercise had been done.

The Figure of Light

This is contained in the talk Gold Spirals and Blue Circles
and is recorded on cassette tape

When I was first given the Figure of Light I did not know what it was, I only knew that it was not my higher self, nor that it had anything to do with me. Later the revelation came that it is the reality of the Holy Spirit, the very vibration of the light of the Christ, His universal presence.

When we make a contact with our feet with the Figure of Light, we are making one with the living emanation of the Christ. It is as though He left His emanation here. It is His resurrection body thought into activity, but it is not there unless we put it there. When we make this contact we are connected with the living energy of His body, His eternal vibration which, through His love for us, He left behind Him.

It is an individual revelation, and slowly our receptivity does make it a real knowledge. The earthing of this knowledge comes from His cosmic mind. An illumination that is only in the mind tends to make us retreat from the world and become mystics. We put the Light at our feet so that they may be planted in stability. It also helps us to have a right judgement in all things. "Be a Light unto my feet." (Psalms)

No reference to Light in the New Testament is symbolic. There has always been this knowledge of Light, but it is only now when there are enough of us to receive it, that it can become a universal thing. The Albigenses had a very great knowledge of Light.

Light is not a recurring principle, so never look for repetition of experience on any of the exercises. If something happens while you are doing one of the exercises that is rather wonderful, and it does not happen again, it does not mean that you have fallen back.

The Figure of Light
Talk given 11th October 1938

I want to make it clear from the outset that this Technique in Light was given through me, and has nothing to do with me, it has no personal interpretation. This transcendental condition in Light is the infinite end of wireless; to get a wireless programme you need the personal contact, so we must tune in to listen to the voice of God. The human body was designed in the first place to be the perfect wireless receiving set. The first insulation between man and God came when man tuned in to the wavelength of power. We read that in the beginning Adam walked and talked with God in the garden. Then he tuned in to another wavelength and could not get back his original contact with the mind of God - he was no longer in tune with it. Now the human race is slowly returning to that first contact.

We have to learn a dual condition - one of complete awareness and yet of complete selflessness. To be empty of our own personalities is not a comparative condition as no one person can be emptier than another. By means of this Technique we tune in to wisdom; we do not acquire knowledge. When knowledge is needed, it will be broadcast into us.

The most difficult thing for a human being to do is to surrender his mind. In this Technique we do not have to make our minds a blank, nor do we have to concentrate or meditate. This is a technique in Light, and light is a spark, a flash. We have to learn to tune in to the wavelength of God, whatever the conditions. We have to learn to live in the thick of everything, yet be tuned in to the mind of Christ. This is the Christian Initiation - how to become a Christ. "Let this mind be in you that was also in Christ Jesus." If we have the same vibration of thought which He has, and become part of Him, we function as He does, because He is in us. I assure you, this is no memorial service - He *is* alive.

We have finished with the past, we have now to *be*. He is the Law made flesh. The soul does not have to function on a separate wavelength from the body. The purpose of the incarnation was so that His body should be able to receive into His blood that Light which was life. Scientists are coming recently to the understanding that life is Light.

The time of resigning ourselves and bowing down to a will which we do not understand, is past. We are His friends, and are ready to receive this knowledge. We have only to learn to receive, for when we do receive we have no power to withhold. The difference between the old initiation and the new, lies in this matter of transmission. Jesus could not withhold knowledge. The old masters of Israel were angry with Him because He taught the common people knowledge which they had kept among themselves. They were a sort of clique who gave out or withheld knowledge at the discretion of their own minds. But if you are in contact with a strong current you cannot keep it to yourself. That is the law of spiritual power - when the truth comes direct into you from the Source.

You know how often people tune in to other people's minds; sometimes they are so much like blotting paper that you can tell from their ideas of the moment, whom they were with last. Yet we ourselves do not believe that we can receive the truth. We look round the world and see every nation and every group of people holding a different wavelength of thought, and all based on fear.

When we tune in to Light we find that fear goes, for when we are the Light, we cannot fear at the same time. This technique is a method whereby we learn to discard our fears. The process must always be an individual one. It does not matter what a person believes, for Light and life are universal conditions and everyone can receive truth. Do not think you have to be clever or psychic - for that often hinders rather than helps. People who are psychic are apt to be like a public telephone on which all wavelengths impinge; unless we have private lines tuned in to the truth. The Technique in Light teaches us how to discern truth, for so many mistakes come from false interpretation.

I must explain that the physical body is composed of substance receptive to spiritual power, in the blood and in the cells. It is not our body so much as the processes of our mind which insulate us from truth. We shut our minds to what we do not believe, and along those lines we can receive nothing. I do not ask you to believe what I say, but I do ask you to go through this process of the Technique so that you may receive this wavelength of truth that I receive. We have to stop knowing one thing and being another, and *be* what we think, and that is hard to achieve. Whatever fears we have will be brought up into the Light, for that is a natural process along the lines of the Technique.

People usually come to the Technique because they want so much to be able to heal, or to help someone else. I can only teach you how to *be* health, and the radiations will go out from you as they went out from the Christ, and that is what will heal. You must take trouble with yourself first if you want to help others. You try to love humanity but when we have tuned in to the vibration of Love, and *are* love, it just happens. Here we get the unity of mind and heart and that is the resurrection body. We have to learn how to have our resurrection bodies here on earth; Christ was the only initiate who took His resurrection body back with Him.

People say there is nothing new in Christianity and quote legends of the virgin birth etc. taken from older religions, but there has never been another resurrection and ascension. That is the New Covenant, which is beginning now, and there shall be a new heaven and a new earth brought about by the human race. But God can only manifest on earth through us, so that we must learn to be the Law, and in learning it, be certain of its power to function through us. We must understand that this condition of receptivity is a direct contact with the Christ.

The first step in the Technique is the visualising of the circle of Light. It is necessary to be in a position of complete relaxation because if we are tense, we cannot receive.

The circle of Light is the circle of life which we all touch with our heads.

When you think a thing in Light *it is*, just as when you draw a circle with a pencil on paper it is done, and you do not have to draw it again. Do not try to reason about what you are doing. Just carry out the formula as it is given. We learn by experience that the things that happen to us in the Technique are real. If we could imagine that we do it perfectly, we should do so; but it is curious how many people who see all kinds of lights round them, still cannot do this Technique - so it is not just imagination, but very real.

When you come to the Conscious Breathing, think the breath down, do not breathe it down. With it you establish a harmony of thought and action.

Get your own picture of the Point of Radiance above you. I see mine as a break in the clouds. A small schoolboy who had asked for the Technique once wrote to me and said I was quite wrong about this point of light - it was a star. He was quite right, but I was not quite wrong. Our focal point of radiance becomes an individual thing.

Remember you do not have to pump the breath all the way up to the Point of Radiance. There is a great breath ray playing down upon the earth - the breath of God - and all we have to do is to send our breath up, and the fusing is inevitable as an explosion if we put a lighted match near petrol.

Physical breath is unconscious - this is conscious and it will change the condition of your mind, because we cannot do anything else while we are thinking our breath up and down. For a fraction of time we harmonise soul and body as we make our contact with Light.

Do not go on doing the Conscious Breathing till you develop a special condition of mind, for that is useless. Limit yourself to say, six breaths. We must get used to being interrupted and re-make our contact, and go straight on again. No noise or personal interruption can sever that contact which is your right to make, and continually re-make. When you are tired and have a difficult interview, or something unpleasant to do, do not say you are tired, because that only makes it worse. Be still for a minute and make your contact with Light and with energy in this first step, and you will find that as you concentrate to make your contact, your tiredness goes from your mind and so from your body. Just do the Technique quite simply and have the experience of it in this next fortnight. It is no good hurrying through this first part - you must get your foundations firm.

Send your mind up on this breath and send your fears up. Make a contact with His mind in which there is no fear. It can never let one down. We have to learn to be true to the inspiration which comes when we tune in to Him. We deceive ourselves so much; we all have to get rid of our illusions along this way.

This is an impersonal teaching, so no one can be hurt by it. Do understand that no one who is here today need feel that they must come again. It is the law that we cannot miss the thing we are ready for. Do not worry about those people who cannot be here today; if it is right for anyone to have the Technique, they cannot miss it.

This Technique is our spiritual food and you will find you would no more miss it than you would miss out your breakfast. You will get wonderful strength from the Technique to deal with the difficulties of your everyday life. This is to understand the law of life. For Jesus said, "I have meat to eat that ye know not of." We have the power to receive direct from His body. That is why the Christ has been the dominant figure ever since He lived on earth. He was different in His light vibration. He was the manifestation of harmony with all living things, because He was whole, and so was the means of making other people whole. We tune in direct to the life force. One reads in

Genesis how man became insulated from God and could no longer walk and talk with Him in the garden and so it became necessary for the Son of God to incarnate, that He, being in the flesh yet keeping His direct contact with the Father, would broadcast on a wavelength to which all men could tune in. They, tuning in to Him, are relayed on to the Father.

It is a fact that "No man cometh unto the Father but by me." That is a tuning in to the very substance of the body of Christ. In Him is that energy which is purely constructive. If we tune in to truth, we can never tune in to depression again.

You know, our fears are not always as real as they look. Think of a child who breaks a treasured toy, and they are heart-broken; the grown-up knows that tomorrow they will feel different about it. When you yourself tune in to, and therefore are the Light, no human fear can dominate the future.

I do not want at this moment, to start a political discussion, but you may be sure of one thing. The tide of peace has turned, and once a tide has turned it does not go in and out. We have not had peace and goodwill on this earth, and we do not know the law along which it operates. But do not believe whatever you hear and read from pessimistic minds because they are basing the future on the past. A new law is in operation, and no man knows how it will work.

The Figure of Light
Talk given Wednesday 3rd November 1954

I have had a new understanding recently of the vast importance of the Figure of Light. Hitherto we have been conscious of its existence at foot level, and I am now made to understand that we must definitely identify it with every one of the exercises we do so that we are earthed in it.

The Figure of Light is the ghost of ourselves which we shall leave behind when we leave the earth, and in it we can earth our physical freedom, and we shall pick it up in our next incarnation. We should in future, identify the reconditioning of our physical body with the Figure of Light and unify ourselves with it as we carry out our exercises. It must be a conscious process, so that at death we may leave behind this reconstructed body for others to pick up its reconditioned radiations; and for ourselves to pick up when we come again. Christ left behind the earthing of His reconstructed body and it is meant to be a universal process, so that we may come with Him when He comes again. That is what is meant by the statement, "the dead in Christ shall rise first." If we die consciously to every part of our earthly bondage, we shall leave no bondage in our Figure of Light. Above all we must be free in our heads or minds, for it is our thought limitations which hold us in bondage when we come again. It is the veil of mental limitation which was rent at the crucifixion; it is our minds which veil us from the knowledge of the truth.

Mere intentions have no power to implement themselves on the other side, and only activity can bring results. There is a great difference between mental prayer and real activity. Christ never gave complicated instructions, but one simple prayer which must be lived all day in activity. The repetition of ideas is not necessary, and time has no importance with Him, but only the spontaneous sparking of the heart. Our remembering of Him must be a non-stop condition accompanying all our activity. The resurrection achieves for us a timeless reconstruction of mind and body, and we may, and should, wash out the past, and live from now in this timeless dimension. It is a dimension which is dominated by the activity of the heart. The power of the mind over matter is a real one, and has been known and practised from earliest times, but the power of the heart over matter is a thousand times greater, and has never been demonstrated except by Christ and His disciples. It supersedes entirely the force of mind and does not work on a time basis. The heart is the unification of all dimensional activity. The world places far too high a value on intellectual power, but it is infinitely more important in the scale of values to manifest love. We cannot truly serve our neighbours only on the mental plane, but need both mind and heart, with the heart predominant.

All that our bodies receive in the exercises of the Technique must be embodied also in the Figure of Light, and it should become brilliant with all the kinds and qualities of light which our bodies have absorbed. Christ came to give this possibility to the whole world as a universal capacity. If we can achieve it in this incarnation we shall be forever free, and able to pick up complete freedom when we come again. We are often afraid of freedom and stick to orthodoxy lest we should offend authority, but it is possible for us to earth absolute certainty and truth in our Figure of Light.

THE NEEDS
This talk is recorded on cassette tape

The Technique in Light is a method of praying, of being prayer, and not just thinking with your mind about it, but being the very essence, as it were, of the beingness of God; for prayer is an energy. It is not just the sound of our voices in petition, asking for, or sometimes demanding something which we have not got, but it is uniting ourselves with God, substance for substance. Therefore we have got to understand the difference between praying with our minds and praying with the whole of ourselves, from our hearts.

We think that our minds are ourselves until we find that our body is a separate condition from our mind. However much we think we are well and delude ourselves into saying we are well, if we have very definite pains and infirmities, we recognise the weakness of the power of thought radiation, and it is that weakness we have to recognise in ourselves.

The sun shines on the just and on the unjust. There is no difference in nature, and the bounties of God's givingness are enjoyed by everybody to the same extent. That is the justice of God. Why is He equally good to the unjust and the wicked, and why do they appear to flourish like a bay tree?

According to our discrimination we give to the good and withhold from the wicked. Why is God so different? What is this energy that proceeds from God and is of equal distribution, taking no account of deserts?

We have to understand the law of what love really is and what we have come into this world to learn about love. It is a givingness without discrimination, and that is a very hard thing for a critical, *self-conscious* person to understand. We are very discriminating and we classify everything according to what we feel we must have and what we want. It seems that the people with the greatest power to grab get the most; but that is not true because there is just as much for the good as for the wicked. Why do we not get it, and what is the matter with us that we are so poor, ill, unhappy and deficient in glandular reaction that we find life miserable; why is it?

"Ye have not because ye ask not; ask and ye shall receive." I am going to give you an exercise in Light whereby we can all learn to ask for things which we must and should have. It is just learning how to ask, because we do not know. We all have different manners, and a lot of us have very putting-off manners as regards one to another. God is not put off from us, and does not stop giving because we are ungrateful. He has no personal reaction towards the just or the unjust and He has no discrimination. Discrimination comes from the individual who will have nothing to do with God nor ask or unite themselves with Him.

We do not know Him - it is not a matter of words and thoughts but of substance. Either we are in substance with Him, or we are separated from Him in substance and do not know how to get near Him. God is the same for ever and is not a temperamental entity; but man is never the same from one minute to another. One minute he has an ecstasy of understanding with God and is at peace, but in the next moment he can get drawn away in argument from this union with the All-givingness. We have to understand that God is All-givingness and you and I do not know what love is in terms of all-givingness.

We come into this world and take on a body of flesh and blood for one purpose only - to learn to unite ourselves with love. Most of us think that we come into this world to *be* loved, and that all we can know of love is what is given to us. We may be loved for our personality and yet know nothing at all about the substance of love.

If only we can understand that God is all time, all conditions of radiation and the substance that He radiates out is Light, we can then comprehend how to receive His All-givingness. If we ask in Light we must receive what we ask for because it is an instant sparking and He cannot refuse it. Whatever your motive is, the moment you spark into God, you become one with Him. "They think that they will be heard for their much-speaking." We take His Name in vain with our mouth and get nothing; but one person with their heart tuned in to His heart gets the abundance of all-givingness and cannot miss it.

One day in the early days of my training I became aware of a brilliant rim of light round my heart, and saw that it was a chalice sunk into my heart, though I only saw the rim. Then I was taught what prayer was and that I was to put into the chalice in my heart all my needs, everything that I needed on the material plane. Do not be discriminating and say that it is not right to ask God for material needs, but that He can give those to us if He wants us to have them. That is not true, and He cannot give them unless you are willing to put yourself into the position

191

of asking, and give a receptacle into which He can put them and radiate them. There is nothing in the material world we should not have if we ask from our heart; but when you put a standard of what you should ask for and what God should give you or anybody else, you are not functioning according to the law of the beingness of God, who makes the sun to shine on the just and the unjust.

The unjust close their hearts to God, and you and I close our hearts when we open our minds to philosophies. You can today get academic minds with little understanding of the human heart; scientists and professional men who know the body and the mind but who have no understanding of the immutability of the law of God, this all-givingness of the law of God which, if we unite ourselves with it, we must receive. There is no withholding in God's nature and no standard by which He prefers to give to you and me rather than to a person whom we condemn as a bad citizen or neighbour. If anyone has a spark of love in his heart he must receive into his being that which God is always showering onto the world. It is not a question of good behaviour, but of living selflessly, and the only place where you will not find yourself is in your own heart. You will find yourself duplicated in your mind and you will find every angle of yourself there, but in your heart you will find those you

love, and so it is essential that we understand what praying to God is.

It is giving Him the receptacle of our hearts to pour His abundance into and not trying to understand Him from the mental point of view. It is not according to our understanding of Him, but according to our receptivity. There is such a wastage of love in this world that is giving this condition of death, destruction and disease, because the individual does not know how to ask for and to receive material, spiritual and mental perfection, beauty and abundance.

In all our life we have suffered what man has given to man, and now comes the simplicity of knowing that if we will ask God from our heart there is nothing in this world He is unable to transmit to us and that there is no substance in this world that is not in the substance of God, because it has come from Him. "It is He who made us and not we ourselves," and if He made us, He must have done so out of the substance of Himself. He has an abundance of all, and so, in the privacy of your room make your requests known to Him, and ask that you may receive this day all that you need. I am not talking of desires, but of needs, and He knows our needs and will always supply them, but you must know what you want. You have to know your life and yourself in pure consciousness, and consciously co-operate with His power to give and He will not be discriminating in giving. It is like putting a cup into a rushing stream and you will get your cup filled in the space of a moment. Send up your chalice on a Conscious Breath and you are only the distance of a breath away from your abundance.

We must get the freedom of givingness so established in us that we do not stop to think, but find ourselves doing it gladly because it is something that we can do. It may be only a word, for no one will ask for what you have not got, but for understanding, a solution you can have at any moment of the day when you ask for it. Once you have given a thing to Him you must not retain it; the moment you send your needs up, put them out of your mind. If you send your worries up and find they are still on your mind, you have not made a proper contact with the givingness of God, but have only got as far as a thought and not as far as your heart which takes you to infinity in a flash.

There is such abundance in this world which we can have; and pray also that you may share in that abundance with others whose needs you put in the chalice. Do not leave yourself out, for we have to love our neighbour as ourselves, and unless we have some substance in ourselves with which to love our neighbour, how can we do it? We have to get this heartbeat of God into our heart and realise that He has never wanted us to be poor, miserable and ill. If we unite with Him we get everything He has to give us, but if we separate ourselves from Him we only have what man has to give us.

God can never give anything but beauty, abundance and all that He has created. If we look to man's giving we shall be poor for we are only getting back what we have inflicted on others. It is not unjust, for we draw to ourselves what we are and what we have got. If our heart has been closed all our life and our brain has been active, we have drawn mental misery and a thwarting of life into the being of our flesh and blood. The substance of God is all radiance, but ours is a grievous condition of absence of Light.

E.O. LIHUM

This is a mental exercise for it is one which passes through the brain. The **E.O. Lihum** takes the place of water and has the most extraordinary cleansing light in it. It washes the brain and can be flashed through at any moment. When I was given it, I was made to take a glass of water outside and hold it up against the midday sun. It is not a white light, but has a sparkling quality of lightness and darkness in it.

This exercise is rather like stringing beads on a chain, and is only for the cooling and cleansing of the mind. When we do it, we give to those we desire to help a gift of eternal value, for when we pass the crystal light through their heads we earth in their bodies a condition of serenity and peace. The **E.O. Lihum** is done in the morning and follows after The Needs. It can however, be done at any other time if it is required. It can change every part of the mind, so do it without any reluctance, in the knowledge of the power of clarification that it can give to others and to yourself.

The linking up in this exercise is one of profound importance to those who have passed on, for they have no contact on this plane except through us. When we go abroad there are travel agents to help people and to serve their needs, and we must look upon ourselves in that same capacity and give them this help so that they can make use of us while we, on our part, are enabled to link up with them. If we do this linking up, we will most likely find what we may call a series of co-incidences happen to us. We may for instance, be brought into contact with someone they know or love, and be able to do them a service.

The quality of unity of all minds is love. All mental love has the quality of light. It is that crystal light which St. John saw round the throne. When you get this unity of mind between two people who love, then you get this crystal spiral. *We* do the exercise, *they* see our prayer operating as we see sunlight sparkling on water.

Through it we can be the agent for cutting karma at any moment. Take the example of the depression which comes over us when we read of some tragedy in the newspapers. Instead of adding to the general depression, we should do this exercise for those we are reading about. Just flash the light through their heads and send it up. We need only do it three times and there our responsibility ends.

This exercise can always be done when we desire to clear our brains. It can be done round a table at a committee meeting for instance; before or during an examination or interview; or at any time we desire to get a clear understanding on any subject.

E.O. LIHUM

This talk is recorded on cassette tape

The quality of our mind is important to all of us and the way in which the mind works and turns is particularly important in facing our own lives and problems. In a circle of thought we have development of different levels or planes of energy. At first the child is taught mental discipline, but as we grow older, our minds change and waver.

We have to realise however, that through the Technique of Light our minds are no longer of first importance because we learn to contact direct the mind of Christ. Christ incarnated to give us this new capacity. The Christian Initiate has to learn how to receive truth and he cannot do it on his own wavelength. From books we may get knowledge, but from Christ we receive by direct transmission wisdom itself; for Christ was the Word made flesh, the Word through which the creation of the world was brought about.

Today our minds often acts automatically; really in an attempt to escape boredom, but Christ had no boredom at all in His mind. Our minds too are unstable, but His is the expression of perfect stability and perfect equilibrium, and we must learn to identify ourselves with it. This however, we cannot do by meditation or concentration for these are mental processes and are therefore tinged with our own characters.

How we can do it, is by flashing through our head in this exercise this particular crystal clear quality and texture of light, for it is a form of light which makes a direct contact with discarnate truth. In the term 'discarnate' you may include all those minds of the invisible great ones who now provide in the spheres a relaying station of truth, but the fountain-head is Christ. "No man cometh unto the Father but by me," He told His disciples. In other words, "It is I that relay you to the Father."

In this new exercise therefore, it is the ear level that is important. We listen to rumour, false opinion, false values, all

195

day long. Now we have the chance to listen to truth and true values. This true listening comes only through Christ and results in receiving true values, not for our own lives only, but for other people of all kinds and in all parts of the world.

As you say **E**, you make a contact with the transparent substance which is the clear crystal light of the Christ. It must go through yourself and the people you are wishing to help. So picture them standing in front of you and begin. The **E** comes into the left ear, passes through the head and out of the right ear. On the sound **O**, the light flashes on through the heads of those you are helping; and on the **Lihum**, spirals back in front of your own face and up to the Father. You may visualise one individual, or a row of them, and flash the light through them all in succession. You may also help those whom you wish to see changed in public affairs. For instance you can focus this light on prime ministers, on dictators and on agitators, and you may be certain they will receive the flash and that it is bound to make an impression if done continually. This is a marvellous sharing exercise. We no longer have egocentric minds but can give those we wish to help an incalculable gift by washing away their mental obscurities.

Now do the exercise a second time, visualising the heads of those you know who have passed on. You were linked with them once, and the **E.O. Lihum** is an exercise in the communion of saints and you are linked with them once again. You may, if you like pick out a favourite saint and do it with Him as the link, but the light always goes back to Christ, and direct through Him the link is more powerful.

The third time we may do the exercise for ourselves. We visualise the head of Christ, knowing that He still makes a personal contribution to this world by washing away our mental obscurity through the light of His wisdom. We all have obscure mental conditions, especially in regard to true spiritual values. Our minds are full of compromise. All this thinking, wondering, balancing of values and mental fear causes loss of vital power; but this exercise will set us free, giving us vitality without fear or doubt, freedom from neurasthenia and mental strain, and utter clarity of vision by our contact with the crystal clear mind of the Christ. You may say I am too old to change my thought habits; age does not signify as the brain can receive new life and capacity for the individual life, and also be a link to all minds dedicated to the service of humanity.

St. John saw this crystal light around

196

the throne, the focal point of the majesty of God. It was circulating round the throne and was the light of pure knowledge. St. John was linked through love to Christ and the light that he saw was the mind of Christ, luminous, enchanting, sparkling. This mind never cuts across another persons ideals or their hopes, but it helps them by being a kernel of stillness in the midst of great activity.

We have so many exercises to help us along this mental way. We must know what we are doing, for we have put our hands to the plough and we shall not be allowed to let go. The need of the world for peace is so great; rather than for a lot of busy workers. It is quietness and stillness that are needed and being willing to be nothing; though not with a show of nothingness.

It is so difficult to distinguish between humility and servility. When you touch so great a fellowship as that of Christ we need to have no sense of depreciation, for every empty vehicle is worthy. It is not a question of worthiness and virtue. Our power to love is only what Christ can manifest through us. We know nothing of love beyond what He can feel through us, and we know nothing except what He knows through us. There is nothing in any of us that need be a hindrance to the performance of help and service. There is no deed we are not capable of doing in fellowship with Christ as long as we leave "I" out of it. Do not be afraid of looking that fact in the face, or think that what happens through you is a thing for depreciation. The most wonderful experience of all is when you know someone who has had bondage of spirit, can be set free through you. You will just *have* these experiences. You will not have to look for them. When it looks as if we are alone and have no results, do not believe it. The experience of being His manifestation will be given to us. Every step in this Technique is for His glory and for the knowledge of the truth that once He was the Light of the world, and He is going to be that Light again.

In this exercise the **E.O.** goes right through the head from left to right and the **Lihum** is a flash that circles round in front of the face. I get His head above mine, so that it takes an elliptical shape. It goes like lightning on **Lihum** and I know it is flashed up there.

It is the essence of prayer for it is the dedication our brains and the identification of our minds with the mind of the Father. We are learning in detail what has been since the world began. We are seeing the things that always happen. When you get a mind tuned in to the Father, on the other side, you see this condition of light pouring up to Him. Along the crystal light the mind travels when it is one in vibration with His mind.

In the next world, harmony is seen functioning as a visible condition. What we think of as a nice thought, they see as substance. Thought is seen as a lovely coloured light. Your soul must radiate out the quality of the self. You see people passing and know them to be love and wisdom because you see it radiating out. So you know people's thoughts and being, by the radiation of their personality. We want to become

so that the radiation of our soul shall have no obstruction through the radiation of our mind and we shall not impose a false condition because we feel it is up to us to produce something. We must not pretend. We must have complete integrity of spirit. You must not control, you must transmute. Controlling a thought is the old way. Transmuting a thought is the new way, for then it is done away with, but when thoughts are controlled they are still there. If you transmute them into something you do not mind looking at, then you will have no rubbish.

Talk Given 24th March 1938

In the New Testament we are taught to ask for, and receive, the divine energy, which is our right. It does not mean that we need consider matter as 'error', but that we should try to understand the balance of the two without prejudice or instinctive rejection.

We need to understand the link between instinct and inspiration.

Instinct is the human side based on long experience of earth life, during which we have instinctively picked up natural law.

Through inspiration, we pick up the laws of the the higher planes.

If instinct and inspiration were perfect in us, picking up true natural law and not debased ritualised law, there could be no friction; and with each half of our nature following the highest, there would no longer be a pull in opposite directions, but instinct would be transcended by inspiration, which is divine.

Instinct contacts earth, from which we receive it, but inspiration can intercept it before it reaches the earth. Instinct is good in its place and can teach us natural law, but there should be a fusion between the two energies through which it will be possible for natural law to be revealed to us when we need the knowledge.

We should be the link between the Creator and the creature, and not be governed by the latter; then we may become healers. As we are trained and aspire to be useful, so must our integrity of spirit grow with us.

Remember that the temptation of Jesus came to Him on the very threshold of His ministry, and that as we overcome the personal self, so experiences are bound to occur to upset our balance; for all power, even that which functions in the deepest humility, has its attendant pride.

Tests are sure to come and we must not be afraid, nor feel it outrageous that we should be subjected to such petty conditions. Big things can be done by the bigness of our minds, but the tiny things have infinite power to upset and unbalance us, just as small pieces of grit can damage a perfect machine, no matter how large.

Our experiences will come in petty, irritating ways. Think of the maddening pettiness and pin-pricks from intellectual minds with which Jesus was surrounded. What a relief for Him if He could have given them some demonstration to silence them once and for all! Jesus resisted any such temptation and His mind never once betrayed the soul.

THE TRANSMUTING LIGHT
This talk is recorded on cassette tape

Most of us are taught from early youth how to give. Now we have a new Technique, which teaches us how to receive, because giving and receiving are the one action, not two. The difference between us and the Christ was that He received from the Father the power to transmit into the world that which He had received. Many of us are people who have missed the turning in life of happiness, and we have to learn how to receive joy, life and love - receiving love not as an emotion but as a creative energy.

We can do none of these things purely on the mental side. We have been taught that the brain is the most important part of the body and that we are of real service if we are clever. This is true as far as knowledge has gone hitherto, but now the person who is of the greatest use is the one who uses the brain as a receiving instrument and not as a generating instrument. The thoughts of the most brilliant mind do not compare with those of the mind of Christ. He received the truth of the law of the creative energy in Light, and He transmitted it out making perfect bodies where ever He went. Your soul body is an eternal condition because it is in harmony with Love.

The point at which the world could stop its disharmony would be when it came into contact with a condition of harmony and active peace. The human body was designed as a channel to receive this energy of Light, which is love.

In the beginning there was a race of beings in this world who were in perfect harmony with the substance of this world. They lived in beauty and in an ecstasy of happiness, until that moment when the human race became insulated from the perfect vibration of Light which it was created to receive and transmit again.

The mass picture which the mind of man has produced of the incalculable cruelty of nature as the handiwork of God, is false. The cruelty of nature is built upon the emanation of the cruelty in man. If the race had never sinned, nature would have been in harmony with the Creator. Our brains transmitted that condition of disharmony which nature absorbed. When we are *love* then, through us, love will be transmitted again into the world with no condition of destruction. All conditions of destruction have come through the mental side of humanity; but the scheme of reconstruction has started and is no longer a dream but is becoming a reality. Hitherto, all the races and civilisations have taken more from the earth than they have given back because of man's greed.

It needed one perfect human soul to incarnate and take on the low vibration of flesh. The fact that Jesus was born into a carpenter's family who worked with their hands is an important point. Your hands and feet are the transmitters of energy and not your brain, for it can only receive energy but not transmit it. The great condition of receptivity of which we are all capable does not depend upon our mentality but only upon simplicity of spirit, an absence of self-analysis and self-importance and of desire for power.

It is a paradox, because of necessity through long hereditary conditioning, that our minds have become accustomed to think that it is up to us to develop ourselves and our capacities, that we have got to show a good front, which is not ourselves, rather than be humble enough to acknowledge our weaknesses. It is not courage to appear different from what we are; courage is to know that we have got nothing.

Our weakness is the material for our transformation. We may be lonely, nervous and afraid, and we have a synthetic power to appear different.

This is possible to every living entity and it is a power which we have greatly developed for we present to the world a facade which we hope deceives. When we are unhappy we are also liable to do this in order to get sympathy; often we are not so unhappy as we would like to believe.

This Technique is a method of showing ourselves to ourselves, and most of us cannot bear to look at ourselves. We can never become empty to receive until this process of emptying the old vessel to receive the new life is carried out. This Technique can and will do it, but not through great mental deliberation or meditation. Do not meditate, for the mind reverts to the ego. We must train our minds to the speed of light, which is a flash. As you do the Technique with the speed of light the result in you is of lightning effect, so quick that we are unable to register it.

Nothing comes in a sensational way. Knowledge is dropped into one's mind, and problems are solved so quietly and naturally that it seems incredible that it has not always been part of our being. This emptying process to receive direct the knowledge, science, wisdom and love of the Father can never be imagined. It will come unexpectedly and not because at some moment we are ready; it will come when we are busy and without time, when we are not thinking of ourselves. At that moment the supreme understanding will be flashed in and become part of us, and we shall hear ourselves saying things which we did not know we knew until the moment when it was necessary for us to know. People have drawn out of me knowledge that I did not know existed and then, on speaking, I have known it to be the truth. It was never there until the need comes to know it.

The teaching of Jesus was not in His mind until the people were there who were ready. All the miracles were done in the same way. It was never organised that people should be hungry with only a few loaves - it was a spontaneous expression. Whatever their need, He was the agent to supply it. This is what He lived to demonstrate.

The human body must be the agent for supplying needs. God manifests through the human body. What does the world know of love except through human beings? What does it know of hate except through the individual? We do not know what the world was like before the race lived; we only see the result of the lives of human beings.

In the days to come, when the New Covenant is fulfilled, when, as Christ said, "All men shall know me, and no man shall teach his brother," then every person will have direct revelation into their own mind, receiving and transmitting.

In the old days the priests were the trained receivers, and their sin was the withholding of knowledge. Jesus gave a new technique of receiving and giving through the heart. They only gave out through the brain, which is of little value. The heart has blood which holds light and life. The blood of Jesus received and transmitted more light and life than the blood of any other human being. The heart contains this magnetic substance, and the brain has very little of it. All the teaching in the New Testament concerning the blood of Jesus is transcendental, not sentimental, for phraseology has led to this misunderstanding. We can receive the same substance into our blood as He received.

The Technique takes the place of food for spiritual energy. We do not forget our meals and our light body should be replenished just as regularly and carefully.

You can do the Transmuting Light not only for yourself but for other people. If a person who is wrought up or who looks ill comes to talk to you, while you are listening draw in the Transmuting Light first for yourself and then to them, and they

202

will be given the power to relax, and as it happens, you have got to relax also to do this. Relaxing is receiving and tensing is shutting off and comes from a condition of self.

The more you acknowledge your weaknesses so the greater the help that will be poured in. Mentally we cannot change, but if we receive, it is done for us and the responsibility is no longer ours. We are never helpless now for we can do something for those in need. Draw the Light into them rather than saying things, and they will have more hope because they have tuned in to you who have got something to give them.

THE NAME

I want to go back to the exercise of The Name because the protection of the blue light is so important. Not for a moment is the mind blank; you are preparing it to receive His thought, and the blue triangle is His sanity and stability.

To have a mind that does not change with every opinion that is expressed; to have a reliable mind that would not be upset by truth, even truth about oneself; to have that feeling of certainty - that is what comes when we do the **Dyè-Thu-Th**.

Then when one's head is the chalice, there comes such a degree of quietness, and absence of all thinking power because you cannot think when you are in the act of receiving; all that one's mind can hold is a great down-pouring of Love. One has no thought, only a feeling of utter peace......

When you do The Name remember that it is Love you are tuning into - Love as an energy, as a well-being, as an absence of all hurt. The more we do The Name, the quicker will come into our lives the readjustment we are waiting for, the happy, peaceful conditions. Do not think that we have to go through a long time of paying back before the happiness comes. Now we only have to ask, and to ask is to receive - that is the transcendental action of the law; so send up your request for happiness and peace, which are our right. We have destroyed our own, and so we ask for, and receive, His. We must receive them, if we have no fear; it is only fear which insulates us from the good things. Belief in one's power to receive is the prelude to the faith we have when we have received. We are the only barriers to our own happiness.

Do this exercise with joy. Build it into your new self and it will transcend the fearfulness of our minds.

THE NAME
Talk given 7th March 1939

On the last day of the term it is I think, better to go over the work already done rather than have a new exercise, therefore I am giving you this very important exercise today. I know that the one you had last Tuesday may have been difficult and I had meant to go over it again with you, but I felt absolutely forced to give you this one instead, rather than leave it for next term.

Last Tuesday, it was I know, a difficult comprehension of the duality of substance and this reality of the functioning power of Light. And here I want to say that if any of you hold pre-conceived ideas as to where this training in the Technique of Light is leading you, do give them up as you will be disappointed, since it cannot conform with the imagination of the human mind.

This exercise which I am giving you today is one, which when I received it, I felt was entirely unique and personal, and that it was very definitely not one which would be possible to pass on to anyone. Now I know that it is not possible for anyone to come here and *not* have it: it is the very foundation stone of the Technique in Light, this understanding of the Name of Jesus Christ. We have been given in the morning exercise the vibration of our own Christian name as a condition of protection. The Name of Jesus has a completely different vibration to any other in its individual vibration by the purity of His ego, and we must of necessity try to understand the utter perfection of sound, rhythm, shape and expression that is united in this word, His Name.

The sound of His Name is **Dyè-Thu-Th**, the rhythm is three syllables and the shape is a triangle. I was made to understand that the ability to tune in to this vibration of perfectness lay along the path of selfless love. He was incarnate love, and the whole vibration of His personality demonstrated the reality of love, and the three syllables of His Name hold the three attributes necessary for the perfection of love on earth. The triangle is a symbol of perfect equilibrium - that is done on the sound **Dyè**. The chalice is perfect receptivity, and that is done on the sound **Thu**, and the **Th** is a breath-sound of perfect givingness. These three conditions in perfection are His perfect love and are incorporated in the Name of Jesus.

205

Some time after I had been teaching this Technique of Light, one member of the class, a man who was an exceptionally good linguist was discussing with me the possibility of picking up old past vibrations, and we talked of the wonderful instrument which has not yet come out but which was tried at the Queen's Hall and succeeded in picking up the sounds of a concert held there seven years before. This is quite possible since all sounds are eternal vibrations, and a co-ordination of receptivity must enable one to hear the transmission of any sound earthed. This was my own experience when visiting an old Roman village near Shrewsbury. I made contact with some Roman ladies on their way to their bathrooms, and heard them talking and laughing, and shared their repartee. These things prove definitely that there is no condition of the elements which can cut off sound; storms do not matter, they can sweep over and leave the vibrations untouched.

This clever linguist then realised that if ever it became possible to tune in to the Christ's words here on earth, no one would be able to understand what He said; therefore he learned Aramaic. A little later he said to me that the Name of Jesus in Aramaic is **Dyè-Thu-Th**. This was thrilling corroboration for me of the truth of the teaching in Light, since I had years before been given this sound of His Name, and now it was, years later, corroborated on the human side.

The human mind must now apprehend the reality of those attributes He earthed here for us, this perfect equilibrium, perfect givingness and perfect receptivity, which He received direct from the Father. We have always looked for love in the human heart, and when we have given ours we are so hurt when we do not get it back again - that true heart's vibration which we know to be love - and we are so hurt when we get the synthetic condition instead. We know in our very being what real love is and feel so let down by those who give what they call love when it is not true at all. We shall not find it in the human heart, because the human heart does not know how to receive, so can only give one personal love, which is never satisfying, since we are looking for the harmony of our soul's knowledge.

This new race on earth will learn through us, not by us, a tranquil condition of healing, of service and joy such as the world has not yet received. We can have this capacity if we will only learn to receive, as He did, right into us this power of perfect love, and with it, perfect transmission, perfect givingness.

I want you to visualise at the back of your head this triangle of vivid blue, coming from above the head on the right hand side, bringing it down and then across the nape of the neck and flashing it back to the point above the head again. It is a brilliant blue, the Christ blue, and is the individual vibration of perfect love on earth, which He earthed in the Name of Jesus - He achieved the Christ condition through His perfect humanity. He is Jesus the Christ, through whom perfect human love was expressed when He received it from the Father and absorbed it and made it real in His personality; this healing and perfection of love which those who only understood mental love found impossible ever to receive.

When we are individually tuned in to Jesus we become for a flash at *one* with Him, not separate on our own wavelength, but united on His. When we are able to do everything in His Name we shall function as He did, in perfect equilibrium, perfect receptivity and perfect transmission. We learn to visualise these three conditions by bringing them into our very being, into our heads, radiating through our brains, colouring our thoughts. We tune into to this blue triangle halo on the first syllable, on a beat of three **Dyè-è-è** which is on an outbreath.

Then with our inner eye of vision, draw a chalice of the same lovely blue, beginning on the left side above the head, the top of the head being the base of the chalice. Do this on the sound **Thu** on an inbreath and the blueness of the chalice is at once filled with a great white radiance. It is never empty, but it is filled with the radiance which is the will of the Father. Then on the sound of **Th**, which is not a hiss but a breath, a vivid line of white shot with blue, drops through the body from the chalice and pulses in the left side just under the skin, where it ends in a spiral pulsating gently. This starts, but only starts, our condition of givingness.

This spiral is in our left side, just where He was pierced at the crucifixion. When He was pierced from His side came water and blood, and the red and white condition of His body was earthed in the ground, and the vibration of His humanity and divinity were then earthed for all time. The earth could not have received this condition of Light and life had He not incarnated in a human body, and with His blood, earthed it as an eternal condition for all of us.

What the mind vibrates, lives on the astral plane; what the body vibrates, lives on for ever on earth. A fusion of soul and body must come here on earth if you want to be free for ever of the karmic law and the bondage of flesh which is the broken law here. He came to earth a law of harmony and love for all time, to which we should be able to tune in as one can tune in to sound. Our blood can tune in to His blood because it is here for ever. Receive on this wavelength your own revelation of truth on His Name. I know in my soul and mind only that truth which, when I am one with Him, I can then receive. There is no difference between my capacity and yours; we all have the same capacity to tune in to perfect receptivity. Why we have suffered so much in the past is because we have only had the capacity to tune in to others. They have given us so often not love, but hate and disharmony and cruelty, since they could only give what they were, and they in turn have suffered because of us.

We must try to know our imperfections, and to have and to hold love instead. How often have we searched for even one person to love us - somebody with whom to live and love in harmony, and have not found them. Now we can be free of that search once we are tuned in to Him, since we cannot miss them. When we are one with Him the vibrations of the love of Jesus Christ extends to the uttermost parts of the earth, and those who are tuned in to the same divine wavelength will be joined and it will be utterly impossible to keep them apart. The only thing which keeps people apart is absence of love - the only parting condition is lack of love, and the one thing that draws them together for all eternity, is love.

This is not a virtue, this loving, it is a necessity. To express ourselves in love is not virtue; we are not good when we tune in to Him, only happy. Again this is not a comparative condition, no one is more worthy. It is not a condition of worthiness to be able to go to Him, indeed, worthy people are often very much away from Him! Their sense of worthiness keeps them away because they cannot share the understanding of what love really is; they have put love on a pedestal and look up to it at a remote height. We are learning that love is here in the inner most parts of our being, that we may have the power to heal through receiving, and not from having standards of human behaviour.

My mistake in the beginning was that I thought it was an individual gift to me, this knowledge of how to become one with Him, and that I could not pass it on. Now I realise that no one could come here and not have it - this new understanding of what His love really is, and how to *be* love and not just look for, but never be separated from it again. All pain and suffering can finish when we have these three - perfect equilibrium, perfect receptivity and perfect givingness. There is no time limit in this connection, nor is it a comparative condition as each one of us has different points of insulation. Whatever our past conditions have been, realise that all insulation comes from the mind, and our mental conditions have closed the door to this peace and harmony because our hearts have been so hurt.

All bitterness comes through mental stress, and broken hearts through broken law; we must learn to look in a different direction for the healing of that shattered condition. We feel we can never again be happy because of that agent who caused that heartache, and we might look for ever and never be free, unless we give up looking here and learn instead to look for His light and love. We can only be hurt through the power of memory and this will vanish when we live tuned in to Him; the past will have no dominion over us and we shall be free because we are receiving love all day unceasingly.

It could happen - but doesn't - in the 'twinkling of an eye'. Our tough hearts do not yield so soon to this process of freedom which we are undergoing now. The *knowledge* of how to do it is quite different to *doing* it! To give up your pre-conceived ideas and acquire this freedom must

be an individual experience and it will not happen unless you desire it. This humility is a growing condition and begins when we first apprehend that knowledge is not the same as *being*; and that the process of becoming, is quite different to the apprehension of knowledge. It is not necessary for this process to be slow, but I have found it so; it may happen to you in this 'twinkling of an eye'. That it will happen eventually is certain, if you will learn to receive, and this resurrection body will be yours - it is bound to be.

Feel this pulsation in your side; it is like a current running in water. It is there and you cannot make it function, it does its own work. Let your mind follow it and know that the shape is a spiral curling round in your side - this is the beginning of your ability to give.

We are only now learning to receive as He received; and to give as He gave. It is not like our ordinary giving at all, but it is a natural thing. This exercise must be done once a day, but do it often, and from now, do everything in His Name.

Do not pass this exercise on. It is your right to have it now but you must not give it, it is a privilege we have no right to pass on - any more than you can tell anyone to call me by my Christian name, which is a sign of personal friendship. This friendship we are acquiring with Him gives us the right to use His Name in all we do and makes us one in this greatest of intimacies, one with Him in every vibration of our being.

Those of us who have difficulty in knowing the harmony and peace of this state of equilibrium are those who have not realised the destructive power of those agents of disharmony, who must destroy, until we are one with His vibration.

Not once did His state of equilibrium fail, even in those pre-crucifixion days. Peter was outraged, you will remember, and drew his sword and cut off the soldier's ear, but Christ immediately healed him. Peter's resentment for his friend made him flare up, but Jesus then demonstrated His complete equilibrium. This understanding of equilibrium holds all dignity, all poise regarding action and events.

Some people find it so difficult to receive, and we have been taught that 'It is more blessed to give than to receive' and we like to give, it soothes our sense of pride. We do not realise that until we first learn to receive we cannot give, because we have nothing worth giving - we must learn to receive without pride.

If, when you visualise the chalice, such a flow of light pours in that you feel the top of your head disappears; let it flood through your mind and do not bother to put the top of your head back again! Let it do what it likes, and know as we do it, that the quality of our minds will be changed by our voluntary action of receiving.

We have no idea as yet of the result of real prayer. One member who was learning with me from the beginning said to me once: "How devastating it is to have one's prayer answered." As long as there are still warring conditions within us, the perfect condition of equilibrium cannot function perfectly. We cannot serve self and be one with Christ in givingness. It depends on our own condition of receptivity and the elimination of ourselves.

We do not know what it is to give as He gave, in that effortless spontaneous condition of being. He gave and gave, and if we can only give like that, there will be none of those conditions of pain and restraint in our giving that there has been hitherto. None of that feeling of, "Why should we give to so and so, they haven't deserved it by their bad behaviour." We judge with our minds; but when we achieve His condition we shall not use human judgement and discrimination, we shall have inspired givingness. We shall not be the prey of all beggars - do realise this - nor shall we give through a weary yielding of 'Let us give and be done with it'.

We shall achieve an exquisite condition of discrimination according to the real needs of those who come our way. When we give according to His standards we shall be able to help and supply where before we were unable to do so.

Do not worry if the chalice is actually touching the point of the triangle or not - it is difficult to put these exercises on paper. You cannot really make a mistake in Light; there is no concussion in Light, the shapes take place in perfect proportion. Thinking of it makes it in its perfection, and the colours do not mix, they are always inviolably their own colour. There is a fusion, but not a blending.

Do tune in to His Name very often, and you will achieve a new wholeness, a rebirth.

THE NAME

Last time I gave you The Name - His Name which signifies perfect equilibrium, giving and receiving; and today I want to talk about these two latter conditions.

If we get a perfect balance of these two, the givingness and receptivity, equilibrium is the natural result. Pain and suffering come from the separation of these two in the mind, and the consequent lack of balance. They are one in the heart, and it is there that we should look for them. The mind says, "Withhold," but the heart says, "Give"; and His heart was always in the perfect state of harmony and balance.

If you allow your brain to dominate you, you get inflation of the ego. There is no true wisdom in the brain, but only in the power to receive. We may think we have originated some idea, but this is not really possible. There is no true originality in any of us, we merely have the power to absorb it out of the atmosphere, the power to receive it from hearsay, books or other human minds.

Now we are learning a very different thing - how to receive, not echoes of past knowledge, but the very mind of

Jesus Christ Himself. He came to give it to the world 2,000 years ago, but so few of us had "ears to hear". He could not have given His radiation to the world at all had He not had it in His flesh and blood, and so, by the shedding of His blood, it was earthed here for us for all time. He came to teach us how to become perfect flesh and blood. We have lost sight of this truth and disregarded our human bodies and have taken so little care of them; far less care very often than that which we lavish on our cars! We have to realise that our bodies must be transmuted with His light until they become "like unto His body". We cannot get rid of our bodies however irksome we have let them become through our past ignorance. We have had our way of escape in former lives by dwelling in the realms of the mind and producing a condition of unreality. Now we have to get down to the reality of flesh and blood, and of becoming a harmonious whole.

He came to bring the world of Light here on earth as it is in heaven. It has been absent here for so long and the result is written in our nerves, our bodily disharmony, for we *are* our knowledge, and it is this ignorance of the law of light and love which He came to give us. We have looked elsewhere for it during so many lives when all the time the key to unlock the door of our ignorance is there before us, if we would only cease to look back.

In this simple technique we have all the wisdom and understanding that we need. We were given the model of perfection 2,000 years ago. Brain and mind had reached a very high standard of perfection in those days, but not the balancing condition of flesh and blood. Now we must have the whole body, hands, feet, eyes, the very marrow of our bones, all must reach the same perfection of knowledge and understanding as our minds. In His Name is this perfect equilibrium in all forms of matter and substance, and our capacity to receive this perfection can be increased day by day if we are only faithful in the drawing in of His light.

We must make this surrender of our brains which in the past we have thought were so valuable. Many people are suffering now in their whole bodies, because they are separated from their hearts, working only with pure mentality so that their hearts cease to function properly. None of us will get the true fusion of mind and body unless we take Him as the one pure model, and absorb, as He did, not only the letter of the law which we have done with our minds, but the spirit also which was His in His flesh and blood. The mind receives the pattern, and the heart

212

gives the substance.

He was the Law made flesh, the living Word here. He said, "I am with you always," and He earthed His law of contact with His presence here for ever. All this wisdom and beauty could be a universal condition instead of our present state of disharmony and disease. We have got to become "like unto Him" and share our becoming.

Nobody can keep anything to themselves, we cannot insulate ourselves, but we pass on our diseases and distresses, whether we wish to or no. Our very sound vibrates for ever and it is an eternal continuity of ourselves. You know how each season of the year seems to have its diseases which are recurrent, and you know how we were told that sin and suffering would continue "unto the third and fourth generation of them that hate me." In hate there is no cancellation, but love can eliminate all our diseases of mind and body, and if we *become* this light and love, there will be a new race on earth who will know no illness or unhappiness, no self-pity, but will be radiant in themselves, and in their radiations of loveliness make that new heaven on earth which we have been promised.

We cannot achieve this through our own vibrations but only through the knowledge of Christ and His perfection. We go on struggling in this appalling state of fighting and killing through our ignorance of Him and our blindness of heart. Let us learn to contact Him and find out what He really needs of us each day; we shall be very much surprised when we come to know His requirements. They will not be the things we have given in the past.

He has no difficult and hard and objectionable plans for us. He came to bring us joy and "eye hath not seen" the glories and wonders He has for us if we will only learn to ask, and to receive. In the past we have been bewildered and have not known how to ask. We have been told this by one person and that by another, and have believed it, and then been very dissatisfied. But have gone doggedly on, trying to believe as a sort of insurance for our fear of the future. Now we know that fear is the root of all evil and unhappiness, and it is indeed the real truth that "Perfect love casteth out fear." There was no fear whatsoever in Jesus Christ, and when you make this blue triangle of light at the back of your head to the sound of His Name, realise that it is the very essence of His presence, and do it in perfect integrity no matter where you are. Eliminate your mind and receive His will as your own experience, not taking anyone else's point of view but getting your own interpretation from Him.

When we know that we have this marvellous privilege to receive Him for ourselves so that we may radiate Him out into the world, let us do it as He did when He healed the sick, let us do it in silence and not chatter about it. Remember how He told them to "Tell no man." When we do become the Light, we do not have to talk about it. People came to Him, were drawn to Him, and He gave Himself to them. If we tune in to Him we shall be enabled to be a channel for Him to radiate His light everywhere here on earth. No matter where it may be, in a theatre, a bus or shops, or in the street, anywhere and everywhere we can be the means of His presence. We must not be self-conscious about it, but Christ-conscious. The moment we ourselves come into the picture, He has to stand aside. We can never know when He gives to us, it must always be when we are unselfconscious.

Let us fast in Lent on our own personalities. In the past we have imposed various abstinences on ourselves according to the letter of the law. Now let us fast in the spirit of the law, giving Him the substance of ourselves wholly so that through us He may feed the world. Let us fast on our critical faculties, on our judgement of others. If we would only give to Him the time we have hitherto given to ourselves! We are such introverts; had He been an introvert He could never have redeemed the world.

He gave every bit of Himself to the Father; if He had retained the very least part He could not have been the perfect whole. We must make our fasting a happy discarding, not a burdensome affair. We can achieve such happiness when we leave aside our carping, critical ways, when we look for the pleasant side of people, tuning in to Him in all our contacts so that we release Him in their hearts. One used to think that the interesting thing was to tap people's brains, but now we know how exciting it is to tap their hearts, for in our hearts lie true wisdom and intelligence.

The world has such a great need at this time of His agents, so do let us do His Name continually, so that we may be available for His work. If we find that His light reveals very dark patches in ourselves, be of glad it. We cannot root up the tares unless we become aware of them and this darkness is the substance for transmutation. We offer it to Him and in this committal; He changes the darkness into light. When we find how it works in us we begin to know that it can begin to work the same marvel in everyone else. He can never impose perfection on us, but when He was here on earth He took all our imperfections and offered them to the Father, and He taught the twelve to follow in His steps. We have strayed away from them for so long but now we are learning how to commit ourselves to Him.

Do not take any horrors into your minds; if one did that one would become quite unbalanced. Take them into your hearts and commit them to Him and so serve the world as He did, not talking about it, but becoming a vehicle for His divine presence.

We must learn to re-present the Christ, giving Him through our hands and our feet, always *through* us, and then we shall give *Him only,* and not ourselves. If our whole selves become one-pointed in His Name, we shall be able to receive Him and give Him. When we are all receiving and giving, we shall become such a means of union and companionship with the Christ that the whole world could be changed.

RHYTHM OVER THE HEAD

Do not worry if sometimes the exercises go well and the next time they will not go at all. Experiences in Light never repeat themselves. Whether the exercises go well, or not, has nothing to do with our spiritual growth. What we can judge by are our reactions to experiences during the day. If we have lost our equilibrium during the day, we shall find the cutting circles difficult to do at night.

This new exercise, the Rhythm of our Name, is for the protection of our minds. When this exercise first came through I was shown a picture of the boy Jesus in the temple. His mind was being assailed by the cultured minds of the day that could so puzzle and disarm the immature mind. I saw a wonderful light playing round the child in the temple and I knew that those minds that were against Him could not penetrate that light.

We need the same protection. We are up against two thousand years of inherited and acquired knowledge. To present unanswerable questions about Christianity gives, to the sceptical mind, a subtle pleasure. If one is in contact with the mind of Christ and protected from other influences, the answer is flashed to one, outside one's natural reasoning. One learns to fall back on the divine knowledge instead of using one's own.

The exercise needs a little explanation. Do not misunderstand and think that you are being asked to substitute the rhythm of your own name for His protection. The Name of Jesus signifies the highest human vibration. When we surround ourselves with our Christian name, which was given us at the sacrament of baptism, we are surrounding ourselves with the power of that sacrament, as a protection from the impingement of those minds that are apt to destroy our own I-am-ness.

It seems a paradox that while we are learning to empty ourselves, I give you an exercise in which we use the rhythm of our own name. But it is our mind that needs protection. In the earlier exercises we have surrounded ourselves with light; within that vibration of our higher selves we can be invulnerable. Otherwise it may be that we go down to breakfast and somebody does or says something that irritates us, and in a flash is destroyed that which it has just taken us twenty minutes to build up. You see, in this exercise, we are earthing a quality of light for our protection. The hands, the head and the spine are all bathed in this light. We cannot tune in to the mind of the Christ unless we know how, and this training is for the development of our receptivity.

You will find in time that you are not quite so busy in your mind, after this exercise, as you were before.

The greatest power of the world is intellectual; we have all suffered from a sarcastic tongue, and we react, according to our natures, either by a sudden flare-up or by a dull resentment. We also hurt other people with our tongues, and this activity of our tongue has to be transmuted until we no longer want and enjoy the quick intellectual sparking from mind to mind. It looks at first sight as though we were asked to become very dull. I assure you that this is not so. It is no good trying to control our words; the surer way is to be so changed that the temptation to give a quick answer is not the same. Remember, our own mind cannot change our own mind.

Let us use this Lent, not for giving up, but for changing something. Discarding must be a voluntary gesture in this Christian Initiation. The act of sacrifice was a condition that preceded the resurrection. There should be no sacrifice in human nature *after* the crucifixion. The

sacrifice was His and the change into the resurrection body was a joyous condition. We are going to be so much happier that every festival will take on a real festivity.

If we learn this lesson now, from the beginning, we shall short-circuit so much of the pain that must come to us in the ordinary way because of the past. The incarnation of Christ cut the human karma, and so by tuning in to the love of Christ we can cut our karma, which is the inevitable result of past actions — "Though your sins be as scarlet, they shall be white as snow."

If we tune in to this cleansing light, the stain must be washed out. You cannot keep both it and the Light. All these stains of broken law which we have incurred in the past can be short-circuited by tuning in to the mind of Christ. Do not think of the past, for you can remit the past mistakes by the perfectness of the present day. If we carry the load of our past on our shoulders day by day, we inflict it on to ourselves — it is not the will of God. We do not know what the will of God is, but it is not that any of us should suffer, in any finite way, for things committed in ignorance in the past. When we know the law, you cannot break it; when you *are* the law, you step on to a different rhythm of being. Day by day, by right living, we can transmute the past until it is finally done with. What I do know is, that the punishment for the things we commit now, in knowledge, follows us so swiftly that it becomes an instantaneous reaction. The doctrine of reincarnation is really a lovely thing. It brings the past into the present, for what we are now is the highest we have achieved (we can never be less), but the highest must always include the lowest, and the sum total will be the point at which we will start again.

We incarnate in love. We pass on in love. We are constructed out of love, and we can never be less than our highest capacity to love.

This exercise gives us the opportunity not to offend and break the law, and not to be vulnerable to temptation. Long ago I was told that "after revelation, comes temptation," and I have found that it is so. After one is given a new piece of knowledge, one is given the opportunity to know oneself in regard to it.

This Technique offers no thermos of protection against experience. We have put up our own reserves of aloofness and pride, but these are illegitimate protections which are not allowed. One has not got to need pride to fall back on. As we discard our pride so does this protection in Light take its place. That is what the whole hierarchy of the heavens give to the children of Light on earth.

THE RHYTHM OVER THE HEAD

This talk is recorded on cassette tape

Today I want to stress the great importance of the realisation that this Technique in Light is to train us in receptivity, and also the great necessity to grasp the fact that it is a universal pattern. What we draw into ourselves is an individual matter - what we give out, is universal. When we draw Light into ourselves and become channels for pouring out that Light, what we give out then differs not at all from what Jesus gave out. What He gave out was the universal oneness with the Father, and we should be able to do the same when we have learnt to make this intimate contact with the Christ.

Let us get down to what this training means and why we come here to these classes. We cannot keep ourselves to ourselves; we give out our disease and disharmony whether we will or no. The training in Light

218

is to teach us to transmute ourselves so that what we give out is no longer our colds and our germs but a radiant state of harmony, health and happiness. I have learnt as an individual what must be yours and everybody's experience when they tune in to Jesus Christ - that it has to be a continuous process of constant receptivity. We have to learn how to receive His body and blood, how to draw it into ourselves as a constant sparking, an instantaneous contact. We are apt to regard it as a permanent condition and to think once we have made the contact, it "holds good" as it were; but when we receive Him we cannot hold the condition, we cannot grasp it as our possession.

His wisdom is always at our disposal when we tune in, but we cannot store it up; there is always something new every day, and we must always tune in afresh every day as our needs arise. Jesus was able to receive into His being the maximum and He came to give it to the whole world - to the multitude and not merely to a few individuals. He was willing to give it to the Scribes and Pharisees if they had "eyes to see and ears to hear".

He received the law direct from the Father, and every single thing He did, He ascribed to God. He kept nothing for Himself and was able and willing to give to all mankind. He always avoided the personal and stressed that the source of all power and works was the Father, and that what He received could be received by everyone. He never stressed the "I" as we are apt to do, and sternly rebuked Lucifer when he tempted Him to make use of His wonderful powers for His own personal glorification. He was the Law and could have done all things, but of His infinite wisdom He knew that if He turned the universal into the personal, He would break the Law for all time for humanity.

That is what we do; we break the Law when we use the "I" so incessantly. The Technique in Light is to train us to get rid of the bondage of our ego; of this idea that we must "express ourselves". Now we must get rid of all this self-expression and only express His radiance. Step by step our bodies can become free of all the old ignorance and we can all achieve our Sonship. We can, when we tune in, receive everything when we know how to ask and not to *demand* for ourselves, and to make a contact with Him in order to receive and to give.

When we are utterly self-forgetting He can manifest through us and we must never impose arbitrary conditions of time. Time is a human imposition - we are always living in the past - this fatal looking back and remembering!

219

There is no waiting in heaven; every minute is a condition of instant activity and we must learn here to live in the *now*, sparking instantaneously, as the condition of receiving has nothing whatever to do with hours or days or time. Memory is sterile and there is no past in Light. Look on the past as a condition of emptiness, if it is empty of Light.

There is no memory in the mind of God, or of the Christ. He does not remember our past failures and we should not dwell on them or let them be re-lived in our minds. If you want to fill up a jug which has been empty on a shelf for ten years, you are not concerned with its past emptiness, you are only concerned with the filling of it. Memories are a human invention and if we can deal with our past in this life, transmuting them with the Light of God, we shall not take them with us into the next world; but you are bound to take it all with you unless you have learnt to free yourself here on earth.

"Whatsoever is bound on earth is bound in heaven." We bind ourselves only, for bondage is personal and freedom is universal. Jesus Christ came to give us the understanding of universal freedom *here*. We know that the law of perfect freedom operates in heaven, but He earthed it here and we must bring it into manifestation here through this Christian Initiation which teaches us how to put our feet into the Light, walking in His footsteps.

Our spines, the nerves of our bodies, need protection, and they were formed to be receiving centres. Every vertebra has little wing-formations which are magnetic points of attraction; and the very marrow of our bones should be filled with Light. Our spines are formed to transmit perfect harmony and should transmit perfect sound. We should be our own music. The spine should be illuminated every morning.

NOTE

People often asked what Olive Pixley meant when she talked,
frequently, of the Law.
The answer is to be found in Matthew xxii **vv** 36 - 40.

MATTHEW XXII
The King James Version

*36   "Master, which is the great
commandment in the Law?"*

*37   Jesus said unto him, "Thou shalt
love the Lord your God with all thy heart
and with all thy soul and with all thy mind.*

*38   "This is the first and great
commandment.*

*49   "And the second is like unto it,
Thou shalt love your neighbour as thyself.*

*40   "On these two commandments hang
all the Law and the prophets."*

CROSSES ON HANDS AND FEET
This talk is recorded on cassette tape

There must be a time of learning through the mind, and then a time of experience, through the whole of our being - soul and body. It is no good if we go through life only understanding through the mind. Always there comes the experience that proves whether we really know, or only think we do. There is one thing I would like to give you an exercise which will be of tremendous service, because we have learnt enough to understand our stewardship, and it is required of stewards that a man be found faithful.

Faithfulness is not a natural condition of the human race; it is one we have got to acquire. Our souls are always faithful to the environment of heaven and harmony. Our bodies are in a difficult position, poised between two worlds, tuning into the material world, being certain of the conditions there, and then suddenly tuning into the other world and not quite knowing which is the real condition because both are becoming familiar.

We have to understand that the laws which govern the world of Light are the same laws which govern this world, but man has never believed it. There are all those sayings of Jesus regarding material things, that if a man asks for your coat, give your cloak as well; and if you are asked to go one mile, go two. We have not understood giving to the uttermost of our being, not just what is asked, but according to the law of the being of God which is giving for ever. As we give we empty ourselves to receive; when we give of our whole being we are in a position to receive with our whole being. We think that when we give we should get something in return and that we have a right to look for it. We do not understand this law of giving - that we receive as naturally as we should give. We should give and be unconscious of giving.

Two things were given me as regards the hands and feet, and I did them regularly, not at first understanding the significance of what I was doing. I want you to do it faithfully, and the understanding of the significance of the sanctification of the feet will come to you.

When Jesus said to His disciples that He was going to wash their feet, and Peter asked that his whole body be washed, Jesus said that if his feet were washed he would be cleansed. If our feet are sanctified when we touch the earth, (which we have trod for many years) along the path of magnetic influences - that is the earthing of His footsteps. When we know the path we cannot stray.

The other thing I am going to give you has to do with the tongue and the hands, because our tongue is the most unsanctified member of our whole being. We can walk and we can think beautiful thoughts, but it is difficult to translate those thoughts into speech, or to refrain from speech when it is God's will that we should be silent. It is a very big step in our sanctification and initiation if we can sanctify our tongues. It must be done through us and for us, for we cannot do it ourselves.

I was made to understand that every morning after I had made the cross with my blood (for one's saliva is the emotional substance of one's own blood) that the radiation of one's humanity, making the symbol on one's feet with the radiation of one's soul, brings about a condition of sanctification. I was told to make a cross on my hands with my tongue so that my speech should every morning go through this ritual of sanctification. If you do this, you have tongue, hands and feet sanctified every day. It will be an act of remembrance, so that if yesterday we forgot that the tongue had been sanctified and said something sharply for which we were afterwards sorry, when we sanctify ourselves today we

have added power given to us by our voluntary act, so that we shall not offend with our tongue. All this ritual is simple, but it is necessary that we understand that the simple things are the greatest things.

You will find on the scientific side that all great inventions are simple to manipulate, and that the process by which the invention is perfected, is difficult. The functioning is simple. What our souls and minds are going through is a complex process brought about by a simple method, so simple that it is hard to believe that it functions. Only one's experience can provide one's own truth.

Remember Christ needs you wherever you are going and whatever you are doing, and one needs to collaborate with Him as to the best way you may be perfected for His work each day. This partnership is as necessary for Him as it is for us. He needs us as much as we need Him. He cannot function on earth without us. The sanctification of our being is an urgent necessity for Him. He cannot entrust us with greater work until we are perfect in these smaller matters of daily routine.

I know that there is nothing too small to be observed by Jesus and to be remedied. It does not matter what your gift is; whatever you have the capacity for doing, He wants to manifest His power to do it more perfectly than before. He must be able to go in every place where there is activity. We are the secret service agents passing through Christ's earth, breathing His Name, having the hands, feet and tongue sanctified, speaking the words He wants us to speak and with no condition of *self*-consciousness. Will you try to get rid of any inferiority complex which makes you feel you can do nothing, that you can be of no use? None of us can do more than receive Christ's power to function through us, and He can do that equally through all of us. If a thing is asked of you, know that it is because He knows He can do it and is asking to use you in that capacity. You hear yourself saying the right thing and going to the right place just to meet one person.

People think it is useless to go to social parties, but how can you judge? Is it not possible that in a crowd someone will be drawn to you because of something or Some One who is drawing them, and you say the one thing they came to the party to hear? I never think it can be a waste of time. There are no values on the social or business side that need limit Christ.

Sometimes people come to you for peace of mind and, if His mind is in you, they will get it and not come in vain. Peace of mind is the most precious condition. "My peace I give unto you. Not as the world gives it, give I unto you." The world has no power to give it for it is not there. If it were, we should feel it and be it. Peace is a radiation and an activity, the most active thing there is; far more active than war, it is a condition that cuts out war. Peace is like a lighthouse and war the angry waves that dash against it, but it stands invulnerable. Peace is built on the rock of certainty of the truth of the law of Love which transcends every other known law.

Fear cannot prevail against love. It can work on the emotions, and if your love is dependent on your emotions, fear will prevail.

The love of Jesus was not founded on emotions. We have only to read about His life to realise that in the trial He knew that this great step in His incarnation for the freedom of the race had to be permitted, that the people would have no power against the quality of His love. This process of destruction must take place because, through it, His love would be manifested in His resurrection body, to prove the futility of the people's power, for they could not destroy Him, but they had to try. Then followed the resurrection and the ascension, so that the power for destruction should be demonstrated to be an inferior condition. That has to be an individual experience of reconstruction.

We have got to prove individually that the power of force has no domination over us, and that the certainty of the love that is our energy will transcend our fury from the ignorance of the human mind, and that it will not touch that which is Christ in us.

THE SOUL BODY
This talk is recorded on cassette tape

I want to pass on to you today what I have been taught about the light body. We are going to get the equilibrium of Light and flesh, of the soul body and the human physical body, and to appreciate this perfect condition of harmony when the two become one, it is necessary to know what the soul body really is.

The soul is a form in Light, a body made completely of light, of the different substances of light, of different colours and different shapes, and it has as definite functioning powers as does the physical body. When little children talk of having seen an angel, they always describe winged beings, and in all the representations we have of angelic forms they have wings. Somebody with an inner eye of vision has at some time seen a soul and what looks like wings are great radiations of light earthed in a column, or trunk, of light. This trunk of light reaches from the throat to the end of the spine, the core as it were, of our soul bodies is this dazzling white light which contains every nerve of colour, all that we know and recognise here with our human eyes, and others which the human tongue cannot describe; a condition you will all have flashed on your consciousness, not yet classified.

This column of brilliance is the I-am-ness of the individual, and corresponds in substance to the great white ray of God's will. From this spinal column of light three wings radiate. On the left side a lovely wing of purest aquamarine light radiates out and up into infinity. This is the wing of universal love, the divine love which is as universal as breath, and it not only radiates this love but gives also the power to receive the energy of love. This is earthed on the side of the heart. On the right side, a wing of equal radiance but of amber colour, brilliant and sparkling as a glass of sherry held up to the sunlight would appear, comes in on our whiteness, and is the wing of wisdom.

The third is a glowing ruby red which spreads out between our shoulders from the spinal column of light and it is the wing of direction, or judgement. So the skeleton of the soul is love, wisdom, direction and individual I-am-ness.

We have been taught to think that the advancement of the soul can be achieved by formlessness and losing of the ego. No one has the same physical body as another; neither the same soul body. What we share universally is the spirit, just as we share breath.

Here on earth souls tuned in to the same quality of love and wisdom will know a companionship, a oneness of great joy and harmony. But the oneness of souls in the Light world is a fusing and union of which we can have no perception. I saw two glowing beings in Light, fusing and becoming one. Their love and wisdom went through, were one, and passed on in complete harmony. There is no concussion in Light. When your light is one, you become one, with a throughness of substance which we can apprehend here but not experience, because of the different vibrations of the human personalities. Here you can meet many people on certain points but on others you might clash, so they are avoided. There is no direction of the

mind in the soul body. You *are* your own vibration and you cannot become one with another soul body in light unless every vibration of love and wisdom is tuned in exactly with theirs.

The quality of our light bodies which are definitely within our human bodies here on earth, is changing all the time. Some people talk of auras of light, and say sometimes that so-and-so has a bad aura; but no one has either a bad aura or a good aura, because our radiations are ever changing. If you hate someone your contact with Love is cut and at that moment the aquamarine wing will be insulated, invisible, and that fact will be discernible to those with X-ray eyes. But the next moment a rush of beauty and colour may come on meeting someone we love, and that too will be equally visible to those who can see our aura. We have no permanent condition. What we feel, so we are.

In the soul body we radiate ourselves, *us*. In the human body we can pretend and say what we do not feel; but on the other side, whatever you are, you cannot keep to yourselves. There is no reserve or facade to protect you; all you are radiates from you, showing every thought. It is the same here, our soul bodies radiate exactly what we are but we are so blind we do not see. We should be able to do so, and we will, then the fusion in us of love and wisdom becomes perfect. Then will our soul bodies radiate out of us, our flesh will become luminous with the Love energy and there will be no opaque condition. The whole object of this perfect equilibrium is to allow the radiation of our soul to come through the facade of our flesh, so changing its substance that there may be no insulation from those great radiations of love and wisdom which, when fusing in the I-am-ness, may stream out from us in uninterrupted radiance.

Often when we are puzzled to know what is right we look to our brains for guidance, but if we try to get it on the mental side we shall be misled. Until we have equilibrium of love and wisdom we have no right direction. When we can empty our minds and receive into ourselves love and wisdom, direction is a natural sequence. It is quite effortless, it *comes*, knowledge comes and *is* - the natural result of love and wisdom blending in perfect harmony.

In the soul love, wisdom and direction is a natural condition of receptivity and transmission. When we become this equilibrium here in ourselves we shall find all those antagonisms of the mind which have destroyed our peace in the past will be transmuted into peace of mind. This is not done through stress or striving, but through the transmutation of substance through receptivity, and only by being able to tune direct into the mind of Christ.

You have to get to the centre point and know where your mind is winging. Do not be uncertain where you get love and wisdom from. You do not receive it out of the ether, and you do not receive it if you try to receive too big a cosmic condition. You can only get to a cosmic condition *through* the Christ. He is the door through which we pass into a greater condition beyond. All those things which He taught were proved because He could not leave anybody unaware of the necessity for accurate knowledge of the Law. He is the Law made flesh and His is Life, Light and Love.

Love is not an emotion - it is a stable condition of receptivity; and giving and wisdom and direction are stable conditions of receptivity. You *receive* direction, you do not direct. I do not want to give anybody a vague idea of the soul as a beautiful butterfly condition. It is a scientific condition and is within the physical body - not an over-shadowing outside, but definitely inside, and the radiation is limitless. At death the radiation is transferred, it leaves the body, and the core wings itself away and the body, the container, is left.

Think only of the soul as brilliance. The greater the development of the soul body, the greater will be the brilliance of its substance; and the more colour it can earth here, the greater the light there. This earthing power is in the blood. You cannot see the form of it, you can only touch the radiation.

When we come into contact with a disagreeable person we usually recoil because we are hit by their radiation. When we begin to become conscious of the power of our soul to function on earth through our humanity there will be such a current of love and wisdom in us that there can be no recoiling from any personality, but we shall meet them with the ability to fuse with the one spark of the divine in them, and thus release in them the Light that is there, but hidden. If we recoil from anyone it is really from ourselves that we recoil, our own vibrations and personality, because we have not yet achieved complete harmony and integrity of soul.

There can be no place where Christ could not walk, through us, and unlock a door. When our souls are functioning in harmony with our bodies there will be no fear left in our minds of any condition, because fear is ignorance of the functioning of the Law. You will walk fearlessly through places when you walk with Him. In the doing of the exercise called the Equilibrium of the Name, you are sparking with the magnetic currents of the earth, and those great cosmic rays; receiving with love and making contact with Light. You are sparking all power on earth and heaven, doing something scientific. You will only record it in an absence of conditions; not a plus condition of power, but an absence of fear and irritability for they will no longer be present. In that sparking when those contrary conditions are not present, then our power to receive the plus condition starts.

We shall learn that peace of mind, equilibrium of soul and body, is an enchanting, vital and lovely thing, and it is creative. When we have achieved this condition of mind we have every moment of the day to create something in - even if it is only creating a smile on someone's face, and laughter and happiness. We shall be used as agents for happiness to make whole broken spirits, to bring happiness into shadowed minds, and to link up again those who have been disconnected with life through death with this amazing current of radiant joy. Where ever you are sent and whatever difficult situation may occur, if you have started the Technique you have

228

started on the path of being His almoner, of giving a condition of happiness and harmony of life.

Do not think that because Jesus came having nothing in His possession that was the standard He imposed. He came owning nothing in order to demonstrate the capacity of every soul for receiving everything; and if He had had everything, He could not have demonstrated how to receive. He had to teach people that there was nothing they could not receive. Do not cut off anything, or look upon wealth, happiness and perfect material conditions as something wrong. If you have the equilibrium of love and wisdom it does not matter how rich or how poor you are because the capacity to receive is yours. Never look upon outside conditions as a standard for good or ill. When we have been faithful over the condition where we now are, we shall be able to be faithful in limitless conditions.

This technique has to be a sparking; not *directed* by the mind, but *received* by the mind. All values and estimates have to be changed, and you have to receive such gifts as He is longing to bestow, which He can only give through the two radiations of love and wisdom, and that means perfect health. We shall learn together how to receive His needs.

We must present our needs to Him and also listen to receive His need, for the transmitting of health into the world.

I know there is a stage that occurs to people who have done the exercises in Light *mentally*, and have not realised right from the beginning that Light is a substance, that Light is love and life and is made visible; that it is a substance with which you can unite yourself. If you only watch and look on with your inner eye at the pattern, it is the same as any other mental process and is not absorbed into your whole body, it is a visionary, mystical condition but not a physical condition. That is why so many minds have been left high and dry and the bodies un-nourished because of the ecstasy of the visionary side of Light.

People have asked me why we make healing more important than other forms of channelhood. What we receive we are bound to give, and as this is the technique of the resurrection of the body, are we not bound to give it in healing of the body? I want the radiation of people's blood and that must be for healing. How can you not heal? It is impossible not to do so if your mind is tuned in to the mind of Christ and you are receiving His body. He gave His body to the world for the healing of the human race. How can we not heal?

What you receive you must give; you have something somebody needs, you have some aspect of the Christ. We are none of us wholly free yet and what we have, we must give. Therefore you are bound to receive something, whether of mind or of body.

You cannot have a mind that does not manifest in your body. We are in our bodies the manifestation of our minds, so why separate mental healing from physical; you cannot heal the mind without healing the body. None of you who follow this training to the end can possibly not heal, but you will only be a *channel* and you will not need to know or comprehend what you are doing. I can register what I receive but I hope I shall never register what I give, because then I register something myself. Do not worry about the different conditions that are going to manifest; where ever He leads you, you will live. Whatever He needs of you, if you give yourself to Him mind and body, He can use the whole of you, but He cannot use just your mind. If your mind accepts the training, your body must do so, but if your mind rejects it, He cannot work through your body.

He cannot and will not impose a single thing, but you can transmit healing through the agency of your heart and mind, even to people at a distance who know nothing, if you commit them to Him and know that they are bound to receive anything you can receive on their behalf.

AH-LAH-HIÈVE
Talk given on 7th February 1939 to Class E

The last exercise given was the Transmuting Light; I hope that you have all been able to *feel* this exercise and to register for yourselves your own sensations when doing it. Some exercises one does quite blindly, but with the Transmuting Light one should know that one *is* different when one draws in that lovely amethyst light, suffusing the whole body; and it is about that, that I want to talk this morning.

It is so important to record in oneself one's own *certainty*. I am appalled sometimes at the vagueness of people's minds as to what they really believe as practical and true in Christ's teaching. I do not mean what has been handed down as His teaching, but the real truth concerning what He spoke and taught and did. People seem to 'shy off' from finding out for themselves their own certainty and truth. So many seem to find it easier to fall back on someone else. This class has only been doing the Technique of Light for quite a short time, but I feel somehow that it is a very responsible class, and I want you all to realise the great importance for the sake of the world's healing, of clear thinking and clear understanding for ourselves; not depending on others for our comfort, nor using them as scapegoats for our muddled thinking! We nearly always make others responsible for our minds; we are apt to think and come to believe that it is all the fault of someone else, some early teaching, or a friend's influence, or that of a parent; then we can blame them. We must do away with all excuses of that sort.

It is essential to understand what you do believe concerning the resurrection body. I do not want you to think *back* when I say this, I want you to be quite clear about what you understand and believe *now*. We are not to make our lives copy-book imitations, but it must come in to our understanding individually, and we must know as individuals the experience of this universal condition - Christ's universal condition.

We know that the process by which He demonstrated universal conditions was an individual thing. His experience proved the law that the body can be reconstructed during one's life time here. And it is going to be done by others by orthodox methods (and by orthodox methods I mean according to law); a perfectly comprehensible condition of a new normality. He demonstrated a new normality; He did not demonstrate it in a super-normal way at all, but on a new plane of experience. No one else ever had a similar experience, and we have felt it to be a condition of the *next* life, and not of this one. We have felt that the demonstration of the resurrection did not take place here but only as the soul *left* the body. That is of course impossible, because when the soul has left the body it no longer has any control over it; it is like a discarded garment that we slip off onto the floor where it lies inanimate, no longer covering our body. When the soul leaves the body it has then no contact with it, so the resurrection of our bodies *must* take place here while the soul is still clothed with it.

This Technique of Light is to teach our generation, and generations to come, how to achieve resurrection so it is not, and must not be a belief in *past* conditions, but a certainty of functioning ever present now. It is happening now, every moment, and it is up to us to train our minds to receive the law enabling us to receive a radiant garment of humanity. So we must eliminate all these doubts, these uncertainties and vaguenesses, all those conditions of instability which belong to the past days of bondage. On this, our road to freedom, we must not bring in old ignorances, we must let them go and bring about a completely new method of thought.

I feel an urge to talk about mind today; it is so important that we should understand ourselves and know ourselves as we really are. I do not want any of us to dwell upon the picture that we have had hitherto of ourselves, that picture which we have held up to others, often hiding the real self from them; that picture of our soul and body as separate entities where there is always conflict between the two. Now we must see a new picture and learn to have the power to bring these two conflicting conditions into perfect harmony *through* the mind, not *by* the mind. We must *surrender* these minds of ours, and by this I do not mean by much thinking or deep meditation, but by learning to receive in a flash, by a process of flashing light, a radiation, a vibration. (Nowadays medical science uses radiation and vibration more than anything else, so that we are becoming used to these terms and know their immense uses.)

Well, radiation must be *timeless*, therefore we must understand how to get rid of time limits with which we have shackled ourselves in the past. We have put down years and allotted to them deeds; we have divided life into childhood, youth, maturity and old age and have expected a certain performance according to years here. Try to eliminate this limiting type of thought because it is such a bondage.

It is a great step forward when we can free our minds and know the reality that truth is a timeless condition in which Jesus Christ worked - "a thousand years is as a day." It is not important whether we are 6 or 60, age has no relationship to the miracle that can take place in us. Christ never said to anyone "you have applied too late, or too soon"; nor is there any limit in His mind either here on earth or in heaven. This harmony between soul and body can take place at any time.

I want you to start trying to eliminate from your minds all 'ifs' and 'buts'; our understanding is clipped by doubts and uncertainty. It was so in my own past, so that I can well understand how it happens, that feeling that we must allow a margin 'for safety'. We must allow such a margin that there are no limitations whatever!

This new mental exercise is a most lovely one, and I want you to have it now before we go any further. It is no good asking anyone to change unless one gives them something to help them to do so.

This is done to the sound **Ah-Lah-Hiève**. The light flashes down on in inbreath to the sound of **Ah-Lah**, from infinity right down in front of the face, and then it pierces the throat and up the back of the head. When it reaches the bulge at the back of the head it rays through and out of the forehead and up again on the sound **Hiève**. When it was first shown to me I saw a brilliant bar of light to which I had to send my own ray, the last thing at night, emptying out all the rubbish, sending it out into infinity to be absorbed into wisdom and knowledge, to the mind of Christ. I then learnt that this vivid bar of light into which the ray went was the brow of the cosmic Christ, and I knew then too the reality of His wavelength. Every individual has got his own wavelength, but Jesus Christ was the first person to earth His body and soul here, earthing that wavelength and so establishing this condition of receptivity, so that all who learn can tune in to His harmony. I obeyed and always sent my ray into this brilliance, to His ray, and felt that I had been in touch with Him definitely. It has now become a certainty, just as much as when you know that you have met and spoken to someone, it *is* so, an incontrovertible fact - so do I know now that I am doing this exercise on the wavelength of the Christ *only*.

I am passing on the knowledge of this contact for you to know for yourselves, so that you will not be sending out this ray vaguely out 'into the blue' for anyone to pick up. For there are others ready to pick up radiations, but when we tune in to the Christ ray there can be no 'interference'. Probably most of you have read papers on psychology and know how it has been proved as a scientific fact that the power of thought is very great, how greatly it can act on feeble-minded persons. Even crimes are committed when a dominating mind controls less strong minds on destructive rays; the person responsible remains free from the consequences of the frightful deeds which they have insinuated into puppet minds dominated by their stronger mental force. If you believe that, as I think you must, you will believe and know that we can all be dominated by spiritual power from the mind of Christ.

If we all trust and record our experiences we will know that we *do* change in ourselves, and are given power to help others because of our changed capacity in receptivity. This is the experience of myself, and that of many others who have been learning along these lines. I want you as an early class to make it yours as quickly as possible. I want you to establish this contact and know it to be true for yourselves, not as my truth, but as your own - it *must* be *yours*.

This capacity for changing brings such great happiness and health into our lives; this resurrection body we are learning to achieve must be radiant. There is no really good person in this world who is not happy; make happiness and peace your standard of goodness; realise that it can be like an epidemic! One happy person at peace with themselves and with all the world can radiate such power that the radiations will be picked up by all who come into contact with them. It should not then be a long time before the world is happy and at peace. Christ said, "My peace I give unto you," but we have not known how to receive it. We have looked for it in other ways; we have looked to money, to material things, to self protection, to give us peace and have been constantly frustrated.

Peace, prosperity and health can only come on the wavelength of Christ; it is all here for us to tune in to, we must go to Him for it. It is no good looking to the Bank of England or to trade - there is no true abundance and peace to be found there. If we seek first 'these things' from Christ, we are bound to be healthy and happy. It may not be easy for you to believe nor do I want you to take it as a 'group belief', the experience can and must come to you as individuals. It can only come into your minds by emptying out all the conditions and taking in completely fresh ones every evening; emptying out the rubbish and receiving new truth. It does not matter whether your mind is humble or arrogant, it makes no difference, it can be emptied just the same.

I am so glad that the people who come to these classes are all capable people of different types of efficiency, not vague or dreamers! You are all people who seek to do things well in various walks of life. In the future you will strive to do things perfectly on a different wavelength to the past. You will perfect the process and fulfilment of your actions now by surrendering your efficiency and not by clutching at it. *Do believe* this. I did not believe it at one time, I thought I had to give it all up and become negative; I could not see that I could become of use to anybody on these lines. Indeed, had I been told in the beginning that I had to teach as I am doing now, I tremble to think what I should have done! It was not a voluntary thing for me to pass on this Technique of Light, but it came to me so gradually that I did not tremble at the idea. Now I feel that it is the one thing I could not bear to lose, the *joy* of passing on this truth and freedom which I can guarantee. But it will not come to any of us in the same way; nor is it any good comparing other people's experience with our own.

I went up in a captive balloon once, and as soon as we had ascended some way up it became impossible to register the comparative heights of either the places we could see below or the height we had come from the earth. Well, that should be the same in spiritual growth; do not make it a comparative condition with friends or relatives. We must be outside any other minds and should only know through our own health and happiness, our harmony in contact with those from whom we have been separated before. Then you will know you are developing, because it is a *uniting* condition with those people and circumstances which seemed so difficult in the past. We shall be on a new wavelength on which He draws people to Him in His harmony and love.

So much of us goes and we are unaware of its gradual leaving, but it cannot remain. We cannot serve two masters; we cannot put ourselves first and yet receive the Light. When we rid ourselves of bad temper, irritability, frustrations, then there is room for new conditions of peace which will repercuss on our bodies and make them whole. We shall achieve our resurrection bodies through harmony of mind when we cease to express disharmony and ill-temper and no longer impose our worries on others. There are few greater sins than that of our desire to impose our sufferings and distresses on other people. Some people seem unable to bear seeing others enjoying happiness, and are filled with a desire to pass on their own woes. Then there are other people who will try to destroy this new found equilibrium of yours, and as long as they *can* destroy it, they will. Do not look upon it as a failure if your peace is at all shaken by their attempts. Look rather upon it as an opportunity to get on a new spiral. Every spiral looks the same, but it is on a new level - we go on and up. Above all, never despair. We must all go through these experiences, and we all have someone in our lives who can destroy our peace of mind. (And it is always their fault, never ours - how often one can hear "I was alright until they said so-and-so!") Look upon them as agents, these causes of our distress; usually they are closely connected with us, friends, relations or it may be servants, as agents to provide us with the necessary experience in the process of reconstruction. We are not free until harmony comes to us in the *worst* conditions.

This exercise of the **Ah-Lah-Hiève** with its flash of cleansing light is of such value in helping us to deal with these difficulties. When the light rushes through the head, coming out of the forehead, keep your head up, not down, so that you send the light upwards to where it will be absorbed in harmony, and it will be transmuted there. Never send it down to earth where so much sadness and evil has already been earthed.

That is really what ghosts are, not the people themselves, but the fragments of their minds which they have left behind. It is their distressing mental condition which is left as an on a gramophone record which people can pick up as the instrument which records the discs. Sounds and vibrations of our voices and our minds are recorded for ever - I shudder to think what one could pick up on golf-courses! All great emotions leave a deep record, and take different forms. Mary Queen of Scots imprinted her distress as if it were a photograph everywhere she slept during those years of her captivity. The emotions were so strong that you can pick them up even today.

Once, many years ago when I was at school in Paris, I went to the Conciergerie and felt quite sick with the miseries I contacted there. Some time ago after I had been doing the Technique in Light, I went back and found that someone had been there who had prayed there, and absorbed all the misery into their love, as it all seemed swept and garnished. It was wonderful, all the suffering had been transmuted, the whole atmosphere changed.

Now that we know through

236

psychology what wavelengths of emotion and ritual the earth can contain, how our thoughts and feelings can be received and picked up, do let us realise what was left behind in the earth 2,000 years ago. His perfect love and peace are there for us to tune in to, to draw into ourselves and radiate out into others to make a new world.

Shakespeare was quite right when he said "the evil that men do lives after them," but he was equally wrong when he added that "the good was oft interred with their bones." Good can be earthed as well as evil, but up to now the evil has a stronger force of reproduction than good, because more evil has been earthed. We have always sent love upwards - evil has gone down, and love and goodness have gone up. One of the reasons that the bulk of suffering and pain continue is because we have always looked for happiness *out* of *this* world. Now we must earth it *here* and transmute and transcend all the past earthing of evil. It is an awful thought really - all the bodies buried in the earth with their diseases and disharmonies radiating into the earth we tread on. Now you see how necessary it is for this world for us to make our resurrection bodies vibrating with love and peace, knowing that we are building up a new race. Possibly it is not extremely enthralling to think of a new race when we have our own lives to lead, but the world is so fraught with pain and suffering that it must be changed, and changed quickly. Do not be limited by these years you have lived, do not be limited by time - this new earth and new heaven can happen to us.

If you will never earth an unkind thought or any miserable condition from now on, (I know this is asking a great deal!) all our past will come into the present and be absorbed into harmonious conditions, and we shall wake up free of yesterday. Do not ever bring any of it back again, it has all gone; all distresses and all failures - we shall be free if we will not bring our past into the now.

When doing this new exercise send all the day's dust out with a *rush*, do not dwell on it or search it over - we do not go through our material dustbins, nor take the contents out again! Keep all that is precious and good only, send away all the rubbish, and wake up knowing it has gone. Never forget to do the **Ah-Lah-Hiève** each night, (it comes after The Spirals). You can do it any time in the day also if you want to clear your mind for any particular reason.

AH-LAH-HIÈVE
This talk is recorded on cassette tape

We want to achieve equilibrium, that perfect balance of heart and mind in our personal reactions to the circumstances of life as we have to live it. We need Christ's light more than ever today in order to keep sane in the midst of the almost universal sufferings of the world. We want to learn to live in a state of constant tuning in and sparking contact with Christ's mind, so that we may live 'on the spur of the moment' in complete harmony with Him - not as we did in our unthinking youth.

We must realise that life is to be lived minute by minute, that decisions must be made in a split second, and that as long as we take those decisions in tune with Christ's mind, there can then be none of those mistakes, no years of remorse. Jesus Christ lived second by second, and was ever in alignment with the Father; He never pondered - He acted instantaneously. As small children do, we must live in the moment; only whereas a child has no conscious sense of direction, we must live in the consciousness of the Christ. So many people having regretted bitterly some spontaneous actions of youth, settle themselves down into an ordered middle-age so planned and organised that they become completely sterile, never getting anywhere, only

sinking devitalised into old age. What fun if instead at 70 we had the spontaneous activity of childhood in our veins; were able to be 'on our toes' with a renewed physical vehicle, instead of having an old silted-up bloodstream! It is only our mental attitudes that bring us all this agedness and frustration; if we truly ask for a condition of eternal life, beauty and harmony, in all selflessness, we can and must achieve it in Light and there will then be nothing to regret. There cannot be any regret where Christ's light is, and when our hearts and minds are so filled with it there will be a happy spontaneity in our actions.

When we do things from our heart there are no regrets; it is those second thoughts which bring infinite regret. We must clear away the rubbish in our minds and hearts, all that waste material which clogs our veins and arteries, slowing our movements, and live instead with the speed of light.

Our minds are so quick to receive fear; but if we keep them free and clear to receive His light and inspiration we need never be afraid again. We can eliminate all fear - fears of circumstances, fears for other people. Do realise that circumstances are universal - pain and suffering come to everyone, frustration and lack of love, and how we suffer from being misunderstood! Our motives are so good and clear to us, but the simplest things we do are taken wrongly and the being misjudged is unbearable. But if we only live in the moment everything will become bearable because all the pain and distress come, not from the living but from the thinking, and if we think with Christ's mind where no pain is, there can only be joy and happiness for us, because we shall be filled with Him and there will be no room for anything else.

I want to pass on to you step by step, this way of Light so that we can live and "bear all things". We cannot do it of ourselves but "with Him all things are possible"; but we must learn to make it an *eternal* "with Him". We must so fill ourselves with His light that we become the very substance of Light, that leaven with which He can do all things. We must earth the light for the Prince of Peace and give Him the substance of ourselves through which He may heal men's minds and bodies.

It is not right to be absent in our minds from the realities of life; it is not being more spiritually-minded to be vague and mystical and so leave undone those practical things which lie to our hands. Instead we must become more aware immediately of them being present, not absent, in our minds from Him. Christ was all-seeing and all-hearing, and acted immediately; He did not let His thoughts outrun His actions by planning ahead what He was going to do next. He knew that He had to represent God to the world and He was ever-present and ready to hear any single cry. He was literally on the spot at every moment and only when the Father called Him aside did He withdraw for a while. We must only withdraw for revelation, not for pondering but a swift tuning in to His will, without any thought of self.

We are so apt to worry at night over all the accumulated frets of the day, and to ponder over all the many problems which present themselves over and over again. This exercise is a method of clearing away all those cobwebs in the mind, and to transmit all the worries and anxieties to the mind of Christ. We are very particular about washing our hair, but you can also wash your mind in Light and keep it absolutely clean and fresh from the day's dust.

This is an exercise to be done every night, but if during the day you are feeling the need for the clarification of some problem, do this exercise as often as you wish. You can do it anywhere as you can make the sound of **Ah-Lah-Hième** silently unless you are alone.

Do remember not to look down when doing this or you will send all your worries back into the earth; look upwards and send it all up to Him.

You cannot do this exercise for other people however much you may feel they may need it; but your own emptiness can be far more helpful, so let us get our minds thoroughly clear at least once in the day and we shall be all the more ready to help with the world's problems which seem so insoluble. This clearness will help us to realise the necessity to achieve reconciliation with our opposites, which is the Law of Peace. Herein lies the solution of the world problems of our time, this Law of the Reconciliation of Opposites.

A new world must be founded upon this principle because there are such vast differences between the nations; not by insisting that they should be brought to our standards, but by recognising what is in them, and in us, which separates us. And it cannot be done merely on the mental level; we have first to reconcile ourselves individually with our opposite, with Jesus Christ, for He is our opposite, being all love, and therein lies all the gulf between Him and the human race.

Two thousand years ago the people preferred Barabbas because they would rather have someone like themselves, it was much easier than reconciling themselves with their opposite.

Let us therefore reconcile our minds with the mind of Christ in absolute oneness, then there will be no limit to what He can use us for - to reconcile families, friends, nations. Each of us must get our own revelation and get rid from our own minds those things which are the cause of variance and separation from our neighbour, whoever he or she may be. When our minds and hearts are cleansed and free for Christ to use, then we shall be *becoming* our resurrection bodies, making them free, as His was free from the bondage of the mind. He gave obedience to Caesar when He dwelt on earth, but when He achieved His resurrection body He was free.

When we never go counter to the Law of Love we shall *be* that law and order; those things which we always long to see in others. When our hearts "dwell in Him and He in us," our hearts will be the very centre of law and order and we shall have got rid of all those self-centred analytical thoughts which so spoil the pattern for every one of us. When we clear our minds overnight we have a joyous awakening free from yesterday's bondage and we need not have those dusty furnishings back again if we have thoroughly cleansed the room in which they have lived.

Take your Figure of Light with you where ever you go; let your feet, hands, throat, glands - every part of you - be filled with light so that there will be a vitalising of your physical self, and a unifying of your soul and body into one wavelength, not a split personality but a complete oneness of being. Above all remember to do His Name and with it start your powers of giving; His Name is your helmet of salvation and in the vibration of the **Dyè-Thu-Th** you get a peace and quietness which is beyond all words. Do not think for a moment that the exercise of the **Ah-Lah-Hiève** is a substitute for The Name. His Name is for the filling of your mind with Christ, the **Ah-Lah-Hiève** is for the swift emptying of our mind.

THE THROAT
Correspondence Course Notes

In the middle of the human throat lies the magnetic centre of the light body. Its activity corresponds to that of the human brain, for it is the focusing point for all the cosmic rays.

Physical food is taken in through the mouth, and spiritual food through the throat. To live in this world it is essential to draw air into the lungs and circulate it through the body. To live in the spirit it is essential to draw light into the soul and circulate it through the light body. Different substances of food nourish the body in special ways; a baby thrives on milk alone, but a grown man requires stronger and more varied nourishment. So it is with our souls. In an undeveloped spiritual consciousness we are content with what is given us. As we grow more aware of our capacities we seek to find what will satisfy our hunger and thirst, Living Water and Bread of Life.

To develop our spiritual brain we must understand its form and its functioning powers. Will you look at the diagram and realise that you have a flower of living light in the centre of your throat? The nine petals are of intense white light and the centre is a glowing ruby light, which is the magnetic point of power. It draws into itself all attributes of divine power, absorbs and transmits them into the blood, so that in time the very substance and rhythm of our blood changes and we become aware in every fibre of our being of a quickened condition of spiritual awareness.

Jesus Christ was able to receive into His transmuted human body every ray of light that proceeds from the being of God the Father. Christ promised that after His ascension He would be able to transmit to His disciples the same power that He Himself had received. He kept His promise at Pentecost, as witness to the whole world. We too can prepare our human bodies that we may receive the current of Love.

Emotion is to Love what foam is to the sea - it can be a lovely ethereal substance, or it can be soiled and contaminated by the flotsam and jetsam of the ocean. It can in no way be confused by the power and grandeur of the ocean itself. And thus it is with Love. We must learn to draw into our being the very substance of God.

Will you quite simply visualise this lovely flower in your throat and know that when we are spiritually unconscious the nine petals are folded over the ruby centre. We must quite consciously unfold them one by one, rhythmically, until when they are all open and the ruby centre receives, according to the ego's development, the cosmic rays of creative power - and then instantly they close up again.

This exercise should be done at mid-day, though any time between 12 noon and 4 p.m. will do. We need to do it as regularly as we eat our midday meal, it should become as much a habit as washing our hands before we eat.

Either stand or sit. Moisten the first finger with the saliva in your mouth. I cannot explain in this exercise what has been revealed concerning the creative qualities of the blood. I was made to understand that saliva is that substance which registers through our emotions the harmony or disharmony of the blood. I was also given the picture of Christ mixing His saliva with the earth when healing a blind man. We can through this exercise develop our capacities to understand all mysteries.

After having moistened the first finger of the right hand, outline the nine petals one by one, starting at the centre going up the inside of the petal and ending in the centre. It is done clockwise - that is to say, from left to right on the following rhythm:-

— - - - — —

for each petal. Moisten the finger between each petal. Each one stays open until all nine are done. Then for a moment in time the ruby centre is fully exposed, draws in all it can receive and then the petals close instantly and remain closed until the ritual is repeated the next day. Every day increases the receptive power.

THE THROAT
This talk is recorded on cassette tape

I wonder if the accuracy of the action of light on the body is understood by those of us who have not yet gone very far in the Technique. Every exercise as it comes along deals with a certain part of the body, with the making of it a temple, a container of energy, a magnet. There are many conditions included in the physical instrument; it has magnetic attraction and the drawing of light into the body is for a very definite purpose. It is not only to feed your vision, but also your physical body. When you draw the Transmuting Light into your heart and right breast, you are definitely making a contact with that part of the body that needs regenerating, and it permeates through the whole of it.

Jesus has been described as the Word made flesh, that is, the materialisation of sound. We can make sounds through our throat but we cannot make substance. We can only put forth a sound but actually the creative condition of sound is to make substance, and Jesus was the manifestation of form, sound and substance. It is so important that we identify ourselves with this process and unless we know that we too can make form and substance through the medium of sound, we shall not begin to go through the experiences of Christ in this Christian Initiation. Therefore we have to identify our physical and mental mystical body as a unit and to do that we have to have a real experience. We cannot do it through the vision only, but we can through an active co-ordination.

The exercise I want to share with you today presents for the first time an understanding of this co-ordination of sound and substance. It has to do with the throat. When you think of your throat, realise that it is a sound box and that you have saliva glands which are governed by the emotions, by your mental body. Whatever your vision is, so will it record on the saliva glands because saliva is that content of the blood which holds the magnetic attraction for energy. It is the watery substance of the blood, and in water is the power to attract light. Therefore it has always been into the white corpuscles, the watery substance of the blood, that the eternal life energy has been attracted.

In order to make the understanding of our capacity real to us, this exercise has been given. I want you to identify it with your thyroid gland. Only lately have I understood how detailed are these exercises for the feeding of every part of the body. We know a person functions according to their glands. Those who lack thyroid, lack energy; and those who have to much, are restless and do not know the meaning of the word repose. So we have to get our balance, as Jesus had the balance of activity and repose. You cannot have peace of mind if your glands are out of order. Mental instability is glandular and the effect of lack of energy of your glands is conveyed all over your body so that you get nerve tension and depletion of all the vital functions of the body. Therefore your throat is a most important part.

You give forth yourself through the medium of sound. The things you say are the expression of your vision and your thought, therefore they go out into activity and finally they will make substance. You will get the reaction from sound back again in to your body as substance. If you are very sharp tongued, ultimately that condition will come back on your nervous system and that sharpness will make you a very angular person. If you have a happy nature and only make sounds of happiness and laughter, that also comes back into your substance. You have a very different sort of body when that sound is integrated in you from the person who is always producing tears and friction to another through the medium of sound.

When the Throat exercise came through I did not understand one half of what I do now. I did not understand the capacity for power that lies within the individual throat; that the paradox of sound and silence is always part of the beingness of the substance of Christ. When sound was demanded of Him by Pilate, the reaction was silence. When sound could only be frustration and destruction, then Christ, in harmony with the Father was silent, and that made the substance of serenity in Him. I want you to understand the vital importance of this exercise. When it first came I was as ignorant as anyone could be about the Technique in Light on myself, or anybody else. I could not know what Christ was trying to get through an ordinary person, for the saving of humanity from their ignorance concerning the law of life and eternal energy.

Visualise a lovely flower of nine pure white petals closing over a ruby centre, which is a power point in your throat. I have talked of the wing of direction coming from the top to the base of the spine, and the power point at the top goes right through to the centre of the throat. As the nine petals open, this strong magnet is exposed and then you draw into your thyroid gland all the energy you can receive, which will be right through your body. We do not have energy because we do not know how to receive it.

This exercise has often been neglected because people have not understood the full significance of it. We have to open the nine white petals with a conscious movement, uniting the substance of our saliva, our own blood, with a rhythmic movement. It is a co-ordination of movement and substance. Your saliva is the most magnetic substance of your blood, and I was shown that Christ needed to use His saliva, mixed with the earth substance, to cure a blind man. He used His own blood content mixed with the earth radiation, and He had a balanced substance. It was the essence of creative radio-active substance with which He anointed the man's eyes and the result was sight, the regenerating of the man's condition which responded in an instant. As darkness responds to light, blindness responded when it had the right content given to it.

We have within us the capacity to receive this energy. I am not going to keep using the word 'divine' because the universal church has blinded us to our infinite capacity, so that we have looked on physical human things as separate. Jesus came to make them one; that His blood and our blood and the blood of God should be one energy, creating wholeness.

When the nine petals are open the magnet is exposed and in that moment the whole of the magnetism of divine energy is received in the physical body. It will vitalise all the glands in the throat and travel into the other glands, and if you have a balance of the thyroid gland you are beginning to have the balance of energy. If you vitalise the thyroid gland every day, you must get rid of the depletion which has been going on all your life. If you put a battery on long enough, you get it up to its proper strength; and if you do this exercise every day, you will get the battery up to normal so that it will then function automatically. The Throat exercise will later on be incorporated in a wonderful condition of energy going right through the body, but unless you have the petals in active operation, the other exercise will not function. You will be able to visualise the pattern, but the substance will not form in your body.

That is the difference between the people who do the Technique in Light and *become* it, and those who treat it from a mental point of view. They think it lovely to visualise light, but they do not connect it with eternal life and the construction of the physical body. I am not concerned with the mental development of an individual

245

because I know that the receptive mind and the one that is in contact with the mind of Christ, must of necessity know infinitely more than the greatest scholar in the world. If you pursue with great energy the written word, you will absorb into your brain the knowledge that is in the written word, but more you cannot absorb and much of it you will forget. A person may be educated or uneducated, intellectual or unintellectual, but an intelligent man knows that a contact with the divine mind is a greater condition than a contact with a human mind, and we can only make a contact with a human mind through the written or spoken word.

We make a contact with truth, true law and true conditions through the mind of Christ because His is the container of true activity and life. You cannot get activity in this world without life, and so you have to go to the source of life before you get pattern or activity. Anything Christ can reveal to you will be of importance to me, and everything He can reveal through me, is of equal importance to anybody else. Therefore we are equal because we have the same capacity but we must have the experience of knowing in our being that that condition of inspiration is available for the human instrument which is developed to receive it. You may, or may not, believe that your capacity for inspiration is equal to that of anybody else; that it has nothing to do with virtue or your past, it has only to do with your present and what we do with our present is of vital importance. If only we can shut out our past with its ignorance, willfulness and self-indulgence, and make up our mind that every capacity we have for receiving truth, we will put into operation, putting that first.

Many people suffer from not realising how to put first things first. They do not think they have put these things second, but it is habitual for the ordinary person to consider that there are many things in their lives that they should put first, such as other people, relations and contacts. If you put them before that which you are able to *receive* for them, if you put their demands before Christ's commands, how are you going to be able to satisfy their demands? You are going to fail, and in that failure comes the disintegration of the physical instrument through wanting to give more than what one has to give. You often hear it said of people that they spend their lives in giving, and die in spending; but it is much more thrilling and interesting to know how people can live receiving, and that is our concern here. Not how people spend, but how they can receive, because giving is not of our choice.

We give according to God's direction, not according to the demands made on us, and we learn to receive this great life energy effortlessly into our being so that receiving and giving become the unity of activity that it was in the beginning; for it was only separated into receiving and giving, or receiving and withholding through the agency of the human mind.

As we receive from Christ, so must we give in a continuity of givingness, and that is what you will find. It is not *your* energy, but the moment you feel strong, happy and radiant, you cannot keep it to yourself. Nobody can keep life energy to themselves, nor can you keep tiredness, or anything depleting to yourself. You know when you hear people walk and talk whether they are well or ill, whether they are receiving or insulating.

If you had X-ray eyes you would see that sparking condition as your contact is made with your finger and the throat, and if we could see, we would know how light functions on the physical body. It produces a spark of light in us which, coming out is invisible to us, but not to those who can see, and they would see receptive people by the radiance of their emanations.

Therefore you have to take it on trust that you are opening the lovely white petals in your throat and the radiance there goes right through to the nape of the neck. It is like a live wire, a strong magnetic contact which is vitalised by the watery substance of your saliva. We are trying to bring the soul body, which is our eternal body of light, into manifestation. It is ethereal here, but becomes concrete on the other side. Light will go through matter here but on the other side light is your substance and matter is ethereal.

Jesus magnetised His reconstructed physical body. He was of the substance of Light and could go through matter. If the door were locked, He could go through it, and because of the love of His disciples, He could draw on their substance for materialisation. Do not be put off in thinking it makes you self-conscious or self-important; it makes you not self-important but important to Christ, which is very different. If we are self-important, we put ourselves first; but if we are important to Him, we put Him first, so that His peace of mind, which passes all understanding, shall come into us and we shall each know it as our own experience.

Talk Given 24th March 1939

In The Throat exercise, that lovely unfolding of the petals, we should, in thinking of the throat, think of the soul. The soul is the light body which has marvellous radiations of love and wisdom, and in the centre of the throat is the beginning of the ruby wing of direction. The soul is the eternal body, and you as an ego, function within your soul body on whatever plane you may be; whatever the outer covering, the light substance is the eternal one.

Our souls incarnate and take on this substance of earth and manifest through the human body. The insulating condition is the brain; this is a filter which can shut off knowledge or receive it, and become one with the soul. St. Paul knew this sense of separation when the flesh warred with the spirit, and it aggravated him beyond measure. Through the Technique of Light the fusion of soul and body takes place in the brain - and that is, as it were, the magnetic centre; and through the Light we are able to receive this eternal life energy into the soul body and radiate it into the human body. The soul is the eternal receiver, the point of magnetism drawing from the cosmos eternal energy.

When we have learnt this divine law, "Which was in the beginning, is now, and ever shall be," the human race will function in their human bodies as Jesus functioned here on earth. Through the top of the wing of direction we draw in light which floods the whole of our being. Making the contact with the saliva (which contains the emotional quality of the blood) our souls and our humanity are equally flooded with this condition of receiving energy. In the saliva is the magnetic quality of Light which is drawn in to the white corpuscles, and this contact and the visualising of the petals which fold over this magnetic ruby centre, becomes the fusion of two opposites which make the perfect whole. This contact between real substance and the substance we see with the inner eye of vision becomes the very germ of energy in Light, and I know that all of us who do this exercise simply, will receive into our minds the knowledge of the real mystery of the blood. Your blood is being charged with energy such as He had, and we can follow in His steps - these are the 20th century footsteps with which we can follow Him.

In the rhythm of The Throat exercise you start in the centre of the throat, outlining the petals in turn from left to right and ending up in the centre again. Do not worry if the petals overlap; and count each one in turn, so that you will then never be troubled as to whether you have left one out or not. The ninth petal is our gift of revelation, and revelation is not a condition we can note down, it is a process and you cannot tell the *process* of knowledge when it is revealed. Nor is this revelation in any way limited - it is an unlimited condition and there is no reason why we should not function as Jesus did when we have rid ourselves of all egotism and the clutch of our minds on ourselves.

THE EQUILIBRIUM OF THE NAME
This talk is recorded on cassette tape

I want to talk about one of the most difficult human attributes that any of us could possibly find to earth on a divine wavelength, and that is equilibrium. How hard it is in these days to maintain our equilibrium, to keep balanced. Mentally I think we can achieve a certain amount of peace of mind under very difficult conditions, and we can always do that by retiring from the conflict, but we Christian Initiates can never retire from the conflict. We have to go right into it and still maintain our divine wavelength. We can go into a place and be apart from travail, we can remain on our knees and let the world go by, but Jesus came into the world to do a world's work which was in the midst of human beings to keep His equilibrium, His contact with God and His fellowship with men.

We are always tossed to and fro on the human and spiritual wavelengths.

Sometimes we are up on the week and have had really rather good results; we may be congratulating ourselves that we have got past the danger lights and all should be different now. Then comes an experience that is beyond human bearing and we lose our equilibrium in the way we always did according to our individual temperament. Some people go cold and hard; others explode. Both are a loss of balance and we suffer accordingly. If we are silent hard people and cannot articulate through resentment but bury it deep down, the reaction will appear in visible manifestation, possibly a long time after. A person who explodes gets the reaction from resentment over quickly.

It is of vital importance that we learn how this condition of equilibrium can be maintained without great mental effort. We have to realise it is our physical condition, and control of our mind is never going to be satisfactory.

There always comes a moment when control is bound to snap. It has got to do so because we have to learn a different way. Our control may serve us adequately for forty or fifty years of our life and then we find that as we grow older and life becomes more difficult we have not got the same control; little things annoy us out of proportion to their size, and we call it the result of the war or stress of nerves, but it is because we have put faith in a method that is bound to let us down.

I want to give you an exercise today that will never let you down, it cannot because it is learning in our humanity to get the equilibrium of our reaction to physical things. This exercise brings into our consciousness a physical movement. You know mentally that if you do anything in the name of Jesus, **Dyè-Thu-Th**, the brilliant blue triangle at the back of the head, the beginning of receptivity on top of the head, and the beginning of the radiation of the blood through our side, it is the start of the understanding of our infinite capacity. But because we are only human we are apt to put that condition of receptivity and givingness onto a mental-spiritual basis and find it very difficult to translate it into the ordinary conditions of everyday life.

Therefore we come down again, as always, to our hands. With the left hand facing up and the right hand facing downwards, the side of the left little finger touching the side of the right first finger; on the sound of **Dyè-è-è**, visualising the triangle at the back of the head, the left hand moves up and the right moves down. Thus receptivity goes towards the source of receptivity and the right hand, the positive member will be drawn down towards the earth. It is not an exaggerated movement but quite gentle. On the sound of **Thu** and visualising the chalice on top of the head, the hands move back again into the original position. As **Th** sparks through the body, the right hand slips over the left with the fingers towards the wrist, and a spark takes place in the two palms as they make contact. That sparking is a real condition of life; you will not see it although you may feel it, but your faith and consciousness will know it has happened. The hands will gently go back into a position with the palms facing outwards to the world, at shoulder level.

I want you to get an understanding of the different movements. The right hand takes the radiation of the earth, and if over-developed, you get what we call eastern magic conditions. They are the earth radiations and if you know how to draw them into yourself without contact with the source of life, you are going to get all those visible manifestations which

250

the channel can exercise as power, and has always done so through the ages. Magicians are only scientific minds that have tapped the world resources in their persons. Our scientists exteriorise in every instrument, except the physical body, to demonstrate the laws of earth radiations. The old magician had not the knowledge of the modern scientist but he knew his body could receive and transmit very magnetic radiations that would have a most powerful effect on ignorant minds who would not know how easy it was to do.

Power coming into you and the inducing of power are irreconcilable experiences. You can either induce powerful radiations, or surrender them and be filled with power. Jesus and Lucifer knew those two opposites, and Jesus is the greater soul because He surrendered personal power, but Lucifer never did so. The conflict goes on to this day in Lucifer's agents and Christ's agents; either channelhood or personal demonstration. That was the temptation of Jesus by Lucifer. "Demonstrate your power; you have got it; you know everything that is to be known about the power of earth radiations. They are greater on this earth than anything you are going to receive; demonstrate it." Lucifer knew that if he could make Jesus demonstrate power he had got Him, and the world, but Jesus put Lucifer behind Him and was able to make His contact and demonstrate finally in the resurrection and ascension the freedom from that unbalance which Lucifer represents; the unbalance of complete worldly power compared with the balance of receptivity and transmission.

Get this clear in your mind. You may come into contact with, or read about, people who have demonstrated the most marvellous miraculous effects and you may be puzzled as the people were in the time of Jesus. Why is one method better than another? They said that if Beelzebub could heal, what was the point of Christ's healing and why did He relate them to the Father, for Beelzebub could do the same things on the earth radiation without contact with the Father? They could not see the difference as the result was apparently the same.

That is where you and I must be able to get our own revelation concerning the source of power because in us is the knowledge of our own potential capacity to exert power. We are all in it and are tempted as Jesus was tempted. Jesus never denied the fact that He was tempted, nor did He say that He was beyond temptation. He went through it and triumphed through it, but never denied that it was temptation. Do not let us deny our potential capacity for temptation to exert power over people who are ignorant concerning the source.

Therefore this exercise, which is very simple will bring about the consciousness in ourselves of our capacity to receive power and our unconscious transmission of it. That is the difference. If you induce power you consciously transmit it; but if you receive power, you unconsciously transmit it. If you know you have been the agent for a manifestation that has perhaps arrested the attention of your friends or acquaintances and they will focus that thing on you, do not receive it because if it has been done through you, it is not you that have done it. If it has been done by you, you have not tapped the Source but you have fallen into the temptation of transmitting power by the influence of your mind.

We have to be so filled with integrity over this condition of channelhood. If a thing is done by us we shall be very aware, but if a thing is done through us we shall not be aware. This condition is the freedom from our egotism and that inherited sense of power which we have all got, whether or not it is derived from the ancient knowledge which we all possess. We would not be following in the path of the Christian Initiation if we had not been through the old initiations. You would not be here if we had not been through the old initiations. You would not be here if subconsciously you did not know the truth concerning the law up to the time of Jesus. Possibly you know it subconsciously in your blood and the moment occurs when that consciousness comes to the fore and temptation will arise to deny Christ and the new path. You will not be tempted as Jesus was, but as we are capable of being tempted. This way is not an imitation of Christ but following in His footsteps along the way of our individual capacity and fulfilment. According to our different environment or past, so will our temptation be. It may come through love, or pride, or any attribute of ourselves, but that temptation is bound to come to all of us.

Therefore this exercise to enable us to receive the equilibrium of emotional reaction must be done in the Name of Jesus because there is no other power of fulfilment or freedom in any name except His. It is in the very radiation of that receptivity and transmission and equilibrium that freedom lies. So once, at some time during the day, will you do this exercise of the Equilibrium of the Name; the left hand always up in the receiving position, the right hand down in the positive direction of earth radiation.

Have them touching, not one more positive, nor the other more receptive than the other.

Many people are mentally and spiritually extremely receptive but positively and practically disconnected. They have not got the balance of the earth radiation and that is what anaemia really is - a lack of balance of the substance of the blood and of the red corpuscles of the blood. You may be extremely intellectually and intelligently receptive but be irritated at the need for equilibrium over the practical conditions of life. Both men and women have the difficulties of the human temperament on that side.

Many men find it difficult to be concerned with the order of life and human existence but are more concerned with the invisible laws of human life. Because we have a knowledge of the perfection of material and spiritual law as it operates in heaven, we are so outraged by the way material law functions on earth. Therefore the instinct of human nature is to go away, and the moment human nature gets away from the earth contact it loses the power of radiation of the red corpuscles and gets an imbalance in the physical condition.

I do not want anybody to force themselves to take a practical view of life but I want this to be a condition of receptivity. We have to inherit the earth in the right hand and to inherit heaven and the cosmic rays in the left hand. Do it in The Name of perfect equilibrium.

That which will come out from our hands at the end of the exercise in a radiation of equilibrium will be an infection for others to pick up. There is no need to do the exercise more than once a day. If you have got a place that is antipathetic to you, or a room in a house where trouble takes place, do the Equilibrium in that room where it is most difficult to keep equilibrium or where people who have contacts need to keep their equilibrium in spite of difficulties.

It is getting the instrument in perfect harmony before you are able to give out. We prefer to bottle our own exasperation and give out what we have not got. We want to give out peace, but we have not first prepared ourselves to receive it. We cannot give more than we receive, but if we are prepared to receive equilibrium, we have something to give. We are giving what we have received, and not our own disharmony.

The moment our positive and receptive terminals have sparked, the immediate result is an unconscious outpouring.

THE INFINITE EIGHT

We have been taught along many lines an apprehension and an understanding of the Law, and suddenly comes the clear conviction that until His will is done on earth as it functions in heaven, there can be no certainty of truth in any individual mind. If our human minds had a certainty of truth we should all be manifesting the Law. We are all trying to comprehend the truth with our minds and trying to direct it into those channels of manifestation which are most congenial to us. We have not arrived at the stark reality that only in our flesh and blood is our law of truth going to be manifested at all.

In future there will be an end of the written word; the Word is to be made flesh and is to dwell among us. We have to *become* this that has been written through all the ages, a living, vibrating law which will be the embodiment of truth. There are those of us who have been satisfied with the fringe of experience and have developed the seeing eye - many of us have it, but this is not enough; there is the necessity to earth the truth in each one of us and that is not possible solely through the eye. I realise that the opening of the eyes and the mouth is the manifestation of truth of the individual personality.

We face the world, each with our individual condition of disharmony, either exposed or secret. There is not one of us who has not some condition of disharmony that may not be manifest to the world but which does exist in our bodies. As long as something is not known to others we feel it is not so true as something that is known; to oneself, one can always refuse to face a fact which is not yet public property. But we have chosen to have our secret disharmonies brought into view for one purpose only, and if there is any condition of separation from the Christ energy, according to the capacity to receive, so will be the capacity to manifest the cause of the disharmony.

The Christ within will bring out into the open the lack of truth in the individual personality; not as a punishment, not through resentment or separation from Himself, but in such a condition of love and with such a desire to give happiness and contentment, that all the things which we are capable of spoiling and mis-understanding must be driven from our hearts until there is no secret condition in our being which we are not willing to bring into the open to be transmuted and finished with. When the truth is manifested in the individual he has no consciousness of it. It comes like a flash of lightning, it suddenly is, and no kind of thought or pleasant behaviour, nor any outward manifestation of the desire for truth will bring that condition about. Only the drastic self-surrender of the substances of our nature which are insulating us at this moment from the Christ love can lead to that emotionless condition of love, and that transcendental stillness which has to be an experience, and not a mental apprehension. At the moment when you are utterly still in yourself, and utterly free in yourself, then that it is when the Christ within becomes a unity of flesh and blood.

It is impossible to pass on an experience, but I must pass on the method by which we achieve this experience, and that which comes through me insists that the only way by which we can become the will of God is by this surrender of the mind. The comprehension of the progressive stages are the revelation of our within-ness, and cannot be gauged or compared or anticipated. I have no idea how the Christ in you would manifest, because for each individual it must always be a most unexpected happening and never an anticipated one.

There is a moment of quickening in the flesh and blood of the body of a child not yet born, and in our rebirth there is a moment of quickening of flesh and blood which has nothing to do with the mind any more than the quickening of the child has anything to do with the mother. She is the channel for that life to become manifest and the parent can do nothing, but only as a channel, fulfil the law. This rebirth of ours follows exactly the same law. We get ready, our limbs are formed, but we have to await full manifestation because our minds are adult and through the centuries have absorbed, and still cling to, so much knowledge concerning the things of this world. The quickening of the soul in the human body takes place when the individual has grown to the stature of reconstruction. We are going through this process of becoming new, and it is not just a vague promise. It is the law and there is no condition of our humanity that cannot and must not follow along this law of reconstruction; but the moment our minds operate and try to assist the law, we hinder and prolong the process.

I feel we have all been led astray by our own desires. We have so wanted to be the will of God, but our minds have misled us. We have done what our minds have suggested and try to justify our desires, and if we have had any supernormal experience we have not waited for the true interpretation of that experience to follow. When an interpretation of an experience is mentally projected by the individual, the law is not made manifest. The experience and the interpretation must be an instantaneous realisation. This realisation is coming to members of our community; some of us have arrived at an understanding of unity with the Will, and through them this wholeness can be made manifest. The trail is earthed and this manifestation is, and will be, a progressive manifestation. We shall find that the law is a condition and once we become the law, there is no separation in mind or experience. It is the most thrilling thing. You do not ask what you can do to bring this about, you simply say, "It happened like this, and I watched it happening."

There has to be an understanding of what this inside watching of our spiritual self really is. We have not got to look outside, but to look in and become one inside, and the exercise that I am giving you will elucidate for you this understanding, and will bring about an effortless fusion. The great shaft of light coming down from the left, going to the right foot, circling back round both feet, then flashing across in front and arching over, comes from infinity; it is earthed by the individual and encircles him. It flashes up and I want you to visualise it travelling round the arc of heaven where it is like a pulse of light. As you bring down the light and send it round

and back again, it is a travelling condition, and we are linked up in consciousness with the brethren in Light.

When the exercise was shown to me I saw the throne and the whole hierarchy of heaven. They were a great group of individuals, and this arc of light passed completely round and down, and I became one with the whole hierarchy of heaven. We do this exercise, and it is not presumption to know that we are made in the likeness of God.

The object of the incarnation was that humanity should return to this sublime condition of the freedom of those who have finished with earth experience. It has been only a separation of experience and now we are to be joined in experience. Eight is the number of the Christ, as above, so below. He was the first incarnate personality who joined in oneness of experience with the Father, and this recognition of our capacity for unity is, and will be, felt on this exercise.

I am only interested in becoming the Technique in such accuracy of formula that the results are inevitable. I do not worry or care about results, they are as inevitable as the pouring of water into a glass, and you do not meditate about pouring it out. I do not meditate about pouring it out. I do not meditate about the fact of the light circling around, and I am joined in oneness of obedience with those making this world a new condition of Light. I cannot direct light, I can only be an agent for it to be earthed, and directed by the Christ to where ever the need is. I am certain that the radiation of His garment was of that quality of light which we are going to earth round our feet. It comes from the Christ and returns to Him. I think the one thing I want to stress is that there is no separation between these two worlds except the separation of experience. Once we experience oneness we are at the disposal of the two worlds. Where ever He wants us to go, or whatever He wants us to do, there is no difference between the will of God functioning there or here; and there is no difference between us and those who have passed over, because all are manifesting and all are obedient to the law.

The need for a new condition of light in the world should help us to understand the need for each one of us to develop our capacity for impersonal service. We are inclined to think over-much of our own personalities and our little egos. I do not want you to have any synthetic condition of false sacrifice of personality, but to realise that the ecstasy of impersonal service transcends anything that can come on a personal wavelength. One does not have to sacrifice the personal wavelength; once one is, and can be used, the old conditions drop away and are discarded.

The joy of effortless agency is a heavenly experience. The body registers tirelessness, happiness and desirelessness - the opposite of all the teachings which insist that a desireless condition should be imposed. Once our desires fall from us we are not conscious of having done anything to bring about that state of happiness. I am surprised to find myself so happy and am not conscious of having done anything or of having given up anything. I have made no effort and yet I know that I think I am the happiest person existing. I cannot share the experiences that have brought me this condition, but it is nothing that I have tried to achieve. I thought I would never be able to achieve the condition, that I was only asked to be the book of the words, and that others would manifest the law. Now I know that this condition cannot be denied to any one of you. Not one of you can say "I will do it quicker than so-and-so." It is not a question of time. I have been the longest, and not the quickest, in this work. Neither is it a question of mental apprehension, and anyone in this class can experience a unity with the Christ. It will not be anything like you expect or as you think it will be. Nothing that has ever been written on the emotional side or the scientific side of what Christ is, bears any resemblance to His capacity to manifest Himself directly to each of us. We shall not be a standard manifestation of truth, but truth will be manifested when we become the law of utter freedom and happiness. How we are all going to express that happiness and freedom must be differentiated. Christ's desire is to create a unity of differences. Two opposites make a whole, and this marvellous unity of differences is so thrilling and exciting and unlike anything that we can imagine. Do not mistake the process for the end; but if we understand that it is not a comparative condition or something we can miss, we can help ourselves and quicken the process.

We may have an idea in our minds that possibly this way is not meant for everybody, or that everybody comes through an experience and is not meant to do anything else. One must not even impose that limitation on the power of Christ to function. Nobody is "not meant" to do anything. If you have been through a dark forest and come out, and then have gone back to show the way, you know you are following a path that leads to a clearing, however dark the wood may seem. I have not worked on a certainty, for one can only receive it.

Your ideas are not true unless you manifest them. One's sense of revelation has to be used for the material, and the understanding of why one had to do a certain thing comes afterwards. This exercise of the Infinite Eight can be done during the day when you feel a great need of unity and to be an agent for earthing the truth. You are there to make it possible for this unity to take place. "Greater love hath no man than this, that a man lay down his life for his friends." Do get the living side. The moment you lay down your personality, you lay down your life, and become one with the tremendous radiance of life.

SAH-VEH

This talk is recorded on cassette tape

The purpose of the Christian Initiation is to allow us to get free in the head, or body, or inside of the body, whatever is due for freedom. You have only to do the Technique, and the Light will work in you according to your need.

You cannot direct the Light. We are so officious and want to direct power: if we feel we are receiving power our instinct is to direct it to where we want it to go. That is the old method of the initiate but is not that of Christ or the Christian Initiate. Christ never directed the power onto the individual; He was the vehicle through whom they drew power, and the difference between drawing and directing is very great. The responsibility lies on the person who draws it in, and not only on the vehicle who receives. Christ was always receiving from the Father and was always ready to be drawn on. He said "Ye have not, because ye ask not." If He had had to direct the power of the Father onto the individual, He would have had a very different mission and life. He could not have done it and people would have accused Him of ignoring them. If the onus had been on Him the failure of the Law would also have been on Him, but He always made the recipient responsible for receiving or not, according to the resistance or non-resistance of their mind.

The only thing that causes non-receptivity is the mental process. If you resist a condition, you cannot receive; resistance precludes receptivity. That is why He was eager that children should come to Him for the childlike mind does not resist, and in many cases gives a better demonstration than the subtle mind which will put up every sort of excuse. I do not suppose there is a human mind which does not do so; the human adult mind reasons out why they are not spiritual and have lost their faith, why they are not very much impressed by Christian living and therefore do not want to emulate the Christian doctrine. When the natural processes are active they are very reasonable. War is accepted as a reasonable condition and the possibility of another war is discussed by people suffering from the last war, and this is still accepted as a possible condition in the near future. Therefore if the mind can accept destructive conditions as normal and reasonable, you can understand how it must resist the mind which precludes war as reasonable and holds that peace of mind and body are a necessity and a possibility.

It is so difficult for us to accept the responsibility of our own mental processes. We are inclined to put them down to inheritance, education, early training, frustrated living, the ingratitude of our friends and colleagues, and all kind of excuses which we make for being ourselves, and not one of them are valid. So it is vitally important to have a technical process which makes it unnecessary for us to reason for ourselves but enables us to get our own certainty without depending on any living soul. Therefore you and I have to face the fact that if we do not achieve it, we render it impossible as a universal condition; but if we do so, we make it possible for everybody else. Thus living becomes an adventure and a crusade comparable to any adventure of the middle ages or crusade of the early centuries.

Today in this ugly modern world we are on the fringe of a new experience, to bring into demonstration a new dimension. What could be more exciting than to be an instrument so receptive to divine contact that we could not fail to manifest it. It must be as natural a condition as breathing, neither abnormal, supernormal nor sensational. There is nothing sensational in healing a person of an incurable disease or taking away grief. There is nothing sensational in committing our frustration to the divine

power, because those things are done in silence and solitude and cannot have a sensational effect. All the great things in Christ's life were done silently, as in the wilderness or Gethsemane. It is difficult to understand why there is a record of these silent conditions, but I am beginning to realise that if a thing has to be recorded, it is done, and the medium for that record must be a human being. When Christ was apparently alone there was still a record of what He said.

In the garden of Gethsemane He was faced with the surrender of His will regarding the pattern of His life, and this has a searching appeal to all Christian Initiates. It makes Him human and a man of the world and gives us an understanding of how He was able to reconstruct His physical substance. He was shown the pattern of reconstruction in that garden, and knew from the world's point of view that it was an impossible situation for His friends to accept. They were looking to Him for great power to be directed into the world and He was being shown a public death.

It was an agony; the whole destruction of His work, with no future on the human side, only a negative condition, death. He who came to give mankind life, and more abundantly than any other human being, was confronted in the prime of His life when all His work lay ahead, with this condition of death and destruction. He could not know whether the pattern was true and whether this obedience to the unseen God would bring about the condition which this God claimed. He had to have complete obedience and confidence. "Go through death and you will be able to reconstruct your physical body." He thought there must be another way and spent hours trying to find the other way in which this world and the next might meet on some line of compromise. He did not care for Himself but for those He left behind and who depended on Him for everything. For them He minded, and then came that wonderful acceptance when all resistance went out of Him. "Not my will, but Thine, be done." How many of us can say that, even in the little things of life?

He was a cosmic figure trying to bring about cosmic reconstruction. If He could do it He could earth the Law and the ability of each individual to take himself back again to God in his physical body. God who was physical demanded the return of His own substance in perfect form as it was created. That was the mission; as He was created so must He return. It had never been done. The mental pattern had been written down on every material substance - wax, paper, stone - but never in flesh. The Law had never been made flesh before and that was His mission, the reconstruction of the physical vehicle, without going through death. Christ had to demonstrate what death was, the resistance of the human mind to love.

You may say that is far fetched and that many people love. There is very little resistance in the human mind to passion, but to love is something quite different. God so loved the world that He sent His Son to die. That is not what we understand. In the war we sent people to be destroyed and die; but what about ourselves, this dying to ourselves and not sending somebody else. Christ went through death Himself for other people. We have not to go through death ourselves for others, but we have to die every day to a bit of our own mental resistance. We have to die on the mental plane and until we have died there, we cannot live on the physical plane. Christ died on the physical plane because He did not have to die on the mental. He had to demonstrate that death was the resistance of the mind to God, and that is always manifested in flesh and blood. Either you resist or you receive. If you receive, you receive life; and if you resist life, which is love, you die.

How can we die on the mental plane effortlessly and happily and bring

261

about a new and living way for all the world? If you can die on the mental plane we can live in the physical world with our neighbour on a perfectly different dimension of power. We shall be 'power' when we have died on the mental plane, but as long as our mind is satisfied with the pattern of the past and the old conditions, and if we have a mind that can direct that power, we are bound to die, not only at the end of our life but to every frustration of our mind. We die when other people oppose us and will not go where we direct them. You have heard it said "something died in me when that catastrophe happened". No true happiness ever dies, for that is eternal; but the frustration of our human will, and the inability to direct power where we want it to go destroys our peace of mind. To be peaceful in our mind is to be happy, but happiness and radiance earthed in us are not affected by our mind at all, they transcend the mind.

Jesus incarnated to give this condition of peace of mind. When we are frustrated by difficulties they can go through us and not hit us, and that is where our freedom lies. I want to give you an exercise to bring that about as an effortless condition.

This is a threefold exercise to be done only at night. At night we add up our daily accounts, and the failure of the day is nearly always heavily paid for at night by thought and remembrance. This exercise will help to transcend mental resistance to pain, whether physical or mental. It will earth a condition greater than your resistance. This was shown me when I was beginning to understand the truth through my own experience.

Wisdom must descend and be earthed by you; and love which was on earth must go through your being and ascend back to Love. Then the brilliant ray comes from your left side, which is the reaction when wisdom is earthed and love ascends, and givingness is an effortless radiation from the left side.

I want to talk about the side. I was made aware that the fusion of love in fourth dimensional beings was a throughness from the side. In the third dimension it is the impact face to face, but love that can pass through and on, is an ecstasy we have known in our being and very seldom experienced, an ecstasy of complete oneness of love. I think we have all known it in our conscious-ness, and the frustration of our human life is caused because when we are in love we think we are going to repeat something divine. It very rarely comes about in the way our vision has expected it because of our mental condition, and the separation of our mind from our heart and the rest of our body. We think that love is the union of two people in perfect oneness, but that does not happen often. It is a natural condition on the other side which is the place of the union of love.

Earth represents the separation of people who love each other from perfection of union, and it is rare to get two people who love perfectly on the mental and physical plane. You may get people attracted more on one plane than the other, and in time, the friction of disharmony on the mental or physical, shatters the heaven they have anticipated. As they no longer care mentally, it causes physical friction, and they think that love is a mistake and an illusion, yet something in them knows it is not and that it can be wonderful, but only when it is the blending of wisdom, love and givingness, those three conditions.

We have the balance of wisdom and love in our beingness and the direction of love becomes an effortless condition when we do this exercise. I think it is because our mind is focused on the gold, the blue and the white, and we are asked to do it three times, making a track of breath for wisdom and love to travel. You may get muddled if you try to do it simultaneously but I want you to be conscious that it is a simultaneous action. On the first time, bring wisdom down on an outbreath to the sound of **Sah**, and on **Veh**, it goes back. The second time visualise the blue chalice at your feet which ascends on an outbreath to the sound of **Sah** and returns on an inbreath on **Veh**; and the third time look at your left side and become aware of the opening and the radiation of white light which is God's will.

The will of God is a white radiance in which is all colour. When we identify ourselves in wisdom and love with the will of the Father, His will is the radiation of our being and we become His will.

We think of will as a mental condition. When you carry out your will you do it physically, therefore you must look upon the will as an active condition, and the activity of the will of God is a white radiation. Our will is the reaction of our desire, and if we want a thing the desire for it reacts on our emotions and then we do it. The pattern comes first into our mind and the reaction comes into visibility. It is the same with the will of God, it is the reaction of a law. The Law of wisdom and love must react in the individual as an absolute certainty. His will will radiate out of you and you will not have to impose it through your mind. It will become your radiation and power that things may be done through His will.

263

When Christ said "Not my will but Thine be done," it was this great radiance that would carry Him right through to the reconstruction of His physical body. He had to do it along the law of His receptivity to wisdom and His love. If He had not had the love of the human world in His heart He could not have done it, for He could not have done it by strength of will. A strong willed person can be destructive, but God who has the strongest will on earth, is a creative condition. His will creates harmony, peace, prosperity, health. This is His will, and when that comes out of you, people will bask in the radiation. It comes because you have surrendered your desire for knowledge with the earthing of divine wisdom.

Wisdom and knowledge are two different things. Knowledge is the result of human desire and is transmitted through the brain. Wisdom is the radiation of divine will, which is the result of individual living experience.

THE RHYTHM OF THE NAME

Correspondence Course Notes and Cassette Tape

We need to understand the law of protection, because to protect or be protected against catastrophe and unwelcome conditions often seems as though we were employing something magical or superstitious.

We need protection from a destructive condition. The answer to darkness is light; the answer to destruction is creative energy. One has always to find something stronger than the force that is against us, and one reason for the incarnation was that Christ should earth a force stronger than magic. He came and He did it, and we have the capacity to understand how He did it.

Christ said "Be of good cheer, I have overcome the world." What did the world represent? The world represented the domination of the human mind over material conditions. There were the magicians who could understand the laws that governed this world; there have always been some scientific minds that have understood the possibilities of natural law dominating material conditions. I dare say you have come across many conditions in your life which you have not understood and may have been frightened about; certain things frighten everybody.

People are sometimes frightened of happiness and do not like to be too happy but must throw a sop to something they do not understand, like touching wood to avoid possible catastrophe.

I came across placation at Stonehenge but it was absent at Avebury where the harmony of the natural forces was earthed. At Stonehenge there was the fear of the moon and the placating of the moon's forces. Through every individual life you will find superstition and inner fear because we are not aware of how to control the forces that may destroy us, our health, happiness, prosperity and security, and we cannot insure against them. You cannot insure against an act of God, and no insurance company will do so.

We know that if we turn on the light the darkness goes, and the light is stronger than any condition of darkness; but we have not that same confidence in the possibility of our spiritual nature being stronger than somebody else's mental domination. It does not follow that we may be strong minded and cope with definite forces of jealousy, revenge and ignorance if they are directed against us. Uneducated people may have great knowledge of conditions that might frighten us.

265

In all countries natural laws about which we know nothing and of which we are afraid, are known by the peasants and handed on by word of mouth from one generation to another. We may come across nature forces in any place and say that it is only superstition with nothing in it, but people who know realise that there is always something at the back of a fear. I have had things given to me to psychometrise because people feared them to be evil.

So today I am going to give you an exercise by which you can cope with every condition of your life, everything that threatens your happiness or security; all those unconscious fears and uncomfortable circumstances that arise at unexpected times. Often when we want to be of use to somebody we find ourselves a prey to some unconscious fear.

The only human being who had no fear in Him was Jesus. I have given you His Name, the **Dyè-Thu-Th**, by which you become part of His fearlessness, but that is not enough because it has really to do with your own personal substance of flesh and blood, that your physical self may tune in to His physical self. Now I am talking of being able to be an agent for people who do not know anything about Him and you want to have some means of protection for their vulnerability and receptivity to adverse conditions. You want it because you love them, whether it is somebody abroad or in the next room, you want to be able to help them. You cannot do it by wishful thinking but you need to know the law.

What made Jesus invulnerable to fear? It was a cosmic condition; He was part of a cosmos that was unafraid. There is no fear outside the human mind and it does not exist except in our mind. It is not a substance outside the mental world but we get it as a pattern of our mind and we can bring it into visible manifestation. When we get a shock our saliva glands dry up, we may lose our colour and long after the event we still bear the stamp of fear. Our body reveals our fear and we cannot prevent it.

We want something which will identify us with a condition of protection and confidence and so the exercise of the Rhythm of the Name was given to me. It is a cosmic condition and concerns world conditions and all the elements, water earth and air. It is a protection against fire and all destructive conditions regarding human beings. We all know here from our experience during the war that it is a protection against all destructive energy. It is not because we did anything, but because we became the agents for earthing a condition which was greater than the power of destruction of matter. By tuning in to creative energy, the body is stronger than the destructive condition. If you will learn to be the agent for it, you can protect every person you care for, and you yourself must be included.

It is His Name earthed on a cosmic wavelength, coming down to your feet because they are a focal point for Him. He needs the earthing of it, and His feet earthed it two thousand years ago. The feet of the disciples earthed it in every part of the world and that was why He sent them out. He knew it must be done through the feet of the disciples and He sent them out two and two. You will get the understanding of how the distribution of this condition must become a world experience.

Visualise the triangle of brilliant blue light of His Name and the white light arching over, and at the moment when you stop doing these arches, the blessing comes and the essence of His love is earthed.

The Rhythm of the Name is for two definite conditions, one for people and the other for places, such as ships or aeroplanes or anything you want to protect. The silver chalice is of a resolving substance and if you have an enemy or someone with whom you have quarrelled, visualise them standing with you in the chalice. There may be a group of people, or only one, but the chalice is large enough to contain that which you want to harmonise with yourself and bring into a condition of harmony. The chalice is of perfectly plain hand-beaten silver, like the old chalices or communion cups. Stand in it and put your disharmony into it, and then bring down this cosmic rhythm. You are now on the threshold of a new experience, and only that experience will be able to convince you of this protection.

Through this exercise you can focus and eliminate noise, and in doing the Rhythm of the Name over any area, know that destruction is not stronger than God. You can shut out everything if you keep your mind focused on Him. It can never be agitating for one feels secure the moment one can throw the Rhythm over. Throw it over your room and your house at night and to every part of the world.

You can do it for people even if they are not in the same place and if you are angry with someone and cannot bear that condition to go on, stand with them in the chalice. If you are throwing protection over a house, visualise the blue triangle (on the sound of **Dyè-è-è**) coming down on your right, running under the foundations and going up on the other side; and then throw the Rhythm over, a dome of light that goes over the top of the roof making a shape of complete protection of light. I have done it over aeroplanes in the battle of Britain and over ships when seeing someone off. It is a condition of protection which nothing can deflect.

You can do it inside a room and since that exercise has been given, it is always done in the room during the lectures because it gives you and me the maximum ability to receive the revelation He needs to radiate through us. It makes us receptive on our cosmic wavelength; everything that happens here is done on the Rhythm of His Name.

Christ knew He had overcome world destruction but the knowledge of how everyone can save the world has been lost. There is the possibility for all of us in the future to be used for creating peace and harmony. Our mind can never be afraid of destruction as we can always concentrate on creative energy. Then by degrees there will be fearless minds, confident of their capacity to earth a new and living way.

It will be so wonderful when we no longer live in the circle of our own fears. The urgency we have put into words of prayer can now be put into deeds by prayer. Every time you put the Rhythm of the Name over a house you are creating a new condition of protection.

Often we do not have the protection we might because we forget to ask for it. Every day must have its own quota of light and energy, life and health, and I cannot give you anything to take you over next week. If you do it today, you must do it again tomorrow. We can all have protection and health every day if we ask for it every day. We are so accustomed to accumulating and expect the doctor to make us well for as long as possible. It was the same with the manna which the people had to have fresh every day; they tried to gather it up and keep it but it went bad. Our health deteriorates because we do not get it afresh every day. The Technique in Light has been given to us for that purpose, to get fresh experience, energy, protection every day, and then we cannot decay and grow old; but we shall grow old and rheumatic and depressed unless we get our joy and vitality every morning and midday, and get our cleansing every night. That is the purpose of the Technique in Light, so that we get our rebirth, our renewal and reconstruction of the old self, and so there comes a time when the old self will have passed away and the new self becomes integrated.

There is no need for memory. What we were yesterday does not concern today and there is no reason to think back or try to mould our life on past exerperience. What one can do today is the most important thing in life; no matter what we were like yesterday we need not fail today.

Do the Rhythm of the Name mostly at night over your friends and send them protection, but it is of great use if you are working in a place where you find the atmosphere is very difficult. It does not matter whether you take those difficult people at night or before you meet in the morning, put them in the chalice then bring down the **Dyè-è-è** three times and send over the **Thu** like a current or movement in light. You can take three breaths for the **Dyè-è-è**, but start it on an outbreath and begin the **Thu** on an inbreath. You can do it inside a room or outside. When you are doing the Rhythm for a place at a distance, visualise that place, not going there yourself or identifying yourself with it, but being the transmitter, as if you were being used as an instrument sending out wavelengths. Thus He can send out a person who cares enough to be of service, a profound condition of protection for all in need.

THE RHYTHM OF THE NAME

I want to give you an exercise you will love, and which you must never do for yourselves alone. It is for world conditions of receptivity and peace - whether the world is the world of your own home, or a school or meeting, or a larger group like a nation. All the previous exercises have been for the preparation of impersonal service and you must have transmuted your personality to a condition of emptiness of self. Do not think it is the same thing as making the mind a blank. There is really no such thing as this for a blank mind has self in it. This is the reverse. It is the emptying of one's own personal reaction to conditions, and the receiving of the vibration of the heart, brain and mind of Christ; transmitting into the body the eternal vibration of the humanity and divinity of the Christ.

It is called the Rhythm of His Name.

You have had The Name and the Equilibrium of the Name, and now comes the Rhythm of the Name, which is a world condition.

Will you visualise a silver chalice which is large enough for you and one other, or a group of others, to stand in. It is the quality of hand-beaten silver light, which must not be confused with any other light. I know that this chalice is made of the inner lining of the esoteric chalice which the church has preserved and which Jesus formed. He gave the understanding to the twelve of this inner lining of the great chalice of the world.

Stand in the chalice and always have someone in it with you, either a friend or neighbour or a public figure or a group of people. They can face you or be facing the same way as you are. When you have visualised the chalice you need not think of it again, for seeing it makes it. I find it dissolves into Light and I am no more conscious of its presence.

Bring down the **Dyè** on the right of you to the ground, on an outbreath. Run it along the back of your feet and send it up on the left side to your Infinite Point of Radiance. You will find you are all standing in a doorway of light. Bring down the side of the triangle and do the base on an outbreath, and send it back on an inbreath: but do not worry too

much about your breath. The triangle is of the blueness of diamonds, which has white in it. Bring it down and leave it to do its work.

The **Thu** is an arc of light with a beat of eight in it which starts from the ground on your left, and arches up and over you and down on the right side. Another arc then comes from the ground at the back of you and crosses over you to the front. This **Thu** is of the same substance in Light but a different rhythm; so it is working like a current of light, arching with an eternal rhythm of eight beats. It crosses above us, arching over the group. Go on doing that **Thu** until you find you no longer need to do it. The utter givingness of His Name comes into us in the moment it happens. You do nothing and it comes. It is His spirit coming into us and the group which we have committed to Him. All you have to remember is to do the **Dyè** and the **Thu**.

We cannot ourselves do the **Th** - the third part of His Name, for then union with His vibration takes place. We can only, as it were, prepare the setting and leave it to Him.

The Rhythm can be done over impersonal things. Bring down the light on the side of the house, along the base and up. Do the Rhythm over the place where your loved ones are, to keep them in the Rhythm of His Name. I do this every night when I am in bed. You need not visualise yourself in connection with it. Visualise any place and bring the Rhythm over it as an arc. You do not need to go on doing it indefinitely. Once you have been the agent for earthing Him, the vibration of His love, it functions and goes on functioning. If you have made that act of contact of the world with His love of the world it must go on vibrating. The only way that Christianity has continued has been through the people who have earthed His love.

Do you realise what power it has? There were only twelve beside Him who knew of this certainty that the human being is the only agent who can earth the love of God; and when once the physical perfection has been lived and earthed that vibration is a living reality because of the service of the individual soul. Shakespeare was quite incorrect when he said, "The evil that men do lives after them, the good is oft interred with their bones." For good lives to a greater degree than evil, and it is a *living* vibration which is picked up. There *is* such a thing as Holy ground, where the feet of an incarnate soul who has been in contact with the

Christ, have trod the earth. People feel happy there though they may not know why, because some soul has earthed in that place a quality of love which has not been spoilt by the egotism of personality.

When we do this exercise we earth the rhythm of impersonal love. We have been given so much, and we are ready to give something to the world. We draw the light down and send it out, but we are nothing. It is not a superior condition, but it is just the beginning of our power to empty ourselves, and use our love for the service of all alike. It is the essence of the power to forgive our enemies. Mentally it is impossible to forgive those who have sinned against our vanity and egotism, and who have hurt us. We ought to forget, but there is no forgetting of a broken law. Bring into the chalice not only those whom you want to protect, but your enemies, and even the people who bore us! See what this can do to open their minds. If people have strong prejudices put them into the Rhythm of His Name, rather than bearing with them.

Never let them know you have done this. The fun of it is that we need never talk about ourselves and make people feel indebted to us. They cannot owe us anything. We can only receive, and be forgiven as we forgive. Therefore if we are given a chance of understanding it is the opening of a door for us - we are not doing them a service. We are providing ourselves with another door to walk through which was locked before our hardness of heart, and the gain is ours. In our forgiveness we can go forward.

I know that some of us have the urge to take people quickly along the Technique, and to give them more than they can receive, and more than is in our power to give. We cannot open doors for other people which are shut to us. To love your neighbour as yourself is first to go through the agony of opening that door, and then we can keep it open. Until we have opened the door of freedom from loss of equilibrium we cannot go through that door and keep it open.

Prepare yourselves by doing the Technique on yourselves. When we have finished with our little selves, then the joy of knowing what an agent's life is really like - the happiest and fullest and healthiest that can be conceived!

When we are worried about our own health, realise that it is only a condition of our mind being brought into physical expression. There must be a leak somewhere; the whole energy of an untroubled mind would go to the reconstruction of the physical body. We destroy our bodies through our mental life; mentally we commit

suicide. Realise that all illness and even accidents that occur, come upon us because that is the way we are going to learn. We must understand that if our mind is transmuted, we can both stop disease that we have, and we can stop making new trouble for the future.

We do away with all luck and get a certainty of direction. No evil need come nigh us, not because we are being protected but because we are invulnerable by our radiation. When this condition has been earthed, all catastrophes will cease. There is no limitation which any of us need sit under. We have been given the power to reconstruct ourselves, and today can include all others as well. Bring all into it, so that this unity of mind and understanding shall be a universal condition. We shall all be one.

At every single class you have ever attended there has been someone doing the Rhythm of the Name for us, uniting our minds in a condition of receiving.

Send the Rhythm on in advance for a difficult interview which you fear, so that the rhythm of peace shall be waiting for you. Do not prepare, but simply earth the Rhythm of love, peace and harmony, and do not let your own mind work to destroy it.

You can leave in safety the result of any circumstance which you have prepared by doing the Rhythm. You will get direction as to what to say and do.

If you are troubled, do not think that any condition is too trivial to be put in the Rhythm. It is for the greatest condition in life, and for the least. I could not function on any line of everyday life unless I knew I could receive His direction, and leave it.

Put those whom you love and are worried about into the Rhythm. Most of one's pain is caused by the inability of those whom we love, to receive, because they do not believe. If you do the Rhythm for them, and then do not measure the result in time, it must work. Do not have a clear idea as to what you think the perfection of the working of the Rhythm of His Name will be. It is always unexpected. Do it at least once a day for other people, and as often as you like.

HI-YOU-MEH
Our Light Bodies

Last time, when we talked about the **Hi-You-Meh**, we mentioned the wing of direction and several people have asked me to say more about it. One cannot talk of it as a thing apart as it is a very important member of the soul body.

I realise that I have always stressed the point that we must earth the light in our physical bodies, and have perhaps neglected the question of the world of Light. I want to make clear to you the points of unity between heaven and earth, especially as we are trying to overcome the mental separation between the old knowledge we have learnt and the new that we tune into. The only difference between this world and the next is the experience which comes through our brains and our minds. It is our reactions to truth which make up experience. Once you know the same angle of truth as someone else, you see things the same way. Your human experience has to be synchronised in time; we are gradually catching up with the truth that has been told to the world for two thousand years.

Our soul, or light body, is a real thing here on earth. It is the eternal container of our spiritual energy, which is directed in our physical body through the brain, and in our soul body through the throat. That energy pours through our soul body, into the wing of direction, and directs our human life according to the amount of energy it receives. Up till now we have been dependent on the direction of our brain, which is of the substance of a receiving set. Receiving and transmitting should be a dual condition but we have turned our brains into transmitting sets without first receiving. So long as the physical brain dominates, we are dependent on how that brain functions. If it is tired, we forget things.

As children, we are taught to concentrate and to remember. In your soul body there is no need for such concentration. The brain is a substance for receiving thoughts, not for originating them. In our light bodies we do not store knowledge, it comes in and is transmitted in a flash.

The outstanding features of our soul body are three great radiations which look like wings. On our left is the aquamarine wing of love, which looks like water. On our right is the amber of wisdom. These emanate from, and are received into a brilliant trunk of white light, which is of the same substance and brilliant whiteness as the will of God - and that is of the substance of the body of God. No person can know its form, or say "we have seen God," but we can all contact it. As we have more of this substance in our soul bodies, so do we become more aware of it. This I-am-ness of the individual does correspond to the I-am-ness of the body of God and of His substance - just as a child is of the same substance as his parents.

From the trunk of white light radiates every imaginable colour. The ruby red of the wing of direction flashes out between the shoulders and gives us the power to function in alignment with His will. Our brain is the thing that can either receive the will or insulate us from it. Through these radiations comes the natural power to receive daily direction, and also an increased awareness of loss of equilibrium, should the power of the ego dominate the power of receptivity. We are learning more and more to act in alignment with His will as a natural condition.

Your soul is a radiant body, and your spirit is of the radiant energy of God which flows into every being, incarnate or discarnate, according to their capacity to receive it. It is flesh which contains the insulator between soul and body because of the mind. In the beginning when conditions here were similar to those of the world of Light, there was no separation between those here and those there. Then came fear and the separation of the substance of the body from God. *That* is original sin, which is only in the mind of man. There is no fear in the being of God, and as we tune in to Him there will be no fear, no sin, in us.

The **Hi-You-Meh** teaches us to feed our wing of direction with the substance of the divine mind, so that knowledge may be instantly received and never withheld. Separation comes through withholding of knowledge. That is the cause of conditions of decay in the body. In the timeless condition created by the fusion of the two bodies all nervous tensions will be healed. The brain will tighten up and insist on trying to work things out for itself instead of relaxing, so that it may receive the inpouring life energy. We shall learn to have no conditions of congestion. All those nerve tensions which result in blindness and deafness, those tightened arteries that bring inactivity - all those things come because the cells, constructed to receive instantly energy they need, are starved of it through the tension created by the brain. All those nervous tensions must work out through the flesh, so that we may seek and know this Light which will spark through us.

You will receive into your soul such light, such knowledge, that every day will see the recuperation of disharmonious conditions. Jesus had to know the law of perfect forgiveness wherein He was made whole, for in forgiveness lies the healing of all conditions of separation from God. The Technique is for the fusion of soul and body; for shutting away the soul energy starves the body and causes disease. Every nerve and cell should receive its energy. That is why we *must* relax, so that we can receive life in our bodies and knowledge in our brains. There is *no* thing that we cannot receive because there is no withholding in the being of God.

It is not true that ill-health is good for people. We can receive our own forgiveness, happiness and freedom, and this will give us the power to become the agents for freeing other people. We may not know the means by which they shall be freed, but through us they will be able to receive their own direction. Each one of us must be free before we can transmit freedom. That is within the capacity of each one of us.

The time is shortening and our karma is slipping away, because there is more Light and Love earthed in the world than there was even last year. We have a much greater capacity for tuning in than we had. It has nothing whatever to do with goodness. If we know the Law, we are wise if we obey it.

It is not a virtue that we should love; we should give love as we receive it. We help because, through us, the need of others is understood. Christ always said, "Why call me good?" So long as He tuned in to the will of the Father that which He did came in and went out of Him unconsciously. We are always aware of our charities and our good deeds because of our brains. We think we are being virtuous when we do not break the law. Let us learn to receive the Light, and then we shall transmit it as normally as we breathe. What really is before us is to be the living, breathing counterpart of the Christ.

The **Hi-You-Meh** focuses our minds on this timeless, sparking condition. It is so light a thing; one cannot be pompous in Light! The two cutting movements of this exercise do quicken us; they go like a flash, more quickly than our minds can go. We become one with this ray of light which is the I-am-ness. You are making direct contact with the aura, the radiation, of God. Your soul receives first, but the reaction on the flesh follows at once. The power of the breath ray, which runs down the arms, is essential for transmitting. We must arrive at a condition when the Infinite Breath will fuse with us, and out of us; so let us get used to visualising breath and light and so *become* their substance.

Revelation will come to every one of us. Do not worry if you have not yet received truth; experience is individual. There is a power of receiving which can only be experienced by a definite emptying, and that is a thing we have to learn how to do. If we would give our minds and brains a rest, we shall be much more efficient, and much more lovable. Stop badgering your minds.

Your capacity is your capacity just where you are and it does not help to worry about it. You will receive just what you can, but remember, your future expectation should never be based on your past, for one day your capacity will exceed your expectations.

You cannot hasten your receptivity; we try to strain too much. Keep simple and happy, and remember that He gives always because it is His nature to give, but we cannot get until we learn how to receive. When you are ready for a different condition, it will happen.

THE CROSS OF BREATH
On Earthing Love - 1938

I want to make clear to you what I mean by the term earthing. What are we doing when this energy of Love flows through our humanity into the earth? Do we really believe that we can change world conditions and, if so, how is it done?

Let me go back for a minute to an experience I had when I was being trained. It was as if I suddenly saw the world as a magnetic centre, the form of which was a network of fine filaments of living wires of energy, like a minute grill, finer than a cobweb, and this was the basic construction of the world beneath the earth. The first principle in the construction of the world was this filament of energy. I understood that the power that it earthed in the world came through the contact of the substance of the human race with the earth energy. I saw the Christ walking on the earth, and where His feet touched the earth every filament of energy leapt into light. Since then the knowledge of cosmic law has been transmitted into my mind ready for the time when it was necessary for it to be given out.

We have got to understand now where we stand, and what we are trying to achieve. I have talked of the forces of the earth and of the cosmic power that is radiated down into the world. When you understand that the construction of the world is of this condition of energy, you will realise that much depends for its replenishment upon the human race, through whom it has to be transmitted. The world would not have survived without this replenishment through the flesh and blood of incarnate souls. When a civilisation draws from the earth more than it transmits into it, there follows a depletion of earth forces, the balance is upset, and catastrophes like earthquakes occur for which the human race is responsible.

Slowly, ever since the Fall, the earth has ceased to be harmoniously replenished through the selfless desire of the human race to be in contact with God. Once a mind is earthbound, then no condition of spiritual energy comes through that individual to be transmitted through the feet - for every current of life which comes through you must make its contact with the world through the feet. Every civilisation must have its own priesthood and religion; they must draw their spiritual energy from God, by whatever name they call Him, and pass it out again through their groups. That is what religion is for; I am talking of a physical condition, not a mental one, of the physical replenishment of all nature, man included.

The dictators of this century are really modern prototypes of the old priests who had power over people, who tuned into their mind and thought. Those people tuned into a dedicated mind, going through the priest to power, instead of going direct to their God. We see a survival of this in dictatorships, who get power through an individual, but they tune into an earthly power which must ultimately bring complete catastrophe. Their way leads to a depletion of the pure spiritual energy, for this can only be received through a mind that does not dominate other minds through mental power.

Jesus was the first person who demonstrated that the Law of Love was the supreme essence of power; that power must be centred in the heart and not in the brain. The brain must be dedicated to receive and the heart to transmit. When you transmit through the heart it must be a conscious condition. You must *know* the Law in order to *become* the Law. In no other condition is it so necessary for individuals to know the Law and become the Law themselves. In dealing with any other powers, only one person need hold and draw the power from other minds, and having got this unity of mind they can forward their condition. When an individual is tuned into the mind of God, getting direction individually for themselves, then there is a unity of mental power, and everybody is a unit, with no mass production. Now that I see what one individual can do to change the whole earth current, I begin to understand the prophecies of Jesus, for the harmony of nature depends on the earthing of the Law of Love. We say that nature is cruel, but it suffers because man is cruel and has not been one in Love. Nature cannot receive the power that one incarnate soul can receive. When that power is being consciously received into the mind and is consciously transmitted through the heart, then it has domination over the waning condition of nature, and is one with all beauty, and is above destruction.

This earthing of spiritual power is our individual responsibility. Through walking the earth we can change its condition into one of peace, through our feet. We must know the Law, and understand that we must not continue to starve the world by just drawing to ourselves the power the world can give us. We must understand that we have only to receive transcendentally the power transmitted from on high;

whereas up to now we have tried to receive power from the earth forces.

We have not only got to understand what emptiness is, we have got to be it. Only by being an empty vessel can this transcendental energy come into us. It is a transcendental filling that fills without any hiatus. As soon as we are empty of self we are filled, and the transmitting follows inevitably. Where we are, where we walk, we shall give out some condition of peace. The transition stage between the old and the new is a definite condition of human nature and in earth conditions, because the emptying of old bottles to contain the new wine is disintegrating, and we always look upon this condition of disintegration as a catastrophe. It is so painful that we cannot believe that it precedes peace and beauty. Only the experience of getting through it can be our guarantee, because it is something which happens apart from our minds and imagination.

We cannot imagine what the Law is like, we can only know through experience. We must hold on to our certainty that the power will function through us. We can be saviours of the world but first we must save ourselves. It is not selfish to learn to swim for then, at a moment's notice, you are ready to help a drowning person. It cannot be selfish to see ourselves as empty channels, able to earth this

energy of Love. This cannot be done without the human body and that is why the human race is so necessary to the earth. We humans are dependent upon the fruits of the earth, and the earth is dependent upon the human race for replenishment from on high, for the energy and life of the world. That mutual love should be the link between us. We must realise that we are giving to the earth something that it needs, and we must not be materialists who take from the earth and give nothing back. The nearer and nearer we get to God, the emptier our minds become and then this great enrichment of ourselves and of the world takes place.

This vibration of breath is the essence of power, and the emptiness of the human being is the zenith of spiritual power on earth. Breath is power. When you are drawing breath into your body, you are receiving the power of the Holy Spirit. You are looking at the inside of yourself, which is empty, and you are sending out through your arms, as the substance of breath, such a power that it must come out through your hands and feet. This cannot be consciously directed. It will in future be the condition of our aura, of our physical selves. Do it once in the middle of the day and at any time when you are feeling rather full of yourself. It is a quiet and peaceful condition, and if only you can take time to do it, it stops an increased ego from taking command. Sometimes we feel on top of our form, and then by tuning into such a condition of energy and peace of mind, we can know all this energy will not be directed into any wasteful channel. No joy and happiness is ever wasted in the world.

Will you in future begin to visualise this great possibility of oneness with nature, which must include oneness with God. Then will taking and giving be a balanced condition and you will get an equilibrium of the earth forces and the cosmic forces meeting in your body. The human will then love life, and will give as much as he takes. Then will there be a new heaven and a new earth. The souls who have loved and tried to live perfectly on earth will make a new heaven, not having failed in their experiences, living in love both here and over there. This is a future within the grasp of each one of us.

A group tuning in to the mind of Christ is a greater force than a majority tuning into the mind of a dictator. Now is the harvest. The wheat and the tares have grown together; now the tares are showing themselves and we can see them. The reaping is going to make the separation. There must be conflict between those who are for world power, and those who are for the Christ; through them the balance will be adjusted. We cannot work it out through our minds; we cannot make people see this condition, for we are not able to show it in words, but only in deeds.

In the ancient mysteries, the ritual for drawing on the power had nothing to do with the heart, but was entirely of the brain, which should be a receptive instrument. They drew, held, stored and transmitted power, but without conscious contact with Love. Jesus came to show that the greatest power was conscious contact with the Father, through the heart and not the brain. We have the formula for how to use earth power, for much power is stationed in the world, but it will not last. It has been earthed through people.

One dedicated person has far greater power than thousands who are undedicated. The new earth will be when what He is giving out to the few becomes the knowledge of the many. We do not know anything, so we must go to the Christ for knowledge. We must go to the one cosmic being who can give it to us. We can earth a change in the condition of the world, which will make for beauty and health, which should be natural conditions.

Because of the past insulation through man, the redemption of the earth must come through him consciously and voluntarily. The feet of the Christ lighted up the grid of the world upon which He walked, and so its current was charged. It is we who are the only insulating condition. If we all did that charging we should have a perfect world. The old civilisations took more than they gave, so one after the other they fell into decay.

THE CROSS OF BREATH
A talk on current events - 30th May 1940

This morning it is most important to get an understanding of the difference between inspiration and imagination. They are things we are vitally concerned with and it is most difficult at the present time to keep our minds free for inspiration, they are so full of pressure, of apprehension. When does our imagination come in and where can we be certain of our inspiration?

Imagination is a process and inspiration is a flashing condition, a spark. We get a flash of inspiration and immediately our minds take up the trail and our imagination starts working on it until in the end we really do not know what has taken place. What was inspiration has definitely ended in imagination.

We have got to understand the law of truth. How can we be absolutely certain a thing is true when we know our minds can provide no condition of certainty? You may think I am hard on the mind and all mental processes, but that is because I have understood their power.

Never in the whole history of the world will we be so close to the reality, the manifestation of the devilishness of the human mind as we are going to be this week, so close to the capacity of individuals for treachery against truth and love and righteousness. Treachery is mental; it does not come through the heart but through the mind. We must understand the capacities of our minds and where we can receive truth.

I have understood it as law that the current or wavelength of that which is real comes, as it were, from north to south - perpendicularly - and that which radiates out as world information, the wavelength of mind, is horizontal. You get the wavelength of truth coming down and the world wavelength coming across. Our bodies are receptive to both these currents, they are both pouring through us and we can no more shut them out than the air can refuse to receive what is broadcast into it. The air has no power of selectivity nor are our minds capable of it, *unless* we have got the wavelength of truth functioning in us. When we *are* truth, all untruth is automatically sparked out - it can make no contact with us at all. I have understood this week the reality of the process which was given long ago for this very purpose of making channels who would be capable of receiving truth in the hour of most urgent need. We must be able to receive the whole truth, not a fragment only with a percentage of lies which have the appearance of truth.

Jesus knew this and foretold the time when it would be possible to deceive even the elect. Things are being projected continually in the air and we do not know how or when we pick them up but when we receive the wavelength of truth, it brings a quietness, a certainty and stillness, and it is on that wavelength we must stand. On the other wavelength we know no certainty, we flinch and go back, change our minds.

Because I know in my own body the capacity for receiving every voltage of light, I know it is possible to stand even against the most appalling revelations of the individual's capacity for wholesale destruction, for acts which one would never have believed the human mind could be capable of, but which are true and which are being projected now in this country. I am only dealing now with conditions as they are in England and with the plans which were formulated months or even years ago to take place in this period of time. These plans of destruction should be brought into being this week and are the essence of mental perfection and ingenuity.

Those of us who *know* can be used to save the world now and it has been revealed to me moment by moment, the perfection of the plan, the things the enemy would have no hesitation in carrying out but which we should be incapable of doing. We are working on a wavelength of love and compassion; the enemy knows no love or compassion and only understands the use of mental power, the domination of mind over matter - force. When we halt, utterly horror-stricken, we have no power to stand, for we have nothing to offer in resistance. Our minds are not capable of dealing with it and we have not the force to counter it, but what we have got are minds capable of receiving truth, and truth is a greater condition than this projection of evil and destruction. It is the power to overcome evil, not by evil but by good.

We are face to face now with the purpose of overcoming evil with good. You may say, who are we to do it, but we have minds and bodies which can be used in world service and our service will be presented to us individually; we shall not have to go and look for it.

Later on I shall hope to give you details of the things which are happening to us now, things which must be secret at present, of the way in which the minds of babes (and we are babes in Light) are being used to frustrate the minds of the enemy. He has chosen very unimportant people to be used but it is the unimportant person, the individual who is used by the enemy to cut contacts and spread confusion; it is the ordinary individual who can cut the enemy's evil contacts and be used for victory. If they can - and it is their plan - render places useless by cutting off the light and telephones and all lines of communication and impersonate harmless people; we can be used to do the same, to cut their contacts and render them impotent. We need not kill them. We can do all this if we do not allow our minds to operate but receive the things which will be shown to us. Things will be done with the speed of light where the inspiration is received and acted on, but if all sorts of

difficulties are put in the way, you may be sure the mind has interfered and your imagination is working.

Above all, do put on your Armour of Light every morning and live in it all day and sleep in it at night. Be absolutely shod with the preparation of the gospel of peace when you put your feet against the feet of the Figure of Light in the morning. That is the first thing which happened in the Technique and next we were given the Cross of Light for our protection and there is our breastplate of righteousness. We also have the Transmuting Light pouring into our hearts and have our breastplate on all the time. When we do it, it is there but it is not put on *for* us, and having put it on, we must *stand*. We can only do that when we are in alignment and the Light is earthed at our feet; if it is not at our feet we can only sway about.

Some of us have only thought it necessary to have the light in their head and heart but that is not enough. If we are to be of service we must have the light at our feet so that we can go swiftly wherever our inspiration takes us. I do not want you only to sit and do the Technique, for evil is here in this world; it has been driven from the higher planes and we are face to face with it on earth. We have thought of evil as a negative thing, an absence of good, but we are now face to face with its reality in terms of flesh and blood. There is no evil now in any other world but this and we must deal with it in a practical way. Mind and body must become of service so that inspiration can come in this hour of terrific need. You may think the danger is far away and you will not know of it until it is over, but it is here on our very doorstep and there must be no imagination about it.

If we are fearless and confident that we can be used, then that which has been projected need not happen. Nothing is inevitable, though all things are possible, but it does depend on the individual that this catastrophe does not materialise. If the issue depends on the brilliant organisation of the enemy, then it is bound to happen; but if it depends on co-operation with the mind of Christ, it cannot take place. Everything depends on making, linking and breaking contacts. That is the whole crisis. Not on force, but on rendering force useless; not on matching force with force, but on getting inspiration on making impotent the forces which are being massed for useless destruction.

I have not talked like this to any other class. Though I have been warned it is only today I feel that there is to be a manifestation to us of the reality of this power and that if we have confidence earthed in our hearts, that manifestation will give way like mist. The mist is real but it can be dispersed. It does depend on the earthing of love and confidence for everything is prepared and only the forces of Light can prevent it from happening.

Do not let your imagination stop you from being used but hold yourself in readiness so that things can be done wherever you are. I have often said, "don't be too busy," but now I say, "service is asked of us today and don't make it unreal." Something was asked of one of us yesterday and it was thought that it was only necessary to do the Rhythm of the Name, but I realised that a journey was involved and that a definite contact had to be made, which was done. What was wanted was a real condition of protection. Do not let shyness or diffidence stand in the way of anything you have to do; do not bother about what other people will think but just do what is asked. We have got our work to do today. I feel that urgent service is required of us which will need fearlessness and confidence. We must get our understanding and stand, and in so doing we shall push back the thing which is descending on us. The only thing which can stop it is for those who know how to, to stand, "and having done all, to stand."

I have not said enough about mind and imagination. The mind will continually fly to unprotected places and people think of every sort of difficulty and danger. If you will have the strength of mind to be and live in the present you will be able to be used, but if your mind is not where your body is, you cannot be used. Therefore if you let your imagination go off along some line where your body cannot follow, you will find yourself in enemy country. If our minds and bodies are in a united condition all the time, then He has agents here who will do His bidding. That is why unity of thought and action must be stressed. There must only be one thought to one action, instead of the usual dozens!

Question: How can we control our thoughts when we are resting?

Answer: Tune in for inspiration and commit all the needs in your heart to Him. "Watch and pray" and realise that though your body is resting, your mind is tuned in to the mind of Christ, so that you are one wavelength. Praying in Light is a united condition. Never have two conditions in you, the mind must always be with the body, whether it is resting or active.

It is not for nothing that we are all living in different places. Go home, and wherever you live *be* the Light; there is nothing to be afraid of except letting your mind betray you. It was the mind of Judas which betrayed the Christ. We have been given flesh and blood for this purpose which is indestructible. We should be joyful and confident. Do believe that this is the very thing of which we have read but have not been able to believe we could receive. As we draw in the light every day to our feet, to our hands, our throat, our heart, and are filled with the Transmuting Light so that all our organs have protection from our emotional reactions, we are receiving His body and blood. There is nothing we cannot receive, "To those who have, all things shall be added unto them, but from those who have not, shall be taken away, even that which they have." Those who have not got the leaven of righteousness will be starved of their power, it will dry up in them. Destruction must overcome those who have no heart whatever, for they do not work on the double ray, only on the black ray of Lucifer. I am talking now of those who have never wanted to receive; those of us who want to, will receive more and more abundantly. That is where victory lies.

Confidence, certainty, stillness are all received through the heart; those of us who have put our trust in the mind have been entangled in the wavelengths of untruth, but if we are willingly receiving truth, it will live in us and spark out all false conditions. Discernment of truth lies in the heart; it is not a reasonable process. It should be a perfectly natural condition.

Some people have felt great reluctance in using the exercise of the cutting circles and that is because the mind is unwilling to give up its own judgement. Unless we are willing to be cut through every night with this light, which is the golden cord of truth, we shall be in a turmoil of mind, not knowing if we really have any capacity for receiving inspiration. We have been prepared and we have the blue circles to protect us, which are part of our Armour of Light.

Do the exercises simply, knowing that it is of vital importance now to keep up our strength and to know how to pray, how to work, how to rest, how to stand.

We shall do all that in Light, through the light at our feet, not in our heads, and we shall be practical people being used in a practical way.

I want to give you an exercise, the Cross of Breath. Will you visualise the great breath ray coming down from infinity through your head, right down to your feet so that you are but a container of breath, completely empty yet filled with the substance of breath, the Holy Spirit. That complete emptiness of self is the greatest relief you can experience. Draw it down on the sound **Fa...** on an inbreath and on **...ther** on an outbreath, it pours out through your arms which should be stretched out, forming a cross.

As you stretch out your arms, think of someone you want to help or of several people, at your right and left, and let the breath pour out to them. The cross symbolises changing conditions. It was in being long before the advent of Christ but He had to take that form because it denotes change, and those who can receive through the cross can have a dynamic condition of selfless service. Christ could not be crucified alone. He had to have the two, on His right and left, to receive that which was pouring out of Him.

If you want to do the exercise where you cannot extend your arms, it does not matter, but do it at least once a day with them stretched out. It is a supreme condition of contact in which we are really of His substance; it is the Creed coming true in a perfectly miraculous way. If we can earth in ourselves the emptiness of His breath, He is breathing through us.

Breath is a greater condition than light,

in this exercise; just as in this world the substance of gold has a greater value than copper. It gives a condition of emptiness which light cannot do. Light transmutes, but breath eliminates. Do get the feeling of your head and body being full of breath; you can do it all day long, and it is essential to get the sensation of giving as the breath pours out of your hands and fingers. Giving is only wonderful when there is nothing of ourselves in it.

Question: Is there any definite colour in it?

Answer: No, it is just breath. Some time ago I was shown all the different colours and there was a colourless interval between them each, they did not merge into each other. They seemed to be individualised by this colourless substance which I know now is breath.

Question: Does it matter that I hardly ever see the blue light, only the gold?

Answer: No, whether we register the colour we visualise or not, doesn't matter at all.

Question: What is the best way to help people?

Answer: It is important to commit people's needs every morning in the Needs exercise, but if they come during the day, just put their need in your heart and send it up in the chalice. We can *do* nothing for people, but in committing them, we put them in alignment so that they can receive.

Question: Is there any other way of getting in touch with people in the next world besides the Needs?

Answer: If you have tuned in to them on the Needs they will be able to get in to touch with you for anything they need during the day. You have made the contact, and it is as natural a law as telephoning.

Question: How do we know how we are to act?

Answer: If no conscious effort is asked of you, go on as you are; if something definite *is* asked you will know it is your moment.

AH-MOU
This talk is recorded on cassette tape

What does it mean to be a child of Light? Light is a flash; its speed leaves no time for calm reflection, and we must receive our divine direction into our brains with the speed of light. We do not have to direct it, only to receive it, and to be in such a condition that the receptivity is quickening and energising. We know how depleting it is to live in a condition of uncertainty, of tuning into other people's minds, of wanting to do the right thing but not knowing how. That is bondage and the world has suffered from it since the Fall.

The Technique has been given to train the mind until it reaches a point of instantaneous receptivity. That is the standard of Jesus. Ever since I first started passing on this Technique to a small group in 1931, I have been told that it would lead to a condition of world service, and yet it has not seemed possible that it could ever be for more than a comparatively small group. The things that have happened lately with the speed of lightning have shown me that we are to be an international group.

The exercise I am going to give you today is one I have always hesitated to pass on until I was certain that those people to whom I was giving it would want only to make a contact with the mind of Christ. Let me make that clear. There are those in this community who have been trained in the past on occult lines. When I was taken through the old initiations I understood how the teaching of the Christ absorbed the old knowledge and revealed so much more. We must discern between the old teaching and the new if we are to be used for world reconstruction. The old teachers were necessary steps in the evolution of the world, in order that the minds of people here shall be opened to things other than the material. Do realise that the old ways which have helped us are only doorways to help us to go direct to the Christ.

If we listen in only to the voice of the world we shall fail to hear His voice. Remember if you tune in on your wireless to Paris no other wavelength will impose itself. So it is with His. We have to chose what we will tune in to. We must have complete integrity of mind; we must submit other voices to the test of that arbitration. We have been taught the Technique for the purpose of receiving direct into our minds the spirit of truth which is the cosmic Christ. His is the mind that can broadcast into every single human receiving set, but He cannot impose it on us, and if we choose to tune into the astral, He will not interfere. He must make the contact with us here and we must be the pioneers to help the whole world to tune in. Our job is to train ourselves to be ready. I am constantly being reminded of the parable of the virgins. You will remember how difficult some of them found it to believe that the bridegroom really would come. We have to have our lamps ready lit; you cannot borrow light, you have to have it in you. That is the large picture, now for the individual one, the exercise.

It is one by which you will be able to make your own contact every day, so that His will may be made known to you. You do not hear on the **Ah-Mou** that which you expect to hear. Perhaps an example will make this clear. There was a time when everything seemed to have failed me, and so I had trained myself to expect nothing. Down on the **Ah-Mou**, day after day, came the word "Expect." At last I began to understand that unless I expected, Christ could not function through me. I had to open the door on the very wavelength that I had shut down. Now it has developed into a certainty of expectation.

Sometimes you will have familiar words from the Bible. Do not think

you have imagined them. Everything you receive on this exercise must be faced up to and not regarded as imagination. The directions come (and go) with the speed of light, and until I had earthed my contact and no longer needed to remember, I used to write down what I received. It is food for the day; the principle is given on which the day is to worked. You will be given that aspect of the Law which the circumstances of the day will bring into experience. We are given our equipment for the day and only if we forget it will the circumstances of the day defeat us. It is our Armour of Light, to be used for our help and protection.

When you do this exercise your mind must follow the travelling ray of light and the returning current as it makes a bowl of light. The voice you will hear will be within. Do not be keyed up but be completely relaxed to receive this ever-changing condition. Your vision must be centred on Christ; follow the light down and His mind will come into yours. Keep your mind here to receive His mind. If nothing comes, do not wait to force it, but go on with the Technique and it may come later in the day. Your mind must be so established that it travels on the **Ah**, and on the **Mou** it comes back ready to receive His directions. The right hand is the light bringer, the left the connecting ray.

REMEMBER ME
Wednesday 24th June 1954

I want to talk about the action and reaction of universal light in relation to the personal radiation of the body of Jesus. This matter is important to the channelhood of Christian Initiates. I have been shown the difference between being a conductor of universal light, and a channel for the personal activity of Christ. The difference is profound.

In the first case the individual taps the universal supply which has come down through the ages wherever the true light worship has been observed. But the coming of Christ brought in a supremely different process which the universalists would not accept at the time, and have not consciously accepted today. Universalists are spiritually minded people who draw on light, and work in it, but they do not make a conscious contact with the mind of Christ. This contact is the only one which can supply the antidote to every known condition of disease and disintegration. The universalists can get most beneficial results along certain lines; but the only supreme contact is with the radiant, divine humanity of Christ, and the Christian Initiates must realise their responsibility for maintaining this contact, and being completely one-pointed about it.

It is difficult for the human brain to sort out the accumulated evidence of centuries of spiritual experience, and because it is really impossible to come to valid conclusions, the only certain way of channelhood is personal experience of personal contact with Christ. The words 'universal' and 'communism' have a profound human appeal because they seem to aim at perfection, but experience shows that these words have no reality, and that the only real approach to perfection is to come through the personal wavelength of Christ to the universal Father. This is the teaching of Christ, but this personal approach has been, and is, sidetracked by millions of other wavelengths claiming to lead to the same universal source. Mentally they do lead there, but physically they do not.

For physical redemption there is no other way except through Christ, and it was on the physical experiences of the twelve, directed personally by Christ, and obtained by a complete focus on His mind, that the Christian church was founded. If the disciples had not done the works, the world would have reverted to the old universal source, and the ancient formulae.

This line of potent experience through

the focus on the mind of Christ is of intense and vital importance at this particular moment of history. I have myself realised the difference between a conductor of universal light, and a Christ channel. The conductor may have no discernment of his source of power, and the reaction on his own body is one of depletion, and affects adversely his heart, veins and arteries. The channel, on the contrary, with his mind tuned in to Christ, cannot have one cell or molecule of his physical self destroyed. Therefore we must focus our minds onto and into, that of Christ, and listen to no sound but that which comes direct from Him.

The whole pattern and process of freedom has now been given out to us channels but, as Lucifer threw it away, so may we. Lucifer chose to express himself, rather than the Father. Christ passed the magnetism of the Father through Himself to the world. The full discernment of this truth is very subtle, but we are at a critical point on the path, for with the pattern of freedom from the self which we have received, comes the possibility of full achievement. Perhaps the only disciple who really achieved in full was John. Peter had a touch of martyrdom in him in the end, when he chose to be crucified upside down; a martyrdom which would never have been required of him.

We must beware of our own desire for martyrdom. God wishes our manifestation to be one of complete radiance, and this it can never be unless our mind touches that of Christ. When we are less than radiant, we may know that we are in some measure separated from Him. We should always use the description the *radiant* mind of Christ, and experience a quite ridiculous joy.

The present physical condition of the world is giving us the greatest opportunity of our lives. Christ has prepared our individual bodies for health under every possible condition. Never fear that you might interfere with the destiny of another person by focusing your mind on Christ on his behalf. But you *must* be certain of your contact. Christ is the only source and cannot deputise His supreme achievement, but He has both the power and the authority to transmit it through all of us. It is for us to follow on one-pointedly, and there is no sacrifice in the process, but fullness the whole way.

There comes to each one of us the point when dying to our old mentality must take place, and a conscious surrender of the old be made, so that it never returns. There should be a sign; a signature of recognition giving us the certainty that we are in touch with Christ.

This must be an individual thing. I see His hair at the back of the head, and realise that the nerves at the back here, should be full of radiance; in Him they were shining. The vital points here must be filled with radiant life in order to transfigure the whole being, and give a feeling of utter freedom at the back of the head.

It is as if He places His hand there, and gives strength and comfort right through me, from back to front, and through the eyes. On the words

Remember Me,

see these points at the back, lit up with gold, and feel the radiance come from the back of the head to the front of the face.

Postscript

The Armour of Light
Trust Council

is the governing body which works on a charitable basis
and has undertaken to continue the dissemination of
the knowledge of the Christian Initiation,
which was revealed through Olive C.B. Pixley.
Currently the published works which are available
to be purchased from the Trust Council are:-

The Armour of Light - Part I
Revised edition containing Volume I and II

The Armour of Light - Part II

The Magnet

Olive Pixley's Spiritual Journey
Comprising - Listening In, The Trail, Human Document

Should the reader require further information, or perhaps wish to
engage in correspondence about any matter which is related to these
works, they are invited to contact:-

The Armour of Light Trust Council
Irena Dean
11 Pathfields
Shere
Surrey GU5 9HP
England
Tel/Fax: 01483-202701

THE ARMOUR OF LIGHT TRUST COUNCIL
TEL/FAX: 01483-202701
irena@armouroflight.fsnet.co.uk
http://www.armouroflight.fsnet.co.uk